HIGH

HIGH

A PARTY GIRL'S GUIDE TO

Peace

TARA BLISS

An audio version of this book can be found at:
http://tarabliss.com.au

Paperback :

ISBN-10: 0994187807

ISBN-13: 978-0 9941878-0-2

Digital:

ISBN-10: 0994187815

ISBN-13: 978-0 9941878-1-9

Printed and bound by CreateSpace

Cover art: Dani Hunt

Photography: Tahl Rinsky

Book design: Sue Balcer of JustYourType.biz

http://tarabliss.com.au

For Missy.
Because I vowed to fit both of our lives into this one.
When you left, I started waking up.

contents

It's early on a Sunday morning and I'm nose-diving into an inevitable come-down, hard and fast. Tomorrow morning, my 6am alarm will set my rattled brain ablaze with dread. I'll make a wobbly attempt at creating a masterpiece out of my hair, travel down the 16 storeys of this apartment building to ground level, jump in my car, weave my scattered ass through peak hour traffic and cut hair all day long under the bright lights of the most elite hair salon in Brisbane. This misery inside of me is unwelcome, but well-deserved, and it's going nowhere.

I look in the mirror. My eyes are sunken, but lit with blackness. Somehow. My lips are swollen and so are my cheeks. I've been crying. It's the day after Future Music Festival, or Summafieldayze, or Parklife, or *whatever*. It's irrel-evant. What's real is that I swallowed pill after meaning-seeking pill last night. I felt the music in me. I danced with the man who only days ago broke it off with me for the third or fourth time. (Again, irrelevant.) I'm plugged in so deep to a world that's built on foundations of how good a high is. Even in this state – a rather messy one – I know it… *I know better.*

No-one's with me now. Not when it matters. Not when I want them. Not when I usually need my crew the most - the day after. I'm thinking about all the times we used to pile up pillows and cushions, and settle ourselves in front of the big screen, as we suffocated our pain with gin and tonic, and Gatorade, and mango and macadamia ice cream. We'd laugh at how ridiculous the whole situation was; how ridiculous *we* were. Our bodies would be trembling, our mouths not able to decipher the garbage clip-clopping around in our spent, exhausted minds. But at least we had each other. Not this morning. I'm sitting beside my bed, knees pulled up to my chest, howling like someone who's grieving the loss of her mother, while rocking myself back and forth, back and forth. I'm looking out over the city of Brisbane, which is still waking up, not caring that at just 21 I'm living a life many envy. All I can think about, all I can feel, is a complete emptiness within me. *The Void.*

I'm lonely. He doesn't want me. My brain is on fire. I can't breathe. I'm starving. *I want out.*

Acknowledgement, acceptance, a feeling of true belonging – we all long for it. As I sob away on this sunny morning, I crave it more than ever. I just need to know, somehow, that I'm loved, or at the very least, that someone gives a damn about me. I want someone to make a pile out of the pillows, tuck me in, grab me some ice cream out of the freezer, and then stroke my hair as I wearily doze off into a world of tangled dreams. Instead, my only companions are my heavy-beating heart (which feels as though it wants to plunge out of me and into the chest of someone more deserving) and silence. The kind of silence that swallows you up and spits you out every few seconds.

And the thoughts. Let's not forget about those. Those haunting echoes of…

"Is this as good as it gets? Is this all there is?"

…repeating over and over and over.

introduction

You're here.
And that's kind of a big deal.

I believe that regardless of how deep you've found yourself in a Party Girl funk – whether you're an addict or simply seeking a little more peace in your life, the very reason that you're here, holding this book in your hands, is enough to tell me that you deeply resonate with the heartache; those feelings of uncertainty that sit right at the base of your belly. The place where despair and discontent combine to create a killer cocktail of complete desperation, much like it did for me in my life.

More importantly, you being here tells me that you're ready to start making some different choices that will impact your life in radical ways.

As much as we Party Girls may 'know better', as often as we continue to ricochet back to the mantra of 'I should be doing more with my life', what keeps us from illuminating our potential is the silence that presents itself when we ask ourselves:

:: *Who am I without this drink in my hand? The drink that makes me feel confident and approachable and interesting?*

:: *Who am I if I'm not the girl who can stay up all night consuming with the crew?*

:: *Who am I without the Party Girl identity that I've spent years manufacturing for myself?*

Most often, the feeling we uncover is one of nakedness. We feel exposed without that drink in hand. We're afraid of feeling boring, vulnerable and uncomfortable. And so - '*barkeep!*' - we order another drink, and down it goes. It feels absurd to even consider what may be lying dormant beneath the agendas we've worn; the ones we've toiled away at wearing properly and with conviction. From as young as we start making decisions for ourselves, we try to forge on forward down a path of difference; of rebellious friction. We'll either do what it takes to fit in, or bend conformity by way of standing out. For many of us, The Party held the ticket for us to make true on our desires and - albeit temporarily - fill The Void.

This isn't a book about fixing what's broke, or righting what's wrong. My definition of peace doesn't dictate that you should become more, do more, or get more. It's not about improving who you are as a person, or striving to become better. To live peacefully, as I've experienced it, is to loosen our grip on the way we think our lives *should* unfold. Peace means embracing surrender *and* inspired action. It's the place where the left and right hemispheres of our brain dance to the rhythm of a life filled with purpose, passion and devotion.

Peace is about letting go. It's about making choices with ease and grace and faith, rather than grinding ahead. It's about embracing who you are as a whole (the light *and* the dark). When we're neck-deep in the grip of our self-made identities, this is certainly easier said than done, but it's the most transformational journey I've taken. Difficult *and* divine. Frustrating *and* fulfilling. And it's beyond worth it.

Oh, the possibilities…

And so, *High* has come into being because the vision I hold in my heart goes a little something like this: I see women the world over waking up on Sunday mornings feeling alive, grateful and filled with energy. They find their drug of choice at the farmers' markets, or on their yoga mats, or while in intimate conversations with their most cherished friends. Their health radiates, their skin glows, and they effortlessly melt into their ideal body shape simply because they've decided to no longer run from themselves; no longer hide from feelings they would rather suppress. These women become magnets who attract beautiful, soulful people into their lives as a result of turning around and recognising the soulful beauty within themselves first. They draw in new, never-before-conceptualised opportunities that align with what's true for them. They feel a constant hovering of support from The Universe as it offers up one spirited signpost after another in the form of divine little nudges and almost-too-good-to-be-true 'chance' encounters. These women are sovereign forces to be reckoned with, giving autopilot responses the heave-ho; instead making wide-awake choices from a place of body awareness and presence. They nurture their bodies, relationships and daily routines by setting intentional boundaries. They make room for pure pleasure - not the type that comes in a bottle marked '7% alcohol', but the type that's constantly available to all of us, at any time, if we could just remain alert enough to notice it. These women release the stuff that's been weighing down on them like a ton of bricks: shame, guilt, regret, envy and a severe case of the 'shoulds'. *You* **are one of the women I envision, sister.**

My journey into The Party

I spent years chasing my choices with a swig of regret. As an inquisitive little girl who craved freedom from the binds of my childhood, it was only a matter of time before I took life by the scruff of the neck and started making my own rules. Like many people who first get a glimpse of independence, rather than celebrating my emancipation with pure happiness vibes, I made a beeline for intense and instant gratification. 'Pleasure' wasn't a concept I was all too familiar with, and I was hungry for a quick fix; a concentrated serving of what it meant to feel truly alive and unchained.

Fast forward a few years, and I wasn't sure how I could carry a conversation if I wasn't half drunk. And as far as establishing relationships with men? Unless I had a belly full of vodka or a nose full of speed, forget about it. 'Real' Tara – confident, accepted, beautiful Tara – only came out to play when she was under the influence. She would creep out from behind the cloak of my day-to-day home base of melancholy and brighten the room with her sass, sense of humour and up-for-anything attitude. And *this* is the very reason why The Party is so damn seductive. How on earth can we let go of the environment that helped us mould and create the type of person we've always aspired to be?

I worked in careers that not only encouraged loose behaviour, but seemed to provoke it: hairdressing, bar-tending and waitressing. To add fuel to the fire, I spent nearly four years travelling the globe, skipping hemispheres in the pursuit of endless winters. Snowboarding and pints unite in a special kind of holy matrimony, so needless to say, my years on the mountains were some of my messiest. My tribe were a team of enablers; each of us holding space for the others to be our most belligerent, chaotic selves. **Happy hour was our church. Hangovers were to be expected.**

My early twenties were bookmarked by a full-throttle lifestyle that swayed between divine highs and such frightening lows that most of the time I barely knew which way was up. In the darkest of moments, I felt as though I were living on my own planet; as if no-one could relate to me, understand me, commiserate with me. And what I sure as hell wasn't expecting was that the post-Party heart-crushing comedowns would be even more painful than the isolation I had felt prior to the arrival of drugs in my life. However, what I've come to learn after working with hundreds of Party Girls is that **our inner struggles are collective**; we all share similar wounds. It's as though the self-destructive Party Girl archetype in all of us binds us in a kindred way. Just as we find solace in our Party crew in those first few years of self-discovery, so too do we find our tribe in the angels who are chanting the anthem of *enough is enough* on repeat in their minds. **This book exists to strengthen that bind between us.**

It took another three years after that opening story, my Festival Comedown From Hell, to discover what 'wanting out' – the alternative option – looked and felt like. Add a further 18 months before I realised that journeying through the fog had supplied me with a story that, while seemingly surface level and *first world* on the outside, was unquestionably significant. All of a sudden, I had something to say about Option B, which in all simplicity is deciding to live a life of conscious choice, rather than one of habit. More important than imparting my own story, though, was how clear it became that there were other young women who were willing to listen up and travel *alongside* me.

Late in 2012, as a 25-year-old, I was sitting on my mum's deck, sipping on my third or fourth glass of pinot grigio. My man was sitting beside me and we were laughing and playing with the puppies. Apparently out of nowhere, I heard 'The Party Girl's Guide to Peaceful Living' clear as day bouncing around the right side of my head. I pulled a *huh?* face and took another sip, half hammered by now. But the idea lingered like a bad smell. So finally, a few days later, I gave it the attention it deserved by allowing all of the fragmented sentences and suggestions that had been showing up in my mind to spill out into my journal. Not long after that, I had a course outline for an online program called *The Party Girl's Guide to Peace*, which I launched from my blog.

Relinquishing my inner Party Girl had been a huge part of my story, even at that point. I'd sworn off drugs and steered clear of the clubs. My marriage was loving and solid (a far cry from the drug-laden lust-fests of the days of yore). And yet there I was, ending each day with a never-ending glass of wine, while preparing an experience for women who were struggling with the very same situation. I felt like a Fakey McFakepants. And yet, I understood that The Party Girl's Guide to Peace was an opportunity to guide others through (and out of) their struggles with Party Girl addiction, while heeding the opportunity to self-heal even further.

Clearly, I had more inner work to do, and it was the sense of purpose and meaning that arose through serving *others* that made my own lifestyle clean-up not only essential, but majorly joy-inducing. Still, I had my moments of crippling self-doubt. I felt intimidated by the idea. I felt inadequate and under-qualified. How could I lend an authoritative voice on the topic when my demons were still rising up from within me? Richard Bach has been quoted as saying 'we teach best what we most need to learn'. Let it be said right here: this book has been and continues to be my medicine, just as it might be yours. I am right there with you, sister girl. In the trenches. Doing the best I can. Taking it day by day.

It has been a privilege and an honour to watch hundreds of young women transform their lives with the help of The Party Girls Guide to Peace. They've accessed their inner joy, lost weight, bravely stepped away from relationships that no longer serve them, attracted new tribes into their lives, and most importantly, they've found an inner peace and acceptance that quite truthfully is difficult to articulate. It's bloody amazing!

When I made the transition from balls-to-the-wall Party Girl, to a woman in the world who prioritises inner peace unapologetically, the journey was a solo one. Unlike today, I was without a mentor, or even a shining example among my peers who'd been brave enough to test the waters of a different, more nourishing life. Blazing a trail of good health and right actions felt risky and uncertain to me. And that's where the irony lies, because if we're honest, we'll admit to risk and uncertainty being the catalyst for our detour into the world of drug and alcohol abuse in the first place. I journeyed alone, but you – like each and every other Party Girl reading this book – don't have to. There's a whole army of us ready to forge ahead with you and cheer you on.

What lies ahead

Everyone's experience with this book will be a different and deeply personal one. I'll just say right here that *your* experience will be made all the richer if you willingly release your need-to-know expectations. This book will impact you in a more dynamic way if you show up to it each and every time with a curious mind, an open heart, and enthusiasm to take action in your life. That being said, I daresay that you can anticipate the following:

:: *You'll find your own story nestled within my own, and the women who have trodden before you.*

:: *You'll begin to unchain yourself from conditioned thinking and limiting behaviour, by virtue of following your curiosities and letting love lead the way.*

:: *You'll start a self-love revolution, after defining your own brand of self-love and what it really means to acknowledge and respect yourself, and be present for who you are beneath The Party facade.*

:: *You'll begin flirting with the word 'no' – a word most Party Girls don't exercise all too often – and you'll discover that this formidable two-letter word is empowering and loving. And you know what? It ropes in results, fast.*

The *Peace Practices* within this book are designed to give you the tools and insights you need to permit yourself to live a little differently. We're going to be slicing through limiting beliefs, questioning the status quo, tapping into your inner rebel and anchoring back into who you are, in a whole, exploratory way. Suffering from a case of FOMO (Fear Of Missing Out) there too? Yep, thought so. We're going to dissolve the obsession with Missing Out by reinforcing that everything you need, want, desire – it's all within you. Until you access it *in there*, you'll be chasing your tail as you hunt for it *out here*. So it would be my utmost privilege to link elbows with you over the next 10 chapters, and lay bare what's possible when you release your attachment to everything you *think* you are; and instead, clear some space to allow the real you to come out to play with the world. If I - a young woman who in the past would chase down her joy in the outside world rather cultivate it within - can find her way through the fog and design a fulfilling, love-fuelled, inspired life, I have no doubt that you can too.

The bones of this book: building it from the base up

Here's how I want you to *feel* as you journey through these pages: **understood and capable**. Though I *am* a coach and mentor, this book is holding space for something a little different. Sure, I'm going to guide you through some practical processes (I can't help myself), but for this experience, I'm primarily here as your friend, your sister girl, your soulie, and my intention isn't to preach, but rather inspire you into your own special kind of action using my stories and memories as the catalyst for change.

And that's precisely why you'll hear plenty about where I've been, what I've done, what I've processed and how I've managed to make it through some difficult times. I heard something once that went something like this: people absorb and implement advice best when it's delivered through story, rather than statistic. That resonated massively with me. We need to feel seen, heard and understood by those we're opening up to. Both you and I are opening up to each other during this process, so my first priority is that you feel a sense of kinship; that you feel *understood*. Once we've set a trusting foundation, this experience is targeted at you finding the courage within to feel *capable* of making changes yourself. You really can become an alchemist of life energy. The good news is it only takes one little choice at a time. This is a No Overwhelm Zone, Party Girl. When you feel capable, you can make shit happen. Period.

Here's the most crucial nugget that I want you to *know*: **you are *not* your Party Girl identity. You've been running away from yourself. And now, it's time**

to come home. Ugh! I know. After all those years you spent creating a Party Persona, I've shown up in your life insisting that this girl you've created isn't the real you; that she's a myth, a figment of your imagination that you plucked out of the ether, onto the earth plane, into your body. Believe it or not, this realisation comes to you signed, sealed and delivered with a message of extreme empowerment. If you're curious enough to investigate what's lying beneath all those false identities, you're bound to experience richness and fulfilment in your life like never before. Ever asked the question, "*Who am I?*" Or, "*What's this all about?*" In this book, we're accessing *that* space– because I don't know about you, but I reckon that's a sweeter space to live in, rather than obsessing over what shoes we're going to wear this weekend. (Am I alone on that one?)

And while you're on this journey with me (and hopefully well into the remainder of your existence), here's what I want you to *do*: **start making considered, wide-awake choices.** Because here's the thing: seeing as I've hacked your life for a living the last few years, I'm willing to wager that you're a creature of habit. (Right?) An extra drink just somehow always *finds* itself into your hand. You keep bumping up against the same issues in relationships. Maybe your inner Party Girl has adorned you with a little reputation? As the weekend rolls around, you find yourself craving The Party, the dance floor, the shenanigans, for no other reason then, *hey, it's the weekend. This is what we do on the weekend.*

I don't mind if you're a seasoned Party Girl, a dabbler, or whether you've turned to this book simply because you fancy a pinch more peace in your life - if we want to transform our lives, we have to transform our rituals, our behaviours, and the actions we take. We have to utilise our God-given gift of decision-making, take a few risks, and bust through a few fears, all in the name of passion and evolution. In the name of growth and fulfilment.

No-one says it better than the great Tony Robbins: "Your life changes the moment you make a new, congruent and committed decision". And girl, from someone who's come out the other end of a few lofty decisions, I've got to tell you, it's delicious. Life's not just *happening* to you; you are co-creating it with The Universe with every moment, breath, thought and choice you make. A show of hands who's ready and willing to choose differently? Atta girl.

Some things you should know before we dive in

High is home to a huge element of memoir, peppered with *how-to* action. I'm teaching through story-telling and experience, not through textbooks, and I'm opening up about times in my life, not because I like the sound of my own voice, but because I believe that these stories will be valuable to you and encourage subtle but powerful shifts within.

The stories that you're about to read from my own life may divert a little from chronological order. This is simply to strengthen the trajectory of the message in a way that'll support you as best I can. Also, the personal experiences that you read here in this book are as I perceived them, and how I 'digested' them through the level of awareness that I had at the time. Apart from Glen, my husband, all names have been changed or withheld, and I'd like to take this opportunity to give deep love and thanks to everyone who is referred to in the coming chapters. With my hand on heart, I mean it when I say that I would willingly embrace anyone mentioned in this book if I passed them in the street. They're all such significant pieces in the puzzle of my life and I wouldn't be the woman I am today without them. **Nothing but love.**

High is not a book to consume passively. Though I have next to no doubt that a little of what feels dark in your life may be brightened simply by being here and reading, like one of my mentors, Marie Forleo, says: "Insight without action is useless". You'll need to put the book down on occasion and play with the ideas, contemplations and suggestions yourself. **You'll get out what you put in.** I recommend that you keep a journal for your journey, or better yet, consider opening up your laptop and starting a video diary. Sometimes, the most effective way we can celebrate and tangibly *see* our progress is to glance back at where we've been and observe the path we've travelled, from a distance. Your journal will allow you the reflective gift of getting to know yourself on a deep level. Turn to it when you feel inspired. For you, that might mean once daily, or weekly, or a couple of times per month. Just give yourself permission to be messy, uncensored, and honest.

Throughout the book, you'll hear me refer to 'The Party'. When you hear this, I want you to take that on board in a way that resonates with you. For example, for you, The Party might simply mean 'The Nightclub' or 'The Booze' or 'The Drugs'. It may even point to 'The Drama'. For me, underneath the umbrella statement of 'The Party' lies anything that suggests I'm running from myself: the excessive alcohol, the drugs, the weekend benders, the men I clung to, the flat-out exhaustion, ill-health, friendships filled with drama and tension, the yo-yoing between excitement and loneliness. And let's not forget the two big elephants in the room: hangovers and comedowns.

Each of us define The Party in our unique way. If I'm truthful with myself, The Party isn't so much about defining my behaviour, and things that *happened*, but rather, it allows me to quickly access the *feelings* stored in my cells from that period of life. And it's an odd combination of surface level joy and anticipation, raging enthusiasm, desire, and adrenaline, stirred in with a deeper presence of intense isolation, sadness and unworthiness.

So when you read the words 'The Party', let them sink into your being in a way that pertains to *you*. Allow those two words to speak to your unique and very personal situation.

Also, I want to speak for a moment about the word 'addiction'. I've got to lay it on the line with full transparency here: this is a word I'm still exploring. I'm not about to put my hand in the air and proclaim that I was or am a drug or alcohol addict, because I've heard so many differing definitions of that word; some that suggest I may not ever have been, and others that imply that I was and always will be. I'm certainly not going to position myself in the world as an addiction expert. That's not my sweet spot.

What I *am* willing to confess to – and it's a confession that has shaped the whole of this book – is that I was addicted to my Party Girl *identity*. I was hooked on the young woman I'd created through the mediums of drugs, alcohol and the perfect house music soundtrack. I crafted her meticulously and strategically, and spent most of my days hungering for her. If I wasn't getting high, or having my belly warmed by a few drinks, I was wishing I could be. And not so much for the high or the buzz but for the person I became with a little help from my friends (read: substances).

I'll share more of my story and my take on Party Girl identity addiction. For now though, just know that when I refer to addiction throughout the book, I'm referencing our mad obsessions with our sense of Self, rather than substances.

Of course, if you need to assimilate that word in its practical term to help il-
luminate any substance addictions that you indeed may have, please, go right
ahead. I'm here to serve you. (And who knows, we may explore addiction in a
future time!)

No matter what your crutch may be, use this as your guide. As you continue reading, you'll see that I'm quite transparent about my hankering for drugs
and men, but if this doesn't vibe with you, apply my stories and suggestions to
your own struggles. For example, the way in which I talk about my difficulties
in attaching to relationships may mirror your association with food or even
social media!

Speaking of addictions and social media, you won't find me on Twitter
or Facebook. I shut those two platforms down because they were kind of de-
stroying my soul. (Too dramatic?) You will, though, find me sitting pretty on
Instagram under the handle @tara_bliss. To crank this message right the way
up, and amplify the sense of community, I encourage you to share your photos
with me throughout your journey (and all of us), using the hashtag:

#highpeace

Are you ready?

**I don't care about how much you drink. I care about how you *feel* the next
day.**
**I'm not concerned with how late you stay out on the weekends. I'm con-
cerned with what *motivates* you to stay out.**
**It's none of my business how you treat yourself. But I'm making it my busi-
ness to reveal a few alternative options, regardless.**

Party Girl, hitting rock bottom can be incredibly useful, but you don't have to
wait until you reach those depths. This is all about breaking the cycle, setting
higher standards for ourselves, and thinking about the type of women we want
to be moving forward.

I don't know about you, but *I'm* ready. I don't want to simply settle anymore. I want to see this life through a lens of total mystery and wonder. I want

to cultivate a connection with my body that's rooted in respect and self-care and deep love. Because when all is said and done, **High: A Party Girl's Guide to Peace is a *love* story.**

Mary Oliver presses us all with this heavenly question:

> *"What will you do with your one wild and precious life?"*
> Mary Oliver

Let's start here. Let's take a deep breath, offer our insides a sly little smile, and turn this page.

You are beautiful. You are remarkably remarkable. Let's help you remember that. Let's peel back some layers, and get to work.

It's so damn good to be here with you.

1.

Curiosity Got You Here,
Curiosity Will Get You Out

*"The voyage of discovery is not in seeking new landscapes
but in having new eyes."*
Marcel Proust

My Party Girl career began at an embarrassingly early age: eight years old, I'm afraid to say. My then-stepsister was 13, and we used to bum-puff cigarettes in the bathroom of my dad's house. That was me as a cute little white-haired thing and I remember feeling pretty badass for two reasons: the image of the thing (all the cool people did it on TV) and I'd achieved a sense of belonging. I adored my big sister and would have done almost anything to ensure that I was granted the privilege of her company.

Image and belonging continued to be the two themes that acted as my Party Girl compass throughout the years, but at the core of that compass has always sat *curiosity* and an ache to escape. Escapism feels as though it's always been lodged deep within the double helix of my DNA. After all, I'm a Piscean in the zodiac and an Enneagram Type 7 (which in a sense is a human personality system), both of which are prone to doing anything – *anything* – to avoid pain (preferably by virtue of getting shit-faced). As long as I can remember, I've played with fire as I searched for where I belonged in this strange world. In my first year of high school, having obviously unlocked my entrepreneurial spirit, I'd steal cigarettes from my mum's friends and sell them to the naughty kids at school who smoked on the oval at lunch time. (Just quietly, I was making a killing.) For a while, I attempted to camouflage in with these kids who so very clearly felt a little alienated from the world, like I did. But as I eventually found out, to them I was nothing but a 'bum-puffing loser', not quite hardcore enough to carry the nicotine right the way back into my lungs.

At 14, I managed to establish meaningful connections with two girls who liked to colour outside the lines, which was exciting to me. We'd have sleepovers, swigging rum of out of the bottle, singing along to Alanis Morissette's *Jagged Little Pill* at the top of our lungs. The scent of nag champa – wafting around the room – would linger in our hair for days. 'I want to die a virgin', Bonnie announced one night when we were bevvied (and probably stoned) out of our minds. She was inimitable like that; comfortable with challenging the status quo, always pushing the envelope in an effort to avoid modelling what the popular girls were doing. It made her beautiful to me. But it also made her *slippery.* I never really felt as though I could keep up with her level of revolt. I mainstreamed into sport and an obsession with being accepted, while she continued rocking on in her own fine way, in spite of everyone.

By the time we graduated high school, we weren't as close (I'll put that down to growing pains), but I still adored her from afar. And at our year 12 graduation, I lit up when I saw her; barefoot with henna tattoos on her ankles, dreadlocked hair, and barely a slick of makeup; divinely feminine and outright captivating. Bonnie didn't remain true to her declaration of celibacy – she gave birth to a baby boy smack bang in the middle of a heroin addiction. Bec, my other friend, fought through an all-out war with crystal meth. I was in my early twenties when I heard about the struggles my besties from years past had faced. Thankfully today, the three of them, including Bonnie's now eight-year-old son, are okay. And Bec is due to give birth to a baby girl any day now.

In my late teens, I felt my best (engaged and confident) when I was well on my way to spew city, pouring down the drinks from every direction in order to chill the hell out and enjoy myself. A glass or two of wine here and there was unheard of for me. Like so many in our culture, I drank to get drunk, and quickly. **There was certainly no time for pussy-footing around**. On my 18th birthday, I got so hammered after only two hours at the bar that I sent myself home and woke up the next morning naked in a puddle of my own piss. *Sexy, I know.*

I was always double-parked, a drink in each hand, always spurring people on to challenge me, to dare me, to bet me I couldn't set a new bingeing personal best, just so I could prove them wrong, and simultaneously prove myself to be 'worthy'. And in my circle at that time, chasing shots of black sambuca with pints of lager meant that I had signed what Jill Stark - author of *High Sobriety* - calls a sacred 'social contract' with kindred friends. Here was a place where we could fly our freak flags and be our messy, narcissistic selves. A place to foster a little more charisma with each and every drink.

If I hadn't already believed that my worthiness depended on how I could handle my booze, one night in particular cemented the confirmation that, yes, in fact, it did.

A seed gets planted

A group of us are sitting outside the bar we work at, enjoying some knock-off drinks, when I decide for some ungodly reason (probably an attempt at drawing attention to myself) to skull as much beer as humanly possible. The decision births me a new nickname - Seven Pots & A Pint Tara - one that goes on to follow me around for the coming months, after I'm cheered on and high-fived for my efforts. My boyfriend, who's still on shift serving drinks, spectates the binge fest from inside. He later wraps his arms around me. "I think I'm in love", he says with a wink.

Drink lots of booze. Remain standing. Keep my shit together. Get approval from the guy. *Got it!*

From there, in what was quite honestly a common and seemingly natural pro-gression, I promoted myself to a drug user. The hospitality industry scooped me into its wasted embrace, drip-feeding me ecstasy to start with. Then once my 'training wheels' came off, in came speed, cocaine, MDMA, GHB, acid and lucky dips of Who Knows What. Drugging revealed a young woman inside of me who I believed was more beautiful and interesting than the one I put to bed before 10pm on a week night. Mostly, I was able to better manage the relation-ships in my life, particularly romantic ones. Having broken up with my high school sweetheart, navigating the strange terrain of men and flirtation and sex felt impossible and awkward before I started getting high. Drugs made me feel present; powerful even. They gave me the courage I'd always craved to act on my curiosities. But they also hoaxed me into believing that I was less of a young woman without them.

Most Party Girls will attest to living some form of double life. Whether it's the swing between the wild child and workplace professional, or the introspective perfectionist who lets it all hang out on a Friday night, there's no question that we feel the weight of the world untether on the weekends, as we make way for our alter egos to explore. **Behind *my* binges hid an aspiring elite athlete.** I worked two jobs (bar-tending and hairdressing) as a way to make ends meet, but my true love was indoor volleyball.

Volleyball made high school bearable. Just like my rum and Alanis sessions with Bonnie and Bec, it gave me an opportunity to feel part of a tribe. The friendships I made on court and while on tour were the type of connections I didn't know existed; whole and perfect, full of hilarity and adventure, and thanks to our collective competitive spirit, laced with determination. On court, we were like fierce goddesses preparing for battle, but once we stepped off, we'd collapse into piles of giggles and story-telling and gossip. Here they were: my girls. The kinds of friendships they write about in books and show on the big screen. The ones that make you feel as though you're skipping through a wheat field in slow motion, in front of a sepia lens.

As someone who was practically born sprinting, with athleticism pumping thick in my blood, jeopardising the health of my body with self-destructive behaviour wasn't exactly a puzzle piece that fit. I remember running warm-up laps of the court at 15, gasping for air, thinking, *"If I want to play volleyball for Australia, I'll need to give up smoking"*. And so I did. I went on to captain the regional and state teams, and donned the green and gold uniform of Australia - my Holy Grail - to represent my country on court by the ripe old age of 16. At 18, high on the possibility of all my most grandiose dreams coming true, I was scouted by a college in Jacksonville, Florida for an all-expenses-paid collegiate scholarship.

But it was too perfect, too big, too aligned with what I really wanted. So, in the first of many acts of extreme self-sabotage, I declined the scholarship just months before I was due to fly out, having convinced myself that bigger than my dream to become a professional athlete was the desire to, apparently, become a hairdresser. I had opted out of a huge opportunity and could feel the tail between my legs long after. This would be only the first of a chain of events that would see me backing down at the last moment from opportunities ripe with promise. At 20, I did it again. After swallowing sour grapes of regrets for almost two years, I threw myself back into the collegiate application process, with almost immediate success. This time, Ohio reached out. My focus was fixed and I was determined to get on a plane and pursue this damn dream of mine. I was going to own it, and own it good. But I seemed to be forgetting a few minor details: By then, I was transfixed with dirty beats and MDMA and a boy. And so, I pulled the plug, again opting for a life of cocktail-shaking and blowdrying instead, which seemed like the most reasonable and obvious choice. (Ahem.)

My final hurrah was being offered a volleyball scholarship at the Queensland Academy of Sport in my home city of Brisbane, on a program that primed future potential Olympians. I was over the moon; and not only because I could train at an elite level and improve my game, but also, I could do whatever the hell I wanted with the rest of my life. All my bases were covered. Besides, seriously, as if I'd want to accept one of those American offers anyway – with their drinking laws, I wouldn't have been of legal age to enjoy a drink at the bar on the weekends. Thanks but no thanks. *This* was the right decision.

The double life thrilled me, and switching roles between team captain, senior hair stylist, bartender and wild child seemed to energise my egoic craving to charge at life and 'succeed' at *everything*. Showing up at 6am strength and conditioning sessions without getting a single wink of sleep had become somewhat normal to me, but my ability to maintain composure began to buckle. The Tara who used to be assertive on the court and demand more from her teammates, instead became quiet and paranoid; more concerned with not being caught out on last night's antics than progressing as an athlete who, up until now, had shown great promise. I'll never forget the feeling of total emptiness - both of physical energy and spirit - on those mornings I would sit in my car after training, sucking down a protein shake, my whole body convulsing, begging for life force to return to it.

"Tara, is everything okay?" my teammate asks me at training one morning, when I barely managed to wipe off my makeup from the night before. "Yeah totally." She raises an eyebrow. "I'm a little tired I guess." Her eyes say *bullshit*. "You look terrible. I'm worried."

And in the hair salon, after ripping into my second can of Red Bull for the morning, my colleague makes an observation, "Big night, Tara?" "How come?" I defend, forgetting the giveaway can of liquid energy in my hand. After he makes mention that my lips look a little bitten up, that my head's still moving to the beat of last night's soundtrack, and that maybe I could have gone to a little more effort to conceal the glaringly obvious (being that I'm very much still high), I spend my lunchtime in a toilet cubicle, crying with insecurity, feeling suffocated by the four hours that remain between right now and the moment my head finally - *finally* - hits the pillow. My key will turn in the door. My bag will hit the bedroom floor. I'll stand under the shower long enough to rinse the *gross* off me. And then crumble to pieces in bed. Bed. *Bed.*

As human beings programmed with an evolutionary impulse to grow and expand and desire; we are hard-wired perpetual students of the world. And I know you and I have only just met, but I've got you pegged as a *seeker*. Party Girls are seekers on the hunt for meaning, but we're also escapists. And time after time, we'll identify ways to disengage from or avoid pain completely, often using alcohol and drugs as our getaway vehicle. **Curiosity is the force behind the wheel.** It's the 'beginner's mind' that wants to learn for itself, give things a try and to, like, never miss out. On anything.

Imagine that your soul sits in a plastic container. When we're expanding, learning, joyful, present, when we're wide open, there's 'room' for your soul to bend and move; there's flexibility. Other times, the capacity of it outgrows its container until it's pushing up against the plastic walls with no room to free flow. Your fluid, transient energy becomes stagnant. This is the visual metaphor I use for curiosity. When my life situation as I know it has expired, when it's been tried and tested, and the walls of my container start to smother me in a claustrophobic way that threatens my sense of freedom, the only thing that has the strength to push the walls back some at distance is a willingness to see a life of what's possible beyond them. So I take a risk, and clamber up, and peek over the fence.

That's curiosity. *A strong desire to know or learn something,* as defined by the Oxford English Dictionary. That 'something' could mean anything from taking an astrology workshop, to making a three-course meal, to watching David Attenborough documentaries... Or in our case, discovering who we become when we climb the container walls and dive off into a world that feels freer and more daring as a Party Girl.

We raise our hands and ask questions, we trip, we fall, we make mistakes, we experiment, we have three-day benders and one-night stands because, as experiential beings, we want to *grow*. And much of our learning stems from our royal screws ups, whether we consciously acknowledge that or not. We want life to be a visceral, eye-opening affair that shows us what it means to be alive in this world; with heart beating, hormones racing, and brain ablaze. We're not taught how to effectively and purposefully appreciate life in this high def, 3D, blissed-out version. Not in school, or the trenches of university, or the corporate vortex. No way, Party Girl. You were taught to study hard, to work hard, to remember processes and systems and formulas and patterns. You were taught to behave, and to memorise information...

But the freedom that comes with embodying what makes you feel vivacious and grateful? Forget about that! Your unique gifts? What of them! Your essences – the specks of you that spring to effervescent life once acknowledged? Quit daydreaming kid, and get back to your algebra! *That's* what a full and brimming soul container looks like: when the ability to dream becomes ambushed by a nagging sense of compression and resentment sets in. So, we do the only thing we can do when we're on the precipice of imploding; we take a run up, and pole vault our asses over that wall into the spacious unknown, into an identity that we can create for ourselves, one we can influence with a little help from drinks, drugs, loud music and mysterious men with a twinkle in their eye. But here's where it gets juicy: **pursuing a high-risk lifestyle with reckless abandon can cause the outer edges of your soul to reach the very same edges of that plastic container.** Even audacious uncertainty can become boring if we spend enough time chasing it. During the thickest of my involvement with drugs and alcohol, circa 2007-2009, when I had completely abandoned my body in pursuit of unattainable pleasure, still, even then, lived a quiet curiosity within me.

:: *What could life be like if I woke up without ever having to feel this way ever again?*

:: *What would it be like if I didn't chase every gym session with a jug of beer?*

:: *What would it be like if I were with a man who adored me back?*

:: *What would my life be like if I liked - or maybe even loved - who I saw in the mirror?*

And the biggie:

:: *What does a good life full of energy, inspiration and ease feel like?*

This is universal, sister. You know yourself that it's not just me who's prone to stumbling through this game of What Ifs. You have too. It's the echo that materialised this book in your life. It's the force that demands you consider a different life for yourself. **Those two words are game-changers.** Here are some contemplations shared by some of my Peace Girls (girls who participated in The Party Girl's Guide to Peace program).

What would life be like if:

:: *I tried for what I wanted, loved who I wanted, and spent time with people who added to my life instead of robbed me of my goodness?*

:: *I respected myself?*

:: *I had the courage to say 'enough'?*

:: *I'd done this sooner?*

:: *I lived in the now, let go of the past and had no expectations?*

:: Comparison didn't exist?

:: I didn't self-destruct?

:: I had a dream or intention?

:: I could learn to love myself, and be proud of who I am and what I've achieved?

:: I woke up earlier each weekend with a clear head and healthy body, sans red wine hangover?

:: I truly loved myself and could really feel it in each moment?

:: I allowed love to be my guiding light and trusted it?

:: I allowed myself to play and lean into my desires?

And that's where *grace* lives; in that internal dialogue that suggests there might be a better way to do life; in the desire to walk out of the fog and into a wide open expanse of possibility and vibrant health; in gentleness and right little actions. And it lights you up with the spirit of enquiry while melting away the instinct to live life on a reckless edge. Grace allows you to flick the switch of motivation and seek your needs in another way. Let me put this differently: you will always, without a doubt, find a way to quench your thirst. The question moving forward is: *how?* Are you going to continue on with the same tactics and behaviour that brought you to these pages, or are you willing to lean into different strategies?

For me, over the years, instead of seeking the thrill from wondering 'what would happen if I double dropped those pills?' or 'skulled seven pots and a pint?' alternatives like these started taking over…

:: What happens if instead of running away, I stay with this man I love and work it out?

:: What if I honour my creativity and start a blog/paint a canvas/start dancing again?

:: What if I offer my time to women who need support and a sense of community in their life?

:: What if I go to the festival straight as an arrow?

:: What if I write a book about what I know to be true, in the hope I can contribute positively to the world?

These contemplations were risky business. They ignited the same sense of daring and uncertainty as a big night out, and in many ways, made me feel even **more** uncomfortable. But as a human with a heartbeat, challenge is what drives me - it's what drives all of us - and I wanted to taste the sweetness of progress. **Soulful risk-taking became my new drug.**

And so, this book is an invitation to start peeking over the fence again, to expand beyond your current limits, to ask *What If*. This time, though, instead of chasing quick fixes and falling prey to your autopilot impulses, we're going to allow purposeful rebellion to ride up front and lead the way.

Your curiosities got you here, Party Girl, and I'll be damned if they can't get you out. The key to cultivating peace via conscious choice is being just as curious about a life *without* your Party Girl identity as you were with it, before you were in the thick of it. You know what happens when your inquisitive nature takes the lead. You're a force to be reckoned with. You become creativity incarnate. You make your own rules, swerving right where you would normally ease left, jumping the hurdle instead of dawdling around it. You become laser-focused, and eager, and *all-in*. This is the energy I want you to embrace as you progress through this book You'll identify your longings, keep your eyes on the prize and use *that* desire, *that* brand of curiosity to course-correct as you go. You don't have to compromise your integrity, health and dreams by surrendering to the Party Girl mask anymore. We're going to make a statement by taking off the masks, slowly, one by one, with self-enquiry as the launch pad. And here's why: When you're making **considered decisions**, you become an active, awakened player in your life. You create beauty and significance in your reality simply by seeking it out, and choosing to dig for it. Actually, come to think of it, if you're looking to embody *any* type of identity, try this one of for size: Joy Hunter. My job is to inspire you to quit looking for it at the bottom of that bottle of vodka, and instead, freaking **bring it**! Curious folks have a sense of wonder in their eyes. They smile more. They are undoubtedly more beautiful. Those who approach life with a child-like sense of wonder, combined with a potent determination to live *well*, follow the joy - the real joy - the joy that accumulates in the heart and shines out into the world via belly laughs and happy tears. They marvel at their contradictions, rather than judge them.

It comes from within

Think you're more beautiful after a few wines? *You're not*. That beauty has forever been latent within you. Think you're more confident after downing a cosmopolitan? That poise has to come from somewhere. And I guarantee you it hasn't been hiding out in a cocktail shaker. That cocktail unlocks what is already within the bounds of your heart, but booze no longer has to be the key. We'll explore authentic, wholesome ways to experiment with your inner confidence, without alcohol. This does *not* require you to move mountains. We can take the size right out of the process and start where it's easy. Think you're more interesting after slipping on your Party Girl cloak? Here's a truth-bomb for you: you don't need a vodka in your hand for us all to see how fascinating you are. Carrying yourself without your habitual crutch will take resolution and gutsiness, but once *you* feel comfortable in that skin you're in, you'll exude magnetic presence. We're all spellbinding in our own sacred way, including you, and you will undoubtedly shine.

If you revel in the fact that you become more fun, easy-going, dynamic and hilarious while you're on the sauce, it's crucial to recognise that you *are* those very qualities without it. **I'm going to repeat that:**

It's crucial to recognise that you are those very qualities that you're ushering in during happy hour.

Contrary to what we might believe in the drunken moment, we don't get closer to our ideal selves when we're inebriated. We run further away from our essence, convinced that the pinot noir leaving a warm sensation in our bellies makes us sexier than if we were simply to make eye contact and smile. *Any half-awake human will tell you that eye contact and a smile are infinitely sexier than a boozed, inflamed Ego.* **We touch people with our presence, not our party tricks.**

Make a declarative statement

"I'm looking forward to more time for writing, reading, travelling, playing, creating; to having complete power over my choices, and finding more meaning and trying new things; to getting to know myself better and loving myself more", says Claire, a Peace Girl I had the pleasure of working with. She continues, "Imagine being comfortable enough with yourself and your life that you didn't need to get drunk to relax or have fun, to be yourself, to connect, to live and to love. Imagine finding that there is so much more potential for all of these things without booze. That's what I am excited about. Still a little scared, yes. But mainly, just crazy, mega, beautifully excited." *Amen, lady.*

Since declaring her intent (which, by the way, was clearly fuelled by curiosity), Claire's gone on to launch her health coaching business, as well as publish a popular blog (ThisIsLifeblood.com), which feeds her primal need for creativity and connection. She is also a self-care pioneer in the online world. I'm sure every time she presses publish on a blog post, she feels both electric and a little edgy (as I do when I publish mine). The pay-off is huge: **soul connection and service.** Bottom line? She still creates experiences in her life that offer up that pang of excitement, that flutter of uncertainty, but these days she's contributing to both the world and her own personal growth. It's meaningful, inspiring and sustainable. It's the stuff that makes the world go round.

Do this now!

Make your very own declarative statement:

_____

_____

_____

_____

_____

_____

A little note on following your highest held curiosities

Resistance, fear and the sonic _boom!_ of your Ego will inevitably come a-knocking. The more curious (and dedicated) you become about living a peaceful life, the more this detrimental trio will try to side-swipe you. We'll talk about these guys in a later chapter, but from the get-go, know this: every time one of these suckers attempts to seduce you into sabotage city, **take comfort in knowing that you're on the right track**. We resist what is _most_ important - what's sure to serve our higher selves - and this understanding can help us remember to use fear and self-doubt as corrective compasses. One of my mentors, Julie Parker, is known for saying: **if you're not peeing your pants just a little, you don't want it bad enough.** Fear is a blessing in this way. It shows up in our lives with an invitation to move through it and expand our experience, and thus build confidence and trust in our ability to grow.

What are you really thirsty for?

I'm looking up at my vision board; a colourful, organised collage of inspiration and longed-for opportunities. Central to this busy hub of sticky notes, manifestos and BluTac-ed oracle cards is a printed poster labelled: *Core Desired Feelings*. *The Desire Map* is an epic piece of work created by Danielle LaPorte, and few books have revolutionised my life as powerfully as this one. Her brain is stunning; her writing, poetic. And with strength and poise, she truly epitomises the essence of this book: purposeful rebellion. At the core of *The Desire Map* sits this one central question: *How do you want to feel?* Not "*What do you want to do with your life?*" or "*What do you want to achieve?*" or "*How much money do you want to earn?*" She guides us back into our bodies, asking us a powerful question that requires us all take a seat in our hearts, and hush.

Once you've narrowed down your ideal feelings to about three to six words, the idea is that you'll be able to reverse-engineer the goal-setting process and identify the fuel behind your ambition. With this approach, we're able to understand that making six figures isn't the goal - experiencing the core desire of feeling free, or abundant, or lavish (or whatever you've identified as essential) *is*.

This changes everything. Rather than waiting for the faraway goal that's perched five years into the future, we can instead check in with our core desires each and every day, and with creativity, generate experiences in *daily* life to ensure we're getting our needs met. If what we want is always attached to a core visceral longing (which it is), we can cultivate presence by ensuring we're feeling that way *today*, instead of months or years down the track. For example, let's say Anna's goal is to climb Mount Kilimanjaro. She's identified that central to this goal is a core desire to feel *Alive!* with a capital A. Rather than waiting for the great hike until she feels that way, she can instil her days with pursuits that flush her with endorphins of vitality: great sex, a beach run, maybe even a meditation. Of course, she will still pursue her original goal, but the point is she needn't wait for daily hits of aliveness.

I came out of my first Desire Map experience with six Core Desired Feelings: **free, brave, playful, lucid, open, blissful.**

Oh, shit! I think as I continue gazing at my vision wall; an epiphany hitting me square in the chops. I realise in an instant why I was plugged in so deeply to The Party. I wanted to feel *those* feelings. The very words that are helping me create a life worth celebrating today are the ones that had me digging for love in all the wrong places. What's one way to feel blissful, open, brave and free? **Get really, really, really high.**

You're going to get your needs met, but the question is: how are you going to approach the process? After discovering that you want to feel *beautiful*, are you going to polish off a bottle of red and bat your eyelashes, or are you going to instead be gentle and kind to yourself, and smile at your reflection in the mirror? **It's not the end goal you're chasing.** You crave the experience of progress, of forward motion, of crowding out those self-destructive behaviours with rich new habits that feel nourishing.

Desiring to feel better than you felt yesterday is a akin to tender prayer, and tidying up The Party chapter of your life cracks open your true potential. Life itself becomes less noisy. Your skin starts to glow. You discover passions that you feel compelled to pursue simply because your new catalyst for action is a drive to feel good and happy and grateful.

Before we move onto this chapter's Peace Practice, I feel the need to really drive this message home. **You'll find a way - somehow - to get what you want.** To feel the way you want to. *Always.* But moving forward, what's going to be your approach? What are going to place your focus and attention upon? A shot of tequila? Or a few minutes of energised breathing? A chocolate binge? Or a frolic in the ocean? A line of coke? Or an adrenaline-inducing, comfort-zone-expanding adventure (think: hiking, salsa, acro yoga)? Be creative here.

Party Girl, if you're willing to ride on into the horizon with the same levels of bursting curiosity that carried you here, the possibilities are limitless. Infinite joy, inspiration, light? You betcha. Saddle up, lady, and bring your greatest gift - your inquisitive spirit - along for the ride.

Peace Practice

What type of life do you want to give yourself permission to live?
In other words, why is this book in your hands?

What's stopping you from getting it?

From that list, what can you control?
For example: you can choose to surround yourself with different people, or refuse to stock wine or beer in your fridge, etc.

What landed you in The Party? What were your curiosity triggers?
For example: a longing to fit in and belong, rebellion, conditioning (following the example set by your parents, for instance).

What have you been searching for in The Party and through your Party Girl identity?

What have you been running from?

How do you feel when you take the first sip, or when you feel the drug coming on?

Or when you binge, numb or escape, regardless of how (reality television, food, shopping, any others).

What else can you do to feel that way, which instead supports your health and greater vision for yourself?

What positive emotions or experiences do you bring to others as a Party Girl?

For example: confidence, a sense of connection with your friends, bringing the party alive.

How else could you feel or experience these things?

What negative emotions or experiences do you bring to others as a Party Girl?

For example: erratic behaviour, withdrawal, aggression.

What will happen if you don't change?
I'm giving you more space to write here, intentionally. Go for broke. Connect in deeply with the cost of not changing.

What's possible for you if you do change?
Again, don't hold back. Think big and bright.

Peace in Motion

Make a vision board of the life you long to live.

Using the insights from above, get crafty and create a collage of images that evoke within you the sensations you crave. For the purpose of this exercise, forget about the life that you don't want, what holds you back, and what you wish didn't exist in your experience. Cast your mind out into the almost impossible, and with your gaze fixed steadily on the horizon, ask yourself this: what if it *were* possible?

Your body doesn't know the difference between you imagining something and you actually doing it. The same neural pathways in the brain fire off, and the same emotions are cultivated. That means creating a visual reminder of where you're going provides inspiration as well as a cosmic nudge to centre back into your heart's desires, and keep putting one foot in front of the other. So often we focus on what's missing. Our vision boards - especially when hung front and centre - encourage us to face forward.

Once you've created your vision, share it with me and your fellow Party Girls on Instagram by using the hashtag #highpeace and tagging me at @ tara_bliss.

Hopefully by now, you've got that sweet taste in your mouth of all that's within reach. Never forget how powerful it is for you to anchor into those feelings of possibility. When we remain optimistic, we keep moving forward, and it's important that you stay mobile, Party Girl. Stagnation at this point is a no-no. We're going for the deep plunge.

Now that we've dialled up your curiosity, we can pivot a little and investigate our fears, limiting beliefs, the behaviours and conditioning in our cells that hold us back…

2.

Party Girl,
Meet Your Demons

*"You will find peace not by trying to escape your problems,
but by confronting them courageously. You will find peace not
in denial, but in victory."*
J. Donald Walters

A dozen of us are sitting around, weary, wide-eyed and wired, having returned from the club a few hours ago. We're settling in for what I'll soon learn is a typical recovery session. Opposite me sits my brand new boyfriend (of whom I'm adoringly in awe). He's a man – a real man – not a boy like the others I've dated. He's popular and hilarious, with that perfectly perfect amount of goofiness in him for good measure. My appetite for him is insatiable. I simply can't get too much. He gives me just enough attention to keep me swooning, and keeps just enough distance between us to keep me desperately grappling for more. My very first drug, that's what he is. The pills and speed may have come before him, but I'll take this guy over the lot of it any chance I can get.

Combine said popular and super-charming boyfriend with a relatively new flirtation with drugs, and right now, as the sun creeps its way into the lounge room after a night of euphoric beats and awesome chats, I feel pretty spectacular.

But something's not quite right. I look over at him, and he's fiddling around with weird-looking paraphernalia that is unfamiliar to me. He's about to take some type of drug. Obviously. But… *which one*, exactly? He's using different tools and gadgets to what I'm used to seeing with these 19-year-old eyes of mine – which are still learning to adjust to this landscape – and seems more focused than I've ever witnessed him. He's anticipating something. I can tell because he simmers with enthusiasm. There's a pipe. There's a lighter. There's a wingman on hand, steadying his aim as he closes in on the contraption in his hand. What on earth is he smoking? *It's not heroin*, I think, doing my best with the few deductive skills I've gained up to this point in my life about how drugs are taken. *I wonder what is it, that white stuff that's turning to smoke in the pipe…*

My curiosity quickly turns to paled dread as I hear someone utter the word *ice*. A wave of recognition floods me. Despite knowing very little about ice (let's be honest, I know very little about any drug), what's uncoiling in my mind is an episode of *Oprah* that aired years ago, when I was a teenager. The episode featured families that had been torn apart by crystal meth, by *ice*, by that thing that my shiny new perfect boyfriend is currently smoking opposite me.

I look at him shyly, a little uncomfortable. He raises his eyebrows, and tilts the pipe my way, as if to say, "*Hey babe, want some?*" The shake of my head says, "*Nah, I'm good, thanks anyway though*". I feel a lump harden in my throat as I suppress the instinct that tells me I should pull him aside and give him a *Hey, that's stuff's really bad for you, you know?* talking to. Instead, I play it cool. All I know about drugs is that I very much like the ones I've tried. But as I sit cross-legged on the carpet, watching people I care about go back for hit after hit, I make an intuitive promise to myself to never, ever touch crystal meth. And not just because of what Oprah had said about it on TV. There's an unmistakable stirring within me. That stuff is bad. *Very bad.* I can just feel it.

Suffice it to say that the next two-and-a-bit years of my life were a rapturous and tumultuous few years with a man who had trouble deciding on whether he loved me or the pipe more. We were on. We were off. Hot and cold. All in, or nothing. And while I take full responsibility for my behaviour, which undoubtedly played a huge role in repelling him, it was also clear that meth was the pesky little prick that seemed to successfully keep us apart. Some days, when my ducks felt as though they were adequately in a row, I could manage my emotions with inner talk. *Chill Tara, it's all good. He's just having a little fun with his friends!* And that voice was right, because he *was* okay. His friends, the sweethearts that they were, were okay too. They'd dust themselves off after a long weekend, pull themselves together and head to work, as any other 'responsible' adult would. They were as perfectly functional as they could be for men in their mid-twenties who got high every weekend on one thing or another. They weren't junkies, and some days, that would be enough for me. With high hopes, I clung to the belief that sooner or later, they'd have a wake-up call; some type of glorious life-altering moment, and grow out of it. *It'd just be a matter of time, right?*

But other days, I swear I could have lit up the night sky with my rage. Anger would swell inside me as my meth GPS instinctively scanned the environment like a smartphone looking for wifi signal. I could tell when it was in the room, when he was on it, when he was on it and lying that he wasn't. I had an acute sense of it around me and often I'd harden into a rigid, frigid version of myself that I hated; a ferocious, numb creature who was silenced on the outside, but burning up within. It was the unpredictability of it all that drove me mad; his comedowns would sway between vulnerable episodes of cuddle cravings, and such stern *coldness* that he'd do well to not shoot me daggers with his eyes. He was secretive, absorbed, absent. The density in the room on the mornings of his bad comedowns made my heart heavy. He'd sit in front of the television with his arms crossed, a furrow etched into his brow. Sometimes, he would take himself off to bed without saying a word to me. So there I would sit, still high myself, in my boyfriend's lounge room; wired, exhausted, eerily alone in the quiet. I fucking hated him for it. I felt so unbelievably out of control. How the hell could I compete with a substance? Meth was sending *me* crazy, and I wasn't even the one smoking it.

While superficially this life chapter was fun and adventurous, and ultimately a great teacher, I struggled daily with this internal war. That was particularly difficult for me because, despite having landed myself in more than enough cheek, I've always held space in my psyche for the belief that deep down, right at the very core of things, I'm a good girl. There lived a concrete recognition that I'm a good person who deserves to feel loved. That greater awareness of myself has always lingered close by, some days nearer than others of course, but it's been relatively constant. It's the capacity within me that's allowed me to say *No* from a young age. I regularly flexed my No muscle when it came to boys, and later on, men. In fact, every sexual experience I've had (while not always being remembered), eventuated because at one point during the night, I'd made the decision that it was safe and that I'd have a good time. If sparks flew, *eureka!* We'd have a winner. If they didn't, I'd rather polish off a few bottles of red on my couch, solo. I've never allowed myself to feel obliged to act or behave (or put out) in a certain way.

When I was 11 years old and in sixth grade, I punched a dude. Actually, I seemed to be getting into fisty-cuffs regularly with pre-pubescent boys who were throwing around words like 'prostitute' and 'whore' – words that they couldn't define, but I could. "What did you just call me?" I'd snarl. They'd respond with, "You heard me." And, *bam*! Low kick to the balls!

Now, I'm not pro-violence, but I think it's worth mentioning that even as a young girl, I instinctively knew when lines of decency were being crossed. Despite being afraid of even being in the presence of boys – romantically – until I was 17, it seems I had no hesitation in telling them when their behaviour hurt me.

In year 6, I was the tallest of my grade, stick-thin and flat-chested. There were girls in my year level who had started wearing bras. Those who had started developing early obviously needed them. For others, I guess wearing a bra – no matter if it was just pieces of beige material sown together – was a coming-of-age novelty. I slid between the latter option and no bra at all. If there was a clean bra in my wardrobe, I'd wear one to school. If there wasn't, I'd skip it. No biggie.

So this one time, we're messing around at lunch time. I tuck my uniform top into my shorts before throwing myself into a handstand against the wall. The world as I know it transforms into an upside-down, back-to-front kaleidoscope of giggles. But not for long, because suddenly, I feel a pressure against my waist, a whoosh of air on my chest, and then I hear the laughter. I fling my legs down from the wall and quickly smooth my shirt back down, my face flushing with embarrassment and anger. Jake has just revealed my tiny 11-year-old tits to my entire class and I want to tearfully implode. Instead, I punch him in the arm, hard. *Don't fuck with me.*

At 16, same thing. I discover that my first boyfriend cheats on me, and although I feel insecure and heartbroken, I call it off immediately. Saying *see ya later* back then felt like a natural decision. That's what you say to people who hurt you, right? See ya later? Well, that's what I said time and time again, even to members of my family. Growing up in a challenging home environment taught me this. I left home at 16, worked a pizza job, and paid my own way through the final year of high school. *See ya later.*

If only Dad could see me now. His ambitious, independent, gregarious daughter, in love with a man who pulls out a pipe of crystal meth first thing on Monday morning. Staying put. Not saying *see ya later*.

My resilience was dissolving. My smarts were fading. That lanky, flat-chested, 11-year-old little girl had more courage in her than that 20-year-old young woman. I attached my sense of Self – my worth – to a man who I believed I wasn't good enough for. This wasn't the first man in my life that I placed upon a pedestal. And he most certainly wouldn't be the last. For fear of forging my own path and remaining aligned to my values (as skewed and slovenly as they may have been), **I instead rearranged my identity to fit into his world.** My lack of self-love and respect was mirrored back at me, via him, proportionally. I could play the blame game all I liked, but the truth was, I chose day in and day out to listen to and believe in the voice in my head that fed on my obsession with our relationship.

Here's one of the many memorable quotes by the late and great Steve Jobs:

"You can't connect the dots looking forward; you can only connect them looking backward. So you have to trust that the dots will somehow connect in your future. You have to trust in something – your gut, destiny, life, karma, whatever. Because believing that the dots will connect down the road will give you the confidence to follow your heart even when it leads you off the well-worn path; and that will make all the difference."

And that is exactly the reason why we *must* glance back and reconnect with our pains, our low points, our dark nights of the soul, while simultaneously trusting that everything ever written in our history was written with reason: to bring you here, to this time and space, where you have the capacity and inclination to reshape your destiny. You must identify the memories of your habits and actions that leave you feeling a little uncomfortable in order to raise the standards of your present moment, and that bright and vibrant future of yours. Such profound and life-changing lessons lie beneath every tear, hangover, break-up, comedown and meltdown from your past. And I truly believe that's the benefit of stepping back in time: to collect the gifts that we were unaware of back then, and leverage them in the now, in order to create a spectacular life.

In this chapter, you're going to have a Mexican standoff with your demons; with the memories, beliefs, conditioned behaviours and fears that you're not all that proud of, and would quite frankly prefer to avoid. We're going to reveal *why* we follow through with actions that sabotage our joy, and what those triggers are that have dictated your choices. And the best nugget of all is that we'll discover we are *not* our fears, *not* our insecurities, and that our past needn't have *any* control over our current experience. *Demons, be gone.*

What are you afraid of?

Who or what has hurt you? Who or what has let you down, betrayed you, ultimately brought you here? How did you lose yourself in The Party? Whose behaviour - your parents, your peers, the people you idolise - have you been mirroring? What price have you paid - financially, emotionally, physically - in devoting yourself to this lifestyle? Can you pull to mind memories that make you squirm and wriggle in your seat just a little? I bet you can. Heck, I certainly can. I've got a whole damn encyclopaedia in my psyche that I can draw upon whenever I need reminding why I've chosen this journey of peace-seeking.

No matter which way you turn, or which road you take, you'll inevitably front up to fears throughout your life. Some will be bigger and more distracting than others, some will be more valid than others, but there's no denying that fear has most likely been a constant companion of yours for a wee while now. If I were to take a guess, I'd assume that you're afraid of staying the same, and you're just as hesitant and unsure about the uncertainty of change. So, with a little input from women I've worked with over the years, let's look at these fears from both directions.

'I'm scared about putting an end to this lifestyle, because…'

:: *I don't even know who I am without this identity.*

:: *I'll risk losing the friendships I've worked so hard to cultivate.*

:: *I'm going to be judged. I'm going to feel like a loser. I'm going to feel misunderstood.*

:: *I'll be ostracised from all social events in the future.*

:: *What will I do with my time? With my life?! How the bloody hell do I have fun if I'm not partying?*

:: *I have no idea what's next for me. The uncertainty of the future rattles me.*

:: *I find a sense of comfort in alcohol/ drugs/name your poison.*

:: *I'll become boring. I don't want to live a beige life.*

As my friend Alice Nicholls would say: screw beige. The pilgrimage to peace is a bright and vivid one, one that vibrates life! That is if you *decide* for it to be. The fears listed above are nothing but sugar-coated gumdrops of dubiousness, designed to keep you stuck and stagnant. These doubts are a function of our mind that kick into gear when we desire change. They're the birthplace of resistance, a force that has the capacity to pause our wild and precious dreams, and jam on our visionary brakes, unless we muster the courage to see them for what they really are: pissy little doubts.

I don't mean to sound crass. I also don't mean to belittle the very beliefs that may well be responsible for many of your choices. My aim here is to offer up a new perspective. These fears are *never* as big, scary, significant or true as what we believe them to be. A little later on in this chapter, we'll play around with a few fear concepts, and get cosier with the fear-based presence within us; our Ego. For now, though, the aim is to lessen the potency of the *worries* in your life.

By the way, what if those fears weren't just pissy little doubts, but signposts to take action? If our fears are essentially myths (and *most* of them certainly are), then how would our lives be different if we understood that our fears spoke the exact *opposite* of the truth? What if we translated each and every fear with respect and patience? If we tapped into it, *really* listened to it, and instead of allowing ourselves to be sucked up into its black hole of misery and self-pity, we asked it: *What are you here to tell me?*

Now let's take a look at some fears that may manifest when we contemplate ignoring change.

'I'm scared to stay the same, because…'

:: *I've jeopardised my health long enough.*

:: *I've outgrown this lifestyle. I can't keep up. Something doesn't feel right.*

:: *I don't feel as though I'm being authentic.*

:: *There's got to be more to life than this.*

:: *My friendships aren't fulfilling me like they used to.*

:: *I barely recognise myself in the mirror. I feel so disconnected from myself.*

:: *I have nothing to show for myself. No savings. No fulfilling occupation.*

:: *I'm worried I'm developing an addiction/dependency.*

:: *I don't want to tread the same path as my mother/father/uncle.*

:: *I'm sick of putting my body through hell.*

:: *I worry I'll never cultivate an ounce of self-love.*

These fears, Party Girl, are different. These are the fears that come carrying enough gunpowder below them to blow up into real and sustainable change in a hurry. They're not fluffy little insecurities, but rather a call to action. These are the cries from the voice of grace within you; that soft murmur that nurtures you with whispers of *honey, enough is enough, you deserve better than this.*

You know that voice.

Formidable success strategist, Tony Robbins, would suggest that we all leverage these legitimate fears in an attempt to throw ourselves into *right action* that serves us on a soul level. And while I'm an optimist at heart, and I whole-heartedly believe in the power of positivity, I could not agree more.

> *"Pain is the ultimate tool for shifting a belief."*
> Tony Robbins

If you're ever going to choose to hang out in a state of fear, do yourself the favour of **fearing what may or may not happen if you stay the same.** Contemplate the opportunities that could pass you by, the passion and romance you may miss out on, the hikes through South America, the yoga in India, the body you could lovingly sculpt and design, the smiles and belly laughs that could go unexperienced, the sunrises you could miss, the gratitude that could swell from your heart after giving your love and presence and service to the world…

It's important that you know that you don't have to have reached your Holy Grail - your Mother Of All Goals - to feel a sense of happiness and achievement in your life. Our brains, our bodies - **they respond to progress, not perfection**. We respond with sheer delight and amazement when we take small steps towards our right paths, and the fears of what life could look like if we remain unchanged may be just the fuel to boost you towards *progress*.

Selling our Selves

Compromise. We're all too familiar with that word. Weekend after wasted weekend, we make decisions that compromise our joy based on a seedy and in-sidious presence within us that hinges our self-worth on popularity, status and material possessions. We *could* be operating at peak health, with high energy, but we compromise vitality to instead chase a sense of belonging that comes with choosing drinks and drugs as the glue that binds us together as people. We *could* be beacons of sprite and vigour by consistently prioritising a good night's sleep, but our FOMO trumps eight hours of ZZZs, any day of the week.

Who needs sleep when tonight may be the night you meet the guy, bust the move, rock the outfit, or scream *Oh My God It's Like Totally Our Song!* **at full volume?** And we compromise ourselves - our very being-ness - by pivoting away from our true essence, and toward a false perception of who it is we think we really are. We clamour for that identity, finding her at the bottom of each empty glass; a place that feels a little more comfortable, a little safer, a little easier. **Which ultimately makes it feel like a compromise worth making.**

Look, we're women. We want to feel good, we want to like what we see in the mirror, we want to feel like we belong somewhere, and we desire a sense *meaning* in our lives. The thing is, as we well know by now, we're willing to do almost anything to get it, even if it means believing this: *if I'm a Party Girl, then I'm more interesting, captivating and confident. I stand out. I'm accepted. I'm better.* That's one hell of a seductive proposition, particularly in the early stages of our Party Girl careers, but that feel-good feeling is fleeting at best and elusive at worst. **It's nothing but a hallucination.**

In her outstanding book *Sacred Contracts*, Caroline Myss introduces a conversation started by Carl Jung, about spiritual archetypes – the energetic patterns in us that create somewhat of a personalised spiritual blueprint. She believes that every one of us has something in common: we each have a Prostitute archetype. Now, before you tie your face up in knots, relax. Although Caroline's a force to be reckoned with, she's certainly not an 11-year-old jerk throwing around names she knows nothing about (unlike those poor boys who copped my knee to the groin). As a medical intuitive and psychic, this is her area of expertise. Here's an excerpt from *Sacred Contracts*:

> *"The Prostitute's core issue is how much you are willing to sell of yourself – your morals, your integrity, your intellect, your word, your body, or your soul – for the sake of physical security… She dramatically embodies and tests the power of faith. If you have faith, no-one can buy you. You know that you can take care of yourself, and also that the Divine is looking out for you. Without faith, however, you will eventually meet the price you cannot turn down."*

I suggest you go back and read that paragraph again, maybe even a third time. You might feel some memories bubble to the surface that resonate with Caroline's message about the Prostitute. And by the way, this doesn't necessarily have to link in with The Party. In fact, in her work, Caroline has noticed that the Prostitute reveals itself most in the woman who remains in an unloving marriage; in the man who refuses to take a risk and follow his heart, and instead stays put in a job that renders him miserable.

Personally, there are a few chapters of my life that spring to mind where I 'sold out' in the name of physical security. Such as:

:: *Giving up once-in-a-lifetime opportunities in order to tread down a safe path of certainty.*

:: *Silencing myself when what I really wanted to do was speak up!*

:: *Betraying myself by continually showing up for work positions that I was both over-qualified for and had outgrown.*

:: *Staying with a man who smoked a drug I was terrified of.*

:: *Taking a pay cheque over a much-needed rest.*

Remember, the Prostitute (as well as any emotion, experience, pattern or archetype that we perceive as 'negative') comes carrying beautiful gifts with her. As Caroline mentions, the Prostitute's gift is the gift of *faith*. When she has *faith* - when she believes in herself and her mission/path/visions/dream/ the possibility of It All - then nothing can buy her; not a round of drinks at the bar, not free entry into the club, not VIP backstage access, not even a million dollar bill.

Inspect your circumstances for a moment and ask yourself:

In which areas of my life am I compromising my worth? Where am I selling myself short? What price have I paid in the process?

So, the big question is: *why?* Why all this sabotage? Why all this beating around the bush if it's only drawing us further away from our purpose, soul truth, and unlimited joy?

Say hello to your Ego

I was 24 years old when Gabrielle Bernstein found her way onto my laptop screen. Her weekly video blogs on personal growth, Spirit and surrender resonated deeply with me, and I felt as though I'd found someone who understood how valuable and important it was for me to continue to aim true on my quest to clean up my life. We had a lot in common. She was a seeker. She felt compelled to help other women. And she was 25 when she turned her life around, transforming herself from drug addict to self-proclaimed Spirit Junkie, overnight. Today, she's been sober a decade.

What I found most fascinating and compelling about Gabby's videos, were her sermons on the Ego. Up until that point, like most people, I'd associated the word 'ego' with 'egotistical people' – those who displayed an air of arrogance, pigheadedness, self-centredness. Turns out there's more to the word 'ego' than I'd first thought, or heard about growing up. In fact, this tiny three-letter word is practically its own planet and as I soon discovered through plenty of research and self-enquiry, the cause of our suffering.

Attempting to summarise the Ego in the space of a chapter is a lofty task. After all, there are entire texts devoted to this strange and gripping construct of the mind. For the sake of brevity and potency, though, I'm going to break down the Ego for you by offering definitions and insights that speak to *me* the most, with the hope you'll resonate with them too. **The key to transcending the Ego is understanding who and what it is, what its functions are, and how it shows up in our lives.** Knowledge is power, and when we become clued onto its motives and tactics, we can rise above *any* adversity and struggle.

First, some 'definitions' of sorts: **Wikipedia will tell us "Ego is a Latin and Greek work meaning 'I', often used in English to mean the 'self', 'identity', or other related concepts."**

I digest this as understanding the Ego as our *sense* of Self, the sense of who we think and believe we are. For example, if I say to you, "I'm hurt", or "I'm offended", or "I'm frightened", I'm referring to my Ego. You may have heard of the term 'a bruised ego'. The Ego is the part of psyche that has a propensity towards being 'bruised', and also offended and jealous and fearful, among many other states. The Ego is the *I* that this world needs to recognise; it's the identity we need to craft in order to relate to people, to connect on some level, and to give ourselves significance. For example, Tara the yogi. Tara the wife, the life coach, the author of *High: A Party Girl's Guide to Peace*. The Ego is not, in essence, who we *really* are at the core of it all.

One way you can quickly recognise egoic thoughts, behaviours and patterns in your life is by remembering that **the word 'Ego' can be used as an acronym for 'Edging God Out'**. If our thoughts and actions aren't aligned with what's right for us at a soul level, if our motives aren't loving and considered, if we find ourselves focusing mostly on the Self, rather than on service and contribution, we can be assured that we're 'edging God out'; that we're defying our true nature. And just a heads up: there's absolutely no need to panic if you've been edging out a whole heap of godliness. Each and every moment is an opportunity to refocus; to change your perspective. As *A Course in Miracles* says, **"A miracle is a shift in perception".** Nothing more, nothing less. And I think that's pretty rad. We quite literally get a fresh slate to work from every moment.

Now, let's dive into some characteristics of the Ego.

1. It's time-bound.

Best-selling author and spiritual teacher, Eckhart Tolle, teaches us that "the Ego is a dysfunctional relationship with the present moment". That Post-it-Note-worthy sentence has quite literally reshuffled the way my brain works. Whenever I find myself indulging in the past, or future-tripping over what may or may not happen, I know that I've absent-mindedly drifted into my Ego. Just as darkness cannot exist in the light, neither can the Ego exist when our attention rests in the present moment. When we are present and mindful - when the totality of our awareness is on the task/conversation/experience at hand - we're our truest, most open selves. When we allow our mind to *use us,* rather than consciously *using it*, we're allowing our Egos to pull us back into the pain of the past, and tug us forward into the anxiety of the future. The Ego thrives on timelines, deadlines, unmet expectations, and five-year plans. Your soul (or whichever elevated concept sits well with you), on the other hand, knows that the buffer of time is a myth; that it's simply a construct that allows us to process our human experiences; a tool that brings some relativity to the shape of our lives.

2. 'The Ego is, quite literally, a fearful thought' - Marianne Williamson

Just for a moment, think about how fear shows up in your life. What does it feel like? Where does it live in your body? And what situations trigger it? Let's be honest for a second here, because fear isn't just reserved for those grandiose, heart-pumping dreams, or those few seconds before you launch yourself off a bungee bridge. So often, it's the small stuff that gets us sweating. For many of us, it's the day-to-day discomforts that open the fearful floodgates in our physiology, resulting in anything from butterflies in the tummy, to nervous-ness, to social anxiety, to full-blown paranoia. These emotional responses or experiences that seemingly plague you are *not* who you are. You are not defined by them. Fear is to the Ego, what Love is to the Soul. Fear is the Ego's lifeblood, its oxygen, its diet. It is quite literally what feeds and nourishes it. **How fearful you are in your life is directly proportional to the extent to which you identify with your Ego.**

Let me say this another way: if you believe the voice of limitation and dysfunctional fear in your mind, you'll be manifesting fearful experiences on a moment-to-moment basis. When the Ego says 'I'm not good enough', and you believe it, not only are you are living fearfully, but you'll proceed to seek out evidence that proves that statement correct. When the Ego says 'I'm never going to be able to turn my life around', and you believe it, you'll continue to live in fear of your future, and again produce evidence that will keep you stuck in your current patterns. Fear – in its very essence – is *limiting*. It is not *expansive*, like the soul. The Ego uses fear to put a lid on everything, a barrier, a glass ceiling.

By now, you might be thinking, *well, fuck, I'm screwed.* But let's remember for a moment the fundamental teaching here: the Ego represents the opposite of the truth. With this optimistic and solution-focused approach, we recognise that our fears offer us opportunities to break through thresholds and grow as experiential human beings. We learn to accept that it's not our fears that shape or determine our lives, but the ways in which we respond to them. And for that very reason, I reckon we can all cultivate at least a smidge of gratitude for the Ego. In my own practice, I have even learned to love, appreciate and bless that Ego presence in me - it is what makes me feel human and complex. It is the reason I keep seeking.

As Mastin Kipp, the founder of *The Daily Love*, teaches: fear is simply a compass showing us where to go. In other words, when we notice our fears, and lean *into them* with courage and the full awareness that they are *not* who we are, we reshape our destinies. If it helps, **think of them as a pain-in-the-ass reminder that you're onto something very, very good.**

3. It thrives on separation and comparison.

'Oneness' is not a concept that the Ego can deal with. Oh, no. It would much rather take a big old fat slab of 'separation' and wedge it between you and as many people as possible. What might this look like? Take your pick:

:: *Comparing your body to the midriffs that are filed under the #fitspo hashtag on Instagram.*

:: *Giving that girl a once over at the club and deciding that, yep, actually, you are hotter than her.*

:: *Feeling resentful that you don't have as many Facebook likes as others in your industry.*

:: *Instead of admiring and celebrating the success of someone, you choose to think thoughts like, "That's just not possible for me. Why does she have such an incredible life, while mine's so boring and unfulfilling?"*

:: Avoiding eye contact with the homeless person on the street.

:: Idolising someone who you deem 'better' than yourself.

:: Deeming yourself 'better' than others.

The lesson here is that when you find yourself comparing yourself to another, becoming infatuated with a certain somebody, or placing either yourself or someone else on a pedestal, the Ego has stepped in.

The journey back into Peace teaches us to see *ourselves* in everyone we cross paths with. Peace will ask that we become more compassionate, loving, and celebratory of the good fortune of others. The soul recognises that the light in someone else reflects the light that resides within us, and it also acknowledges that what negatively triggers us in another *is present within us.* When we judge others, or separate ourselves from humanity (either 'positively' or 'negatively'), we've made the detour into Ego territory. (More on this is chapter seven.)

4. The Ego has one hell of a poverty consciousness.

Your soul is all kinds of radical - limitless, all-loving, ever-present, illuminated by light. **Its vibration is one of abundance**. The Ego on the other hand doesn't jibe with abundance and possibility; its native tongue is one of limitation and scarcity, which isn't at all helpful if you want to create an awesome life. If you've got dreams of becoming a coach (like I had), your Ego may pipe up with mantras of, *"There's too many coaches out there, why even bother?"* Or *"Who the bloody hell would be silly enough to pay **me** to be their coach?"*

As you might have guessed, scarcity thinking (otherwise known as poverty consciousness or a lack mindset) is acutely linked to separation and comparison. If I compare myself to you, essentially, that means I've decided that I'm competing with you. Then if you and I are in competition, one of us must win and the other must lose. One of the Ego's roles is to try to convince you that there's simply not enough to go around. And let it go on the record right now, that is bullshit. The world really is your oyster and it's ripe for the harvesting. **Competition is a myth**. We're not talking about winning 100-metre sprints here, we're talking about living a good life! Get it out of your head quick smart that you'll be unable to reap your dreams; or more accurately, acknowledge that these thoughts are simply egoic distractions. Notice them for what they are, breathe them away, and remember we live in an abundant Universe with unlimited resources.

5. Gimme, gimme, gimme! (The Ego always wants *more*).

So everything I just mentioned about the Ego believing there's never enough? It's for the very reason that, when it finds something it likes, something it can sink its teeth into and lose itself in, it goes bananas in ensuring it can get lots of it. And fast! Think about that tray of shots that came your table's way that night. Were you not one of the first to slam yours back in the hope that there might be an extra one sitting there with your name on it? Were you ever the first to nosedive back into those lines of coke on the coffee table. I know I was? What about the guy? You know the one. The stud you became infatuated with. The guy you kept going back to for more, more, more. And no matter how many times you quenched your thirst, you could never quite scratch the itch good and right. Addiction, obsession and compulsion are all Ego behaviours and patterns. Behaviours and patterns that can be disrupted and dissolved with awareness, and a willingness to do the inner work. To illustrate what I'm talking about here, this is an awesome excerpt from Steven Pressfield's incredible book, *The War of Art:*

> *"Have you ever wondered why slang terms for intoxication are so demolition-oriented? Stoned, smashed, hammered. It's because they're talking about the Ego. It's the Ego that gets blasted, waxed, plastered. We demolish the Ego to get to the self."*

In other words, **we lose ourselves in an attempt to find ourselves**. You mightn't barely be able to stand your own company sober, but baby, send over a few glasses of killer vintage, and you're fabulous! That right there is the carrot that the Ego dangles; a seductive trap that lulls you into a false sense of happiness and contentment.

Now, before we attempt to set fire to our Egos, it's important to note that any attempt at eradicating it, conquering it, or beating it to a bloody pulp is flat-out foolish. If you take that approach, you will undoubtedly fail, because guess what? Declaring war on the Ego is nothing but the Ego declaring war on itself! Love doesn't fight. Your soul doesn't throw spears to the heart. The Universe isn't a battlefield. So instead, you can lessen the grip that the Ego has on your life by **becoming aware of it, and choosing loving, high-vibing, heart-centred thoughts and actions** instead. We're more potent when we put our energy into actively working on better, more productive ways to respond to doubt and worry. Imagine if you could welcome the arrival of fear with a greater understanding that its very showing up in your life is a suggestion that it's time for you to play bigger! After all, were it not for the fear-stained Ego, how on earth would we know what **courage** feels like?

I understand all too well that right now you might be feeling frustrated, alienated, alone, confused, fed up, defeated, curious, unsure, foggy, empty, and like something's missing. These emotions breed revolutions, sister. So consider yourself in a position of remarkable power. **You are in the right place.** You *are* in the right place. I know you have regrets about where you've been. And I know you have fears about this lifestyle shift; about what may or may not lie ahead of you. But I also trust that you're inspired and willing (and hopefully, after the last chapter, curious as all hell). And right now, that is one of your most effective tools moving forward - your sheer determination to get high on the good stuff.

Before moving onto the next chapter, settle in for the Peace Practice below. It's going to help you shift your perspective of what my dear friend Melissa Ambrosini would call your inner 'Mean Girl', in a profound and incredibly gentle way. I don't want you to fall prey to the Ego any longer, lady. It doesn't have to be that way. With awareness, our Egos are an asset, a guide, a teacher. We just need to unpack it a little and get to know it a little more intimately...

Peace Practice

What are you afraid of?

Grab a pen, take a few deep breaths, and without judging yourself or censoring your answers, stream-of-consciousness riff as you finish these sentences. Again, just to remind you, allow this to be a No Judgment Zone. One of my yoga teachers, Darci, once told me, "The more you realise you have work to do in your practice, the more you progress". What she meant was: do not be afraid of the journey ahead, because it's laden with sweetness.

'I'm scared about putting an end to this lifestyle, because…'

'I know that these fears are downright ridiculous, because…'

'If I use these fears to drive me, call on my courage, and create change in my life, the possibilities are endless. Could it be true that I may indeed be able to...?'

Unravel your dreams and longings here. For example: you might be able to save for that round-the-world trip, invest your newfound energy in starting your own business, improve your health and run a half-marathon...

What price have you paid, Party Girl? Name the relationships that have been built on the foundation of drugs and alcohol? Give specific names.

For example: Sarah and I met at a party and every time we meet, there's alcohol involved.

What dear friendships have dissolved from your life as a result of you detouring into the Party-perfect illusion?

For example: I turned my back on those friends I cherished in high school. I judged them and thought that they weren't fun enough to spend time with.

What travel opportunities have been stifled with the expense of your favourite cocktail or drug?

For example: I've been saying for years now that I've wanted to backpack Central America. Though I always give the 'no money' excuse, I seem to always come up with the cash for a wild weekend.

What precious time have you sacrificed?

Think: experiences, special occasions, good times you truly regret missing out on.

Can you recall any moments in your life that left an 'I just sold my soul' taste in your mouth?

Let's reel this back in, re-calibrate, and face forwards, by crystallising a set of beautiful new intentions.

I would like to see, do and experience…

I want to attract people in my life who…

I want to spend my money on…

I want the relationships in my life to be rich with…

I want to feel in my body like I'm…

When I wake up in the morning, I want to feel naturally...

When I look in the mirror, I want to believe...

I want to celebrate my body by...

Accepting and Transcending the Ego

My Ego's name is...

By giving her a name, you're acknowledging that she's not your true nature. (Try to avoid giving her an awful or offensive name - that'll only cultivate inner tension. Keep it light and bright - a name that won't trigger you.)

Her anthems go a little something like this…

For example: 'I'm not good enough'. 'I'm not pretty enough'. 'I don't deserve to be happy'. 'Just one more drink…'

Her mission is to ensure that I…

For example: compare myself to other women, sabotage my health, wake up hungover on a Sunday morning.

I understand that [name of your Ego] is just a cry for help. If she speaks a language of opposites, then I can choose to translate her like this…

For example: a mantra of 'I'm not good enough' is a signpost that I need to cultivate worthiness from within, rather than seek validation from the outside world.

When I acknowledge that [name of your Ego] is *a part of me*, but that she is *not* me, I feel…

For example: relieved, surprised, grateful.

Moving forward, instead of indulging in the Ego's criticisms, believing her, and getting swept up into her world, I can lovingly silence her, by...
For example: saying internally, 'I choose to see this differently', or 'Thanks but no thanks'. You might simply breathe away her voice and instead focus on how your heart feels, rather than what your mind says.

If I dig deep enough, I can find instances in my life to be grateful for my Ego. These memories come to mind...
For example: she has a great fashion sense. She loves ambition, and achievement- without her, my life would actually be kind of boring!

My Ego is one of my greatest gifts. Here's why:
For example: she's my greatest teacher. She gives me an opportunity to practise radical, sweeping self-forgiveness every day. She allows me to become more courageous. If I listened to what she said and never tried to 'prove her wrong', I'd never overcome my fears.

One of the most important things I can do with this book is to help you fully grasp and understand that you are *not* the voice in your head. This chapter has given you the fundamentals of recognising the Ego, but in the chapters that follow, we'll widen our lens and reveal the stealthy ways in which it can burn us out, and send us into a tailspin of upside-down priorities. Let's nip all that in the bud.

3.

The Candle Burning
At Both Ends

*"It is our best work that God wants, not the dregs of our exhaustion.
I think he must prefer quality over quantity."*
George MacDonald

Work hard, play hard; the motto of those who - with a balls-to-the-wall attitude - throw themselves at life, taking no prisoners, making no excuses. That was me; an oblivious, wired, burnt-out hot mess. I'm not entirely sure how I found the time, let alone the energy to party most nights of the week, while working two jobs and training full-time as an athlete, but my guess is that I was tapping into some serious adrenaline reserves. I thought that by *cramming* I was living a balanced life. I could enthusiastically tick *exercise, hard work* and *social fulfilment* from my checklist. Delirium felt… kind of… *normal*, I suppose.

One thing's for sure: jugs of beers and lines of speed **were my reward system**. My Ego loved to beef-up on feeling bigger and better than I did when I was straight. It had me convinced that, since I was such a gosh-darn hard worker, then dammit, I deserved to let my hair down. Sound familiar?

Weekends were the biggest test of my determination. I'd roll out of bed on Friday morning, my mind overcast and heavy from Thursday night drinks, and I'd dress for work with an unmistakable sense of dread in my belly. On the weekends, I pushed myself to a place even I didn't feel comfortable, but I somehow always managed to justify that the reward - Sunday night - would be worth it. After hairdressing all day on a Friday, I'd scurry to an inner city bar and clock on at 6pm, finally finishing my work shift once the sun had set and risen again at 6am. After a few knock-off drinks, I would step out into the sun, my corneas feeling frazzled in the brightness of the morning, and drive myself home, sleepily. I can still so vividly remember what it felt like to stare at the wall in my shower, my knees aching from bearing the weight of me for close to 24 hours, the water against my shoulders rocking me in and out of micro-sleeps as I'd stand there, in a half-conscious trance, not quite believing that it was time to pull myself together, slather a thick layer of foundation atop the bags under my eyes, find my way to work, and do it all over again.

Saturdays were manic and stressful. Fully booked. Fully frantic. Often I'd have five or six clients in the salon at once - one with a head full of foils, one waiting at the basin for a toner, a few waiting for blow waves, and a couple more that were being welcomed and seated. The weight of the responsibility not only to manage my time and do my job properly on zero sleep, but to cradle the importance of everyone else's physical appearance (pretending as though I actually gave a shit) was enough to make me wish that snapping my fingers would render me invisible. On those days, there was barely enough time to skull a chai latte or chew through a few sticks of liquorice, let alone take a moment to catch my breath.

I'd race out of the salon at 5:30pm with a *thank God that's over!* groan, and begin mentally preparing for yet another sleepless night. Switching environments from the salon to my bar-tending job energised me temporarily, but by midnight, my knees were swollen, my eyes glazed over and my whole body creaking in agony. The words that fell out of my mouth were indecipherable to customers and workmates alike, so I would resort to communicating via eye contact. But by that time, I was almost there. *I can do this.*

There I was again. Another 6am knock-off. Another burn-the-eyes sunrise. Drinks sometimes settled the aches and pains. By the time I made it home, I was so entirely depleted that it was impossible to get to sleep. At home, I lay semi-paralysed on my bed, staring through the spinning fan into nothingness on the ceiling. I've never been diagnosed with anxiety, depression or chronic fatigue, but in those moments, when it felt like my chest was caving in, when it felt like a 50kg rock was inhabiting my skull, when I couldn't feel myself from my waist down, in *those* moments, I was concerned for myself. Tired tears would find their way down my cheek until finally I'd fall into a few hours of disturbed slumber.

It was the whisper of my reward that would wake me. Sunday; the most gorgeous, most perfect day that represented the end of my hairdressing slog from hell, the day I was allowed to sleep a little, and the day that my people and I congregated for yet another instalment of belligerence and memory-making. It was time to reap my reward for being such a hard-working, contributory citizen of the world. (Ahem.) **It was time to wipe myself out.**

The pain becomes the pleasure becomes the pain: that just about sums up my lifestyle in my early to mid-twenties. Whether you can relate to my story in giant doses or little glimpses, I bet that you can resonate with the vicious circle of buying into a reward system that chews you up and spits you out, leaving you feeling grotty and frazzled and disconnect from your body. Which brings me to this next story; one that, today, leaves me scratching my head with an *I can't believe I did that* look on my face. Despite jeopardising my health every which way possible, **I still expected my body to perform and look the way I thought it ought to.** Stacking up my physique against the fitness models in the magazines was a war I couldn't win, but by hook or by crook, I would try. My diet was governed by the statistics in those magazines: perfectly portioned strips of lean chicken breast, no-fat Greek yoghurt, low-carb everything and tinned tuna were the staples of my diet. High-sugar fruit juices were replaced with litres upon litres of Diet Coke. When the whole aspartame issue broke out, causing a ruckus (aspartame is a neurotoxic artificial sweetener added to 'sugar-free' foods), I distinctly remember telling a friend of mine, *"Whatever - I'd rather get cancer than be overweight".* Gulp. I can all but hope that the inner work I've done since then – on my body, mind and approach to life – has erased that noxious statement from the Be Careful What You Wish For archives of The Universe.

It gets worse. Every Tuesday morning I would meet my personal trainer at my gym in the city for a Coming To God 30-minute session of blood, sweat and tears. Most days I'd wobble out of there, drunk on fatigue, and dying for some food to raise my blood sugar. Carrie whooped my ass each and every time. She was one of the best trainers around, often entering into body building competitions, which in itself was a huge, inspirational display of discipline and determination.

But she also liked to party. We shared stories of messy nights out, and I was curious about her approach, seeing as she was so strict and regimented with diet and training. Even I knew that boozing opened the floodgates for a caloric catastrophe, and that drugs suppressed the metabolism, essentially meaning that even though a body laced with narcotics can go days without eating, when it does eventually get fed, it grabs a hold of any nourishment, and holds on for dear life. This, of course, is not at all conducive to ripped muscles and a dangerously low body fat percentage. Was Carrie one of those kooks who could have a rad time on the town while straight as an arrow?

No, it turns out she wasn't. "We take GHB when we go out", she explained to me. I repeated this novelty with a question in my voice. "Yeah, some people call it fantasy…" she said. Her voice hushed a little so no-one in the gym could hear her. Hold on. What? I'd heard of this. *Fantasy fucks people up*. That's what went through my mind. *Like, for real.* "Isn't that dangerous?" I ventured. She explained that it could be, but not if you 'took it right'. A certain amount at the right time would make you feel super-drunk, but without the calories; then because it didn't mess with your metabolism, apparently you still had an appetite to eat. "So it's perfect", she concluded.

And just like that, my friends. *Boom! I was sold.* It's at that point Carrie casually dropped in that GHB was also commonly known as the date rape drug. Thanks to the *Six O'Clock News*, it turned out I knew more about 'G' than I initially realised. *This* was one of the drugs that sexual predators slip into the drinks of innocent, distracted women. And yet - and yet - I was so naive, and so extraordinarily tunnel-visioned, that I was already convinced I wanted it in my life. At that time, Carrie was also good friends with my housemate, who revealed himself as a fan of G too. Not only was this new-to-me drug exciting and easy to access, but it turned out my housemate was distributing the stuff. *Could this be any easier? My stars are lining up.*

I was sound asleep one night when I received a text from Carrie at 1am. "Hey, we decided to go out tonight. Have stuff for you if you'd like to try it?" I shot out of bed like lightning and raced into town for what would be the first of a series of encounters with GHB. No matter that I was tearing my boyfriend a fresh asshole for dabbling in crystal meth - here I was downing one of the date rape drugs just so I could achieve optimal metabolic function and wake up without a hangover. *Fun!* **Can you smell the almighty stench of that hypocrisy?!**

It wasn't my 'drug of choice' by any means, but like so many of the choices I made during my time in The Party, I took it in an attempt to fit in, to belong somewhere, to expand my comfort zone. And to some extent (though I wouldn't blame you scoffing at this), I respected G; this was not a drug to take lightly. All it would have taken was 1ml too much or an extra half a glass of wine to make it a killer cocktail. And you'd be a goner. *Dead.* Thankfully, and with my hand on my heart in a gesture of gratitude and relief, I turned my back on G before any real harm was done. Looking back, it disturbs me that the woman I paid to train my body and make me stronger would take me under her wing and apprentice me on new ways to get high. Then again, as anyone who has a leg up will tell you, the fitness industry is rife with debauchery. And besides, it was *me* who asked Carrie about this drug. It was me who said, "I want to try it". And it was me who put the cash in her hand. She, like me, was just another 20-something out there following the scent of fun. She was on the hunt for herself. She was just trying to find her feet in the world, and for that, I have compassion.

But for the love of all things holy, why on God's green earth do we make delirious decisions such as these? I've always identified as a 'health nut'. Why, then, wasn't I making choices that aligned with the lifestyle that accompanies that identity? Rather than choosing to make simple, holistic choices for the sake of my health, I instead hunted down ways in which I could maintain my lifestyle, without having to 'sacrifice' a thing. I sniffed out the danger. I sprinted for the shortcuts. I prioritised the Quick Fix, rather than establish a sturdy foundation of *real* health.

In the last chapter, we spoke about the energy of compromise. We're going to dive a little deeper now and… **take an inventory on our current reward system**, because I'm curious about something. Do we catch onto the scent of an excuse to party and then leverage it, making it the headline act of our week? Do we set our sights enthusiastically on the weekends because we believe we're worthy of letting our hair down as reward for being 'well-behaved' all week? Do we run those miles, make our green smoothies, take our vitamins and read *Women's Health* magazine to feel a little better about our bingeing? I suspect – at least in my case – that we oscillate between all three. Partying for the sake of partying. Partying for the sake of relief, celebration, reward. And exercising, detoxing and diet-hunting for the sake of guilt-diminished partying. **What a vicious cycle of Ego mania.** Being the media-affected, impressionable beings that we are, particularly as women, you'd be hard pressed to blame us for getting our approach to wellness so severely warped. We've done a great job in creating a pretzel out of the process. Tell us to quit eating gluten, and we'll take the bread off our plates. Tell us that Pilates lengthens our legs and tones our asses, and we'll drag those very asses to the studio. (We may even set our alarm for it.) Tell us to achieve and to please, and we'll excel in the workplace, regardless of whether we're fulfilled or not. We will willingly switch from coffee, to green tea, to green juice. We will take pride in our superfood-laden oatmeal recipe. We will dabble in meditation, and renew our gym memberships, and recite the odd positive affirmation. But at the price of the loose, rambunctious girl we become after the clock strikes five on Fridays? Our self-care regime becomes redundant as we flush our cells with a fresh bunch of toxins. We juggle identities in an attempt to have our cake and eat it too. The rules change. *I've worked so hard. It's time to let my hair down. I deserve this.*

Riddle me this, Party Girl: **Why the healthy Monday to Friday choices?** Your response will undoubtedly land at this: **I want to feel good.** And of course you do. We all do. But hovering ever so close to the desire to feel great is a motivation to **look good.** And so it should, right? We want to feel and look radiant and beautiful and fresh. And it's our birthright to feel that way! Femininity and beauty expressed is perfection. The deal is though, when you're *externally motivated* to create *any* result, whether it's to do with your body, creativity, relationships, or anything else, rather than *intrinsically inspired*, you enter the chasm of comparison. The fray of frustration. The never-ending labyrinth of Not Good Enoughs. You'll continue to weigh up your experience against the measuring stick that you've created; an expectation you've placed upon yourself, which dictates how you should look, live, behave. Then we spiral into harmful waves of jealousy and inner judgment. This does *not* help us to live a celebratory, peaceful, contented life. Plus, it's *exhausting*. It's no wonder we look to the glass as our saviour. We're tired! We're over it! We've had enough. And dammit, we know that when we take that first sip, the day beneath us will dissolve under a cosy blanket of nourishment; warming us from the inside out. But here's where we get a little honest with ourselves. Truthfully now, how long does that nourishment and comfort last? I'm willing to wager an answer of just one single sip. Two, max. **The first sip is always the sweetest.** It feels like a deep breath; like the butterflies in your belly are starting to settle; like the muscles in your body and loosening their grip to the bone; like a weight is pleasantly melting off your shoulders as butter would; like a tsunami of relief. **Thank God the day is over.** That feeling, we can all sympathise with, but it's not the longing for nourishment, or the sweet taste we sensed in our first sip. Nor is it the freeing feeling of *relief* that keeps us going back for glasses four, five and six. **It's the habit of the thing**. It's our inner saboteur. It's that egoic presence of fear and escapism.

Remember how one of the distinctions we made about the Ego was Eckhart Tolle's brilliant one liner, "The Ego is a dysfunctional relationship with the present moment"? On most occasions, we reach for the drink when we decide to not feel the experience of the Now. What would it be like if we could completely shift perspectives? What if our motivation to create nourishing routines wasn't governed by external conditions, but rather an inherent yearning for inner peace? What if *"I am ready and willing to do what it takes to love myself"* became a guiding statement of yours? Can you even imagine the ripples you'd leave in the ether upon committing to the belief that - *oh yeah, that's right, I remember now* - **living life is about *loving* life**?

Maybe we could tear down our reward system – which at this point is nothing but a hamster-wheel of bingeing and deprivation – and start over, this time planting it in fertile, organic soil, making it easy and fun for us to experience joy and celebration without abandoning our health. Maybe we could create some space between the distractions that inhabit our psyche. I'm talking the number of kilometres we can run, the volume of the music that's blasting in our headphones, the repetitions of squats we can manage, the calorie counting, the endless To-Do Lists. When we allow most of that noise, and many of our alter egos to melt away, we're left with a woman (you, me) who perhaps doesn't quite recognise herself anymore. And even though she can identify what she wants out of life, she's unsure of what she *needs* these days. And even then, if she does have a greater awareness of her needs, she's terrified of the climb ahead of her. The gap between here and there? It's too great. There seems simply too much hard work ahead. It feels intimidating when the very thought of embodying freedom and true self-acceptance appears light-years in the future.

I understand, sweet thing, because I've been there. I commiserate with that feeling of being stretched too thin, of knowing what you want out of life, how you want to feel, what you want to experience. Yet somehow, you're not quite able to press the 'pause' button. Here we stand, stifled by dreams that we don't believe we deserve. The first thing we must do in this instance is quit chasing down dreams that belong to others, for fear of designing our own.

As someone who's been blogging for years, I can't tell you how many times I've been asked, either via email or interview questionnaire: *"Can you share with us your morning routine?"* and *"What does a typical day in the life of Tara look like?"* This worries me. It's these types of Perfect Day templates that smother women in guilt and shame, as they compare the messiest moments of their days with the sparkliest snapshots offered in a perfectly edited preview from Internet Person. My job is to inspire, not to teach lifestyle blueprints, which is why I make a habit out of answering such questions with transparency and non-glossed truth. Yes, I have learnt to cultivate an extraordinary relationship with myself through the practice of nourishing routines and healthy reward systems. But I also live a perfectly imperfect life, and some days, I barely manage to clothe myself properly, let alone make it to my yoga mat. And that's the beauty of life – taking each day as it comes and checking in with yourself, rather than falling victim to a rigorous To-Do List of 'shoulds'.

On that note, one of the most powerful decisions you can make on your Peace Pilgrimage is to shun the word 'should' from your vocabulary. It's a terrible, terrible word, which will completely hinge your expectation of yourself on the choices others are making in their lives. Not only is that unsustainable, but it's hell for your nervous system. As we established earlier in this chapter, it's a shortcut to feelings of failure, self-loathing, and exhaustion. Have you ever noticed that you don't say 'should' when you feel spiritually compelled to do something? You say it when you're measuring the difference between your life and that of your contemporaries (or celebrities, or the media). **You say it when you're failing to meet your own (unrealistic, abrasive) expectations.**

Here's where I'm going to contradict myself a little, because while I'm holding steady in the belief that we've already got everything we need within us, I'm no stranger to how beneficial it can be to turn to, or look up to, a role model. Surrounding yourself with positive people (whether that is physically, or by conscious choice of who takes residence in your Facebook feed) is crucial to calling into your life what you desire. Why reinvent the wheel when those who have already trodden the path have illuminated the goodness along the way? My key message here: **choose your role models wisely**. Be diligent, selective, and set high standards for yourself. Remember, this isn't about trying to clone their reality. Yet, if someone you admire credits her bright outlook on life to an attitude of gratitude, then absolutely try your hand at generating glorious amounts of the stuff in that same way. Myself, I credit my newfound bliss to meditation, mentoring and mindfulness. I'd adore for you to explore those things as well! (That's kinda why I wrote this book!) Know this, though: your life needn't look like mine. You don't have to stack up your worth against how 'little' you meditate compared to someone else, how much gluten you eat, or how long you can hold a downward facing dog.

Combine your most heartfelt *aspirations* with a thirst for *authenticity*.

What if your internal culture was one of self-love, rather than self-destruction? What if you created an environment that allowed you the confidence to say no when your body is begging for rest, and to say yes, with authenticity and enthusiasm, when an invitation feels aligned? What if you celebrated (and you make the rules as to when you deserve to celebrate - whether you've been promoted, finished a creative project, or simply made it through a long, difficult day) in a fashion that serves your body, mind and soul in the most nourishing of ways? What if you consulted your vision board and heartfelt aspirations from chapter one before imagining the cool slick of wine sliding habitually down into your belly?

Would any of that change the way you approach your current model of celebration? How would your life be different if, while in the throes of celebration, you exalted in the name of sustainability *and* satisfaction? No hangovers. No comedowns. No walks of shame. And in place of that? A jubilant heart. A thriving body. Integrity intact. A salute to your spirit. Sounds delicious, no? It truly is, sister girl, but before we investigate and play around with wholesome ways in which to have fun without The Party, first we need to understand and own the situations in our lives that make us Party-trigger-happy.

I'd love to share some insights with you now from other Peace Girls and follow up with a few suggestions of holistic replacements. Maybe you can put your thinking cap on and come up with ideas yourself. Let's see if you recognise your story in theirs and can witness the alternatives.

Here's what Jenn has to say:

"I wanted to forget my worries and woes and just concentrate on being me. Deciding to take a drink meant freedom from the constant merry-go-round inside my head and it allowed me, in a bizarre way, to be more present."

Notice how Jenn's reaction to her trigger is to change her inner world with an external resource? She was seeking freedom from her mind, and so, resorted to numbing her body. Obviously, she's not alone here. We're all guilty of this. Let's not forget that the drink *will* provide temporary nourishment, but comfort in the form of instant gratification will only keep us hungry for the next hit.

For anyone I work with these days, whether it be Peace Girls in training, or life-coaching clients, my suggestion for situations where stress and overwhelm dominate them is to draw down their awareness, away from the chaos of their minds, into the certainty and support of their heartbeat. I ask them to place their hands upon their chest, close their eyes, and plug every last inch of their attention into the pounding beneath their rib cage. Try this right now. Notice how you feel as your heart b-b-beats gently into your palms, as you remember, *"Oh, hello heart. Hello heart that beats life into my veins… that serves me every moment of every day. Even though I take you for granted, even though I neglect you, and invest my energy into my thoughts, into my fears, here you are, loving me, beating for me, thriving for me. Thank you for that."* I wonder if this short heartbeat meditation will allow you to free yourself from the merry-go-round inside your head, too.

Next up, Jacky:

"I wanted to be the life of the party. I felt too shy to have fun, so I used booze for Dutch courage to let loose."

Ah, this old chestnut is what was most responsible for my own Party Girl addiction. I wanted my personality to be *bigger*. I wanted to puff myself up in an attempt to better show up, just as Jacky did. I've got a lot more to say about this in later chapters, but for now, I'll pass on this nugget: **allow yourself to feel awkward.** Whether you're feeling shy, awkward, confident or crazy, they're all just sensations in the body that rise up so that they can fall away. Many of us actually don't know what it's like to feel the full experience of awkwardness or shyness. We've already swallowed a few drinks in the hope of dissolving any possibility of it. But a feeling, an emotion, a sensation, it's not going to kill you. In fact, if you're present with the states that your body moves in and out of, you'll grow exponentially, connect more intimately with who you really are, and as a result - *hey presto!* - naturally garner more confidence from within, because of your choice to stay rooted in authenticity.

Treat this as an experiment or game. Next time you notice yourself feeling shy or awkward, ask yourself, *"I wonder how long I can take this for?"* There's no need to make this a heavy experience. **Laugh at yourself! Be amused by the Ego!**

Here's some maths, from Becs:

"Beer = relax."

If relaxation is the goal, let's expand our reward system from one that links alcohol with relief to another that substitutes it with rituals that stimulate the same response. Replace reaching into the fridge for a beer as soon as you get home with a mindful routine. *Off come the shoes and socks, out comes the ponytail. You place your bag and keys down gently. You change into something that makes you feel cosy and comfortable. You wash your face, pour a glass of filtered water, and then…*

What's it going to be that invites a sense of complete and total relaxation? The ritual of boiling a pot of chai tea, strained carefully into your favourite tea cup? A bubble bath, lit up by a vanilla-scented soy candle? A carefully crafted soundtrack, playing softly in the background as you prepare tonight's dinner? Turning your phone on airplane mode and curling up with some fiction? Lying on your bed, taking a few deep, belly breaths, as you consciously release your day?

Let me just say that there's nothing wrong whatsoever about enjoying a drink at the end of your day. What we're trying to do here is cut the cord that links 'I'm tired and I need to relax' with 'I need a drink.'

Tricia shares:

"My trigger was most certainly the reward. I was like, 'Good, the kids are asleep and I've been up since 5.30am. Now time to devour a big bag of chips on the couch and drink half a bottle of wine. This is my quiet time. I've earned it.'"

How much more spritely and ready for her 5:30am start do you think Tricia would be if she turned down the volume of her inner saboteur and instead recited, *"The kids are asleep. Now it's time for me. I love this time of night. I get to sip my tea quietly, watch my favourite television show, and snack on the raw chocolate in the freezer. I can even squeeze in a little journaling and self-reflection. I'm grateful for this time."* Notice how that option feels in your body as you read it. It's empowering. It puts her in the driver's seat. She's no longer a victim of her circumstances, but is cultivating gratitude and healthy habits. Mama Bear self-care is vital!

Meet Kristen:

"I liked the energy I felt surging through my body, and that I could dance until 4am. I drank to get drunk and let loose. And I also remember a time where I had a few wines so that I could open up to a friend who'd hurt my feelings. After two wines, I finally said what I felt I couldn't say sober."

I have so much to say about the surging energy that Kristen mentioned, as well as letting loose, and being vulnerable (while sober!) with those we love in upcoming chapters. And - *squee!* - I'm more than excited to dive into these topics with you. For now, just know that your dance moves and your capacity to feel energy flowing within you are *not* limited to you being drunk or high. Far from it. Neither is your ability to aim true in your convictions, to hold steady for those uncomfortable conversations. In later chapters, I've got you covered.

Here's what Juliet has to say:

"Having a constant drink in my hand meant that I could keep the buzz going all night long. Even if I didn't feel 'drunk' and that wasn't my goal, I could keep up

with the party. Yet I would wake up with a massive hangover, and feel not-so-hot the next day."

I'm sure you've heard of the placebo effect, yes? In fact, I'm sure you've felt the placebo effect in action. Can you call to mind a few memories when you were barely a drink or two into the night, and yet the anticipation of the evening ahead, paired with the knowing that sooner or later you *would* be plastered (or high out of your mind) seemed to create an early onset of drunkenness? An attack of the sillies, a few words prematurely slurred, an unjustifiable extra decibel in your voice? Sometimes, the sheer ritual of the thing can fire off those neurones in our brains, creating the result we're after, without the ingredients that are usually required. It's no different to those clinical trials in which half of the participants are testing a pharmaceutical drug and the other half are swallowing sugar pills. It's staggering to discover how often the sugar pills amass positive progressions for the participants. These minds of ours? They're weapons of mass manifestation.

Seek (or believe) and ye shall find. The same applies to The Party. If you feel as though you need a drink in your hand all night, missy, go right ahead. In fact, I recommend that you ensure a drink is always close by. (My personal favourite is sparkling water with lime.) This way, a simple *'no thank you, I'm good'* as you point to the tumbler in front of you will suffice quite nicely in kindly refusing shouts from your mates. You'll find comfort in your (non-alcoholic) drink, and can utilise the placebo effect if you feel as though you really need to rise to the occasion. Meanwhile, bid *au revoir* to that nasty-ass hangover.

It can be super challenging when we're attempting to change things. So much of the good old-fashioned, flat-out *fun* we experience in our lives is dictated by alcohol (or your poison of choice) being the catalyst. The question is: *where do we dig for pleasure in this afterlife?* How can we experience joy in our lives now, if the binding link as we know it between us and fun is an environment of booze and drugs and sex and men?

When I was making the transition myself, I kept busy. I'd read books, cook up a storm in the kitchen, journal, vision board, recite affirmations, and blog my little heart out. To begin with, it was nothing more than an attempt to distract myself from everything that was happening in the social circles around me. As time passed, my wholesome pursuits filled the gaping hole left in me which was once full of tequila and Jägermeister and drama. Something beautiful began to happen: my attention naturally and habitually started to settle on those pursuits with *struggle*, which made it incredibly easy for me to stay true to my body. Doing what felt salubrious also fulfilled me on a level I hadn't experienced before. **I began to prioritise being present over just another piss up**. I craved meaning. I wanted to 'come home'. And the more I noticed the change in my life – in my body, my emotions, the spaciousness in my mind – the more hooked I became on my new and improved reward system. This new system enabled me to turn into myself for answers, love and connection, rather than resort to escapism. It was becoming clearer by the second that there was in fact *nothing* for me to run away from.

My Peace Girls experienced a similar process of turning inward. When I asked them what 'filled their void', what they exchanged for their old reward systems, what brought them a sense of fun as they stepped out of The Party, here's what they said. (And just a little side note here, these statements make me totally **beam** with pride!)

"What I'm learning so far is that the 'new fun' I'm experiencing is much more about me and what makes me happy, rather than making others happy", says Amy.

And this, from Jackie, *"It's amazing how things have changed in such a short period of time. A beach walk and meditation are my relaxation go-tos, hands down. And as it turns out, I can be very fun without a drink or five. And I embarrass myself far less."*

Mia describes – beautifully – how her attention shifted from The Party to Passion and Purpose, *"For me, it was finding my passion and being able to focus a lot of my energy into that. I realised the main reason I would go out all weekend and get shit-faced was because I had no idea what I wanted to do with my life and it was filling a void. Plus, it was the only thing I could think of that was fun. And getting constant attention from guys was the only thing that made me feel good about myself. I realised when I started becoming interested in health and becoming a health coach that I got sick of going out and getting drunk. I got so much more satisfaction and pleasure out of working towards my goals and connecting with people in this circle."*

I love this enthusiasm from Beth, "*I have taken these nine months and totally dedicated them to me! When I say this, not only have I been discovering what moves me to the max, but also living it! I still think I love to be around the party scene and live vicariously through others. The beauty of that is that I feel amazing in my body in that moment. And the next morning, no hangovers. That is huge for me! Hangovers would trigger my tailspin downward. Now I wallow in the clarity and energy I have all the time.*"

I fist-pumped the air when I read this genius suggestion from Alana, "*I found years ago when I quit my party lifestyle that emphasising 'day' activities as opposed to 'night' activities (e.g. planning weekend road trips, markets, theme parks, day spa, beach days) naturally reduced the chance of drinking, and were still tons of fun. When you have cool stuff to do through the day you're less likely to want to drink all night and sleep the day away.*"

Hell to the yes, sister. I couldn't agree more. I undoubtedly discovered that intending to make the most of my *days*, rather than my nights, was soothing for my soul and kind to my body.

"*Dance! Every form, night or day. It pushes the self-expression buttons*", says Kris. I can practically see those hips of hers shaking from here!

And lovely Corona adds this, "*Spending the time caring for me. It's also been about reaching out and finding other ways to explore and have fun. I went to this amazing evening a couple of weeks ago called Soul Celebrations - dinner, Kirtan and meditation. It was amazing. I didn't miss the alcohol and left on such a better high than any drug or alcohol could provide me with! I've been thinking about doing a creative course like painting or pottery soon, and I'm starting to enjoy my own company more. So if my hubby heads out drinking, I love nothing more to sit in with a good book.*"

Notice how this is not about deprivation? Some of these girls have tried sobriety on for size, been blanketed by the snug warmth of it, and loved it. Others still love to head out, dance up a storm and enjoy the company of their friends. It's all about making more of those delicious, conscious decisions that empower you and enable a sense of control. You might also notice a running theme of 'me' in the girls' feedback above. 'Me-time', 'focusing on me', 'finding my passion'. Swivelling that spotlight around so it shines back in your face is hugely symbolic; this is a very introspective, powerful time, and to make the most of it, you must be comfortable getting a little selfish. Not selfish with a capital 'S'. Selfish with a lower case 's'; a gentler, empowering, healthful version.

Have you ever had the words *the whole world doesn't revolve around you, you know?'* spat at you while you were growing up? You too?! Allow me to evaporate that toxic statement from your psyche, because - shock, horror! – lo and behold! - guess what? - you really *are* the centre of *your* Universe. The world as you know it would cease to exist if you weren't experiencing it through your lens, through your heart. Our world needs to spin on our own sacred axis, so staking a claim on how significant we are from a humble place ignites a fire of purpose within us all.

That's precisely why we've got to quit it with this madness of celebrating the big, beautiful work we do in the world by trashing our bodies and nervous systems. And it's also why I was inspired to start the #SelfCentredSundays revolution on Instagram. Each Sunday, I share snapshots using the hashtag #SelfCentredSundays. My intention from the very beginning was to give every woman out there permission to devote a day entirely to her soul. The trend caught on like wildfire. Every weekend, I revel in witnessing women share pitures of their healthy meals, their sweaty post-run selfies, picnics with their friends, creative projects, and their bathtubs filled with bubbles, waiting for them to slide into. I invite you to join us all for this Sunday ritual of sharing what serves our highest selves. (You can find me at @tara_bliss)

Let's flip this picture the right way up. Let's get our priorities straight. Let's really drive this home.

Here's what's worth it:

:: *Your body. That precious body of yours that carries you, beats for you, breathes for you.*

:: *Pressing up against your passions. Your ability to express yourself creatively.*

:: *Your open-heartedness, which when tended to, ushers in intuitive insight. (Who doesn't want to be more intuitive?)*

:: *The radiance of your skin. The shine of your eyes. The glow of your spirit.*

:: *Vitality. That gorgeous, sacred, bounding energy within you, begging to be unleashed.*

:: *The power of your presence in relationships. Your capacity to give freely, receive willingly and love fiercely.*

What else would feel just plain amazing?

:: *Smiling as your head hits the pillow at night.*

:: *Getting up at 5am on a Monday morning feeling damn grateful to be alive and kicking.*

:: *Losing the weight (in the most loving of ways).*

:: *Falling in love (in the most conscious of ways).*

:: *Dropping the resentment (in the most deliberate of ways).*

:: *Recognising that girl in the mirror once more and remembering how truly astonishing she is (in the most natural and most accepting of ways).*

Let me remind you that this isn't about never having a Friday night drink again, or never toasting your best friend at her wedding. It's about listening in to your body, and giving thanks and cheers in a way that really speaks to you. It's about you making a decision from your heart space, rather than becoming burnt out from socially over-committing. It's about finding the courage to stay in for the night when your eyes are heavy and your poor body's crying out for a break.

Look, I'm the first to admit that sometimes, the only thing that can do a situation justice is to order a damn fine margarita! (Save the sugar, extra lemon, please!) When you make that choice, **make it a conscious one**. Make sure it's a 100% *yes!* Because if it's not, the guilt is going to do more damage on the way down than the tequila itself.

You have permission to celebrate your accomplishments with *class*. You have permission to commiserate your discomfort with *care*. **With your pure desires as the guiding force, you can give yourself the gift of diving into new and beautiful ways to experience what you really want, and to meet those primal needs of yours, without resorting to escapism.**

Peace Practice

What are your triggers? What makes you crave a drink or drug?

What need are you looking to meet?
For example: nourishment, comfort.

How else can you support yourself and meet these needs when these triggers present themselves to you?

What's your current reward system?
For example: for a job well done, I turn to champagne; when I'm tired, it's a bottle of wine on the couch...

What changes would you like to see in your reward system?
For example: more connection, more me-time, more pampering.

Who are the people in your life who will support you with this?

Forget about any routine blueprint you've ever read. What does *your* ideal day look like?

Let's break this right down from the macro to the micro. Be as specific as possible - we're going for an idealistic vision, not because we're shooting for perfection, but rather so that you can start to see that how your day unfolds is largely choice-driven, rather than circumstantial.

What time do you wake up?

What thoughts do you think upon waking?

Who do you wake up next to?

What does your morning routine comprise?
(Movement, meditation, other self-care practices?)

What do you eat for breakfast?

What kind of outfit do you slip into after your shower?

What time do you start work?

What type of work do you do in the world? How do you serve?

Who do you connect with throughout the day?

What's for lunch?

What key feelings will you experience throughout the day?

What time do you finish work?

What do you have energy for after your work day is complete?

What music will you listen to as you're winding down/preparing dinner, etc?

What will you eat for dinner?

What time will you sit for dinner?

What time do you head to bed?

How are you feeling when your head hits the pillow?

Is there anything else you'd like to write about your ideal day?

Which of these experiences can you start implanting immediately?

Peace Performance

Take the insight you've gained from answering the questions above, and this Sunday, join the #SelfCentredSundays movement over on Instagram! Show us your new and improved reward system; how you're treating yourself after a big week. I can't wait to see those hangovers of yours replaced by healthy habits!

It's time to throw everything you've learnt so far into a big puddle of Love. We're going to hold up a magnifying glass to the romantic relationships in your life and investigate the importance of unconditional self-love. Giddy up.

4.

What's Love Got To Do With It?

When you meet someone, remember it is a holy encounter. As you see him, you will see yourself. Never forget this, for in him you will find yourself or lose yourself.
A Course in Miracles

I drive away from Brisbane a 21-year-old on a mission to free myself from the addiction of (what I believe to be) 'love'. I have single-handedly allowed that dizzying on-again off-again merry-go-round to consume my every waking thought. Yet, by some miracle, I'm finally starting to wake up to the notion that it's doing me no good.

A few months ago, a close friend announced she was moving back down to Sydney to pursue further study and my entire body knew in an instant that I'd be making this move with her. In my mind, the only way I can create a life that doesn't revolve around this guy is to pack my bags and hit the highway for a place far enough away that even the most heartfelt text or impatient drunk dial can't be acted upon. I need to know what life can be like without him.

I settle into a share house with four other 20-somethings in Sydney's eastern suburbs, feeling both electrified and overwhelmed to be in a new city by myself. Nervous as I am, I have crystal clear, determined intentions. For starters, I've pledged never to work in a salon again. Instead, I'm going to find a gorgeous cocktail bar to work in as a means to be creative and meet like-minded people. I'm adamant that I'm going to compose myself in the company of men. I want rid of those feelings of powerlessness and obsession that are so deeply rooted in my track record. They can fizzle the hell out, *thank you very much*.

Two weeks of unexpected homesickness pass. I pick up a position at a trendy bar in the inner west, and it's precisely what I had in mind; a bustling hub of creatives, eccentrics, gays and lesbians, and hipsters. When my trial shift comes to an end, I bravely ask my manager if I can take a peek upstairs and check out the cocktail bar. I explain that I've long loved mixology and that cocktail lounges are my favourite environments to work in. "I'll work the rest of this shift for free. I'd just really like to have a crack and see what it's like up there." "Sure!" he beamed. "I'll take you up to meet the guys."

As I follow my manager up the flight of stairs, I feel my energy shift as I draw closer to the middle level of the venue. My body relaxes and welcomes the change in music, the dim glow of the soft pink lights. The bartenders move with poise along with the smooth, flawless electro beats. I levitate. *This bar has my name all over it!* It takes me barely a moment to understand that this – right here – is where I'm gonna find my people in this big, scary city. I'm introduced to both guys working the bar and reach out to shake their hands with an enthusiastic *"Hey!"*

His eyes meet mine. *"G'day!"* he beams. And the butterflies that suddenly take flight in my tummy don't know whether to say *"Oh shit"* or *"Hello, handsome"*. He's present, beyond confident, and looks as though he'll be a lot of fun to hang out with. Somehow I know, just like when I walked into this space, that he will become significant to me in one way or another.

The very next morning, I - *ahem!* - awake next to him, naked and foggy, a little taken aback at the memories that start swooping in; ones that depict *me* making the moves. I'd seen something I wanted, and apparently, gone after it unapologetically. That's a very different approach to take for the girl who up to now has drawn men into her life by sitting in the corner and *willing* them to approach her. It turns into the most un-awkward, most pleasant Morning After ever. We dress, laugh, dive deep into conversations with ease. We bond over our matching greasy breakfasts (chicken burgers with extra chilli, and Coke Zeros).

There are mentions of his ex, and mine. We share that neither of us are ready for relationships; that we need time to explore, to be free, to sort ourselves out a little before committing again, to revel in independence. In a little more than 12 hours, I manage to identify a sacred connection with this guy. And though it isn't necessarily romantic, it's as though an undefinable, unspeakable force has orchestrated our very meeting, perhaps so that we can flesh out what it is that we most want out of our lives. Neither of us are hungry for commitment. And the mutual relief about the safety of that is almost palpable.

After walking me to the bus station, he thanks me for the night, and I climb on board that bus predicting that whatever is about to unfold in my future is going to be an experimental life remix that I'm more than up for. I'm ready to be shaken up.

And did I get shaken up or what? The months that followed were equal parts euphoric and emotional. Utterly bewildering and heart-crushing. Our shared love of the Red Hot Chili Peppers, Indian curry and narcotics meant that we were never far from each other's side, often spending days at the hip - working, playing, sleeping together. There we were - two humans messily manoeuvring their way through a web of friendship and unwavering respect for each other, who happened to occasionally fall into the same bed. For a while, the formula worked. We *got* each other. On the mornings we'd wake after drinking so much that we'd blacked out, he would lighten what would normally have been an awkward mess of *What The Hell Happened Last Night?*, by rolling over to me, collecting me into a sleep-deprived bear hug and suggesting *"breakfast?"* with a freaky enthusiasm. Then we'd laugh over lattes and mushroom omelettes.

What made him so captivating to me was how fully engaged he was. There were times I found the intensity of his eye contact excruciating. His compliments would rattle me, too. Most guys I'd met in the past had been reserved in voicing their observations, but not this one. He was profuse with his praise; often telling me that I was articulate, intelligent, that I was a 'stunning young woman' - words I'd never heard thrown at me until I met him. He was so painstakingly transparent that it made me quiver.

But as the chemistry between us became more potent, it also became more destructive, and more confusing. One night, a regular customer strikes up a conversation with him at the bar. When she notices me, she smiles my way and asks, "Is this your best friend?" He puts his arm around me, and says "She's so much more than that". I stab my lime with my straw and think to myself, *"What the hell does that mean?"*

Another time, after downing way too much vanilla vodka, we lock eyes and talk about a life that might have been were we not in the space we were in right now. "If I were ready for a girlfriend, we'd be the best couple on the planet", he declared. I nodded knowingly, while maintaining a stoic kind of cool, responding with "Yeah, totally".

But it wasn't cool. I was losing control again. So, in an attempt to take back the reins and dictate the flow of our friendship, I tried avoiding situations that would add to the already hovering complication. To protect the friendship, I raised my armour. Only problem was that armour of mine had a few chinks in it. I would drive him home after work at 4am and he'd ask "Coming inside?" "Not tonight. I'll just head home I think." He'd insist, "Come in, I've got a few bottles of wine." I'd shrug and make up some lame excuse about wanting to get home to my creature comforts; to my shower, my pyjamas, my toothbrush. But he'd just shoot me those eyes and say "Tara, I want you to come inside".

Then there were the nights where I tried to gather my wits and leave with a belly full of red wine. But all he'd have to do is say 'stay', and with a silent sigh, I would. Moments and memories like these burned my brain at night. I was brave on the outside, but inside, I was screaming, *"For fuck sake, why are you doing this to me!? Do you love me or not!?"*

Did I love this man? I don't know. I think I loved what our friendship might have been, had I never jumped the gun that first night. But in those moments, I was desperate for answers. I wanted the mess in my mind to become linear and figure-out-able. I was done with all the guesswork. Until, that is, the weekend once again rolled around and it was time to drink and drug our way into oblivion.

On a night where I must have been feeling particularly courageous, I asked him - with big, innocent eyes - if we might ever be together. He took an apprehensive breath. "I know now's the right time", I interject before he gets an answer in, eager to patch up my question. "I just mean... do you think there will ever be a right time for us? Ever?" He closed his eyes and pulled me in. His body language said it all, *"Let's not talk about this right now"*. In other words: ***no.***

The nose dive continued. After swallowing way too many pills and drinking way too many long necks of beer, I got kicked out of a club in Oxford Street for being so high that I was convinced I was a member of staff. After somehow managing to assume position behind the bar and serve a few people drinks, I felt the force of two security guards dragging me out from behind the bar. "Hey guys! It's me. It's Ta's! Put me down." I remember feeling upset and offended that they didn't recognise me - a valued member of their team! They threw me out with a forceful heave-ho. For hours I sat in tears outside, wondering where I was, wondering where *he* was, wondering when he was coming to get me. I have no idea what happened in the following hours, but I remember beating on his door after the sun had come up, having practically stumbled to his house after running out of money for the cab fare. He opened the door wrapped in his bath robe, and for once in his life, he looked like shit. "What happened? Where were you? I was all alone and you didn't come get me..." I was hysterical, and in tears. His eyes told me he was sorry and glad I was okay, but something was up. Something didn't feel right. I moved to push past him, craving a soft pillow to finally collapse onto, but he blocked me. "Ta's, you can't come up." And even in the state I was in, I instantly deduced the presence of a woman in his bed. A woman in his bed while I was crying in the gutter, waiting for my friend to come find me. While my calls went unanswered. While, with mascara running down my face, I begged the security guards to let me back in so I could just *find him* and go home and leave them to get on with their night. Seems he'd been a little preoccupied.

At his door, we hold eye contact for a while. I remember maintaining a few moments of centeredness, because let's be honest here, we'd never *really* opened up into a grand confessional about our feelings for one another. But finally, that armour of mine dropped to the ground. I inched backwards, letting out a little pain on my face. My heart concaved, as I slowly blinked away the welling tears and retreated home on foot a blubbering mess.

All those questions I had, all those emotions I contained beneath our Friend Zone mask, they all seeped out of me now, now I'd been disarmed of my sword. At the time, I thought the tears that found their way out of me that morning were weak and unwarranted. Now, as I look back, I recognise with compassion that, actually, I was just a woman, finally *feeling* the full experience of what can't be explained any other way than: *rejection*. Amidst this fiasco, I asked myself whether I could have slept with anyone while he was in my life. The answer in my body was a resounding no. No, I couldn't. *Motherfucker.* He texted me that very same afternoon. "Hey. Let's hang out. Beers?" And when I arrive at the pub, we embraced in a big hug, as if nothing had happened. I passed him a pill. **We got high**.

I had begun to hate myself for making that first move on him, that drunken night months earlier. I hated that I'd kickstarted an avalanche of friend-sex and flirtation, which I knew was peppered with a deep, friendship-drenched love for each other. I despised knowing that, if only the two of us could have been friends from the beginning, if I could have maintained a little composure on that first night, then everything would've been amazing between us. I'd have had the most caring, beautiful best friend in the world, with whom I could share more openly, and stop playing games. We could've been real with each other, present with each other, *there* for each other. But we were neither here nor there, and the whole thing felt tarnished and soiled.

After years of partying and attaching my worth to how much a man wanted me or not, how he *perceived* me, my experiences began to consistently reflect my inner environment. If I felt I wasn't worthy, I'd seek out the evidence to render my beliefs accurate. If I believed that a man was too good for me, he would carry on acting as though I was nothing but a bump in the road along his path. This mirror - this reflection that our life experiences offer us as a response to our inner world - is *Universal*. Every Party Girl I've ever worked with will tell you that the more they abused alcohol and drugs, the more chaotic their lives would become. That chaos would manifest in their relationships, their self-care practices, their state of mind. It's not rocket science. Finding solace in a coke high - although temporarily inducing you with euphoric sensations of love - is a far cry from the real deal, from love itself, from self-love. When we're feeding our body toxins, how can we expect our lives to manifest as anything but turbulent?

So much of my attention was placed upon how people were identifying with me, how I appeared in the world, how much of a chameleon I could become in social situations, that my relationship with myself was irrelevant. **Mattering to someone else was of highest importance to me.** Making an impact. Being top of mind. As though I were still eight years old, blowing smoke out of my dad's bathroom window, two questions that plagued my subconscious were: *do I* *belong somewhere?* And: *am I crafting an identity that feeds the image in my mind?* The only time I felt connected to myself was when I gave myself permission to cry in moments of solitude; usually in bed, in the shower, or in my car. In those tears, I could finally feel that inner child of mine knocking on my heart. I knew she deserved a better life than the one I was orchestrating, but I was stuck beyond stuck beyond stuck. My idea of making positive change in my life was going on a diet and hitting the gym for a couple of extra sessions a week. If I had even known what self-love was back then, this would have been my definition of it: train hard, eats lots of meat and vegetables, limit booze intake to red wine and vodka lime and sodas, maintain a good tan, and drink soy milk instead of dairy.

When wanting leads to losing

White-knuckling our lives, hooking our happiness onto certain things, people, and experiences is a sure-fire route to what the Buddhists call 'suffering'. I wouldn't dare admit this to myself at the time, but I was deeply attached, not only to this man, but as I've already mentioned, to his perception of me. And so, on a spirited mission to free myself of an addiction, my Soul took the steering wheel and course-corrected.

When we've outgrown an intended learning, we can become uncomfortably unfulfilled; sometimes with resistance, sometimes with bitterness, sadness, or a longing for things to be the way they were before. Regardless, when the lesson is learnt, we naturally start casting our attention back out into the world of possibilities again. I began to wonder what it would feel like to create a life of meaning without him in it. (Those bloody repeating lessons!) The feeling of being able to stand independently on my own two feet again, without using him as a crutch, without wondering whether our friendship was worthy of a cameo on *Dawson's Creek*. I wanted to retreat, and start again, and be alone. I fantasised - albeit a little dramatically - about the promise that accompanied rebirth, of showing up in the world as a big girl again, not one with a lousy, crumpled heart. I knew that, if I were going to be with a man, there couldn't be any question as to whether we loved each other or not. I was through with the abundance of grey, and craved a little more black and white.

So, in one of the greatest acts of self-love of my early twenties, I packed my bags again, and drove to the snow-capped mountains of Australia. Tears rolled down my cheeks for the journey's entirety, as I contemplated whether turning my back on the most significant friendship I'd ever had was a huge mistake. He had held my face in his hands, kissed my forehead and told me to "Be bad, Bliss" before waving me off. My throat - the place where the head meets the heart - thumped in pain for the six hours of that car trip. There was so much that had been left unsaid, and mostly, I just wanted to say, "Thank you for being there for me". But it was all too little, too late. I could see it clearer than ever, as I drove into a silhouette of mountains, the sun setting behind them.

In the pitch blackness, when I was just minutes from the top, snow started falling on my windshield. I consciously slowed down my breathing, and as those wipers flicked the snow from my view, the last of my tears dried up. I'd spend the next three months here. The snowfall reiterated that I was in a different place now, with different rules. The uncertainty of it all comforted me.

There's no such thing as a dysfunctional relationship

Noxious relationships are a fallacy. Every encounter we've ever experienced comes carrying with it a function. Sometimes, we perceive these functions as incredible, wonderful, blissfully life-changing. Like carefully gift-wrapped parcels from The Universe, we serendipitously bump into the man that becomes our lover, and teaches us how much beauty and light lives inside of us simply by how alive we feel in his presence. We cultivate a once-in-a-lifetime friendship with a soul sister, who teaches us how to laugh from the depths of our bellies, who mirrors back at us the generosity we never realised we were capable of, who offers us opportunities to listen not just with our ears, but with the whole of our hearts. These are the functions we welcome into our lives with our arms wide open. Other times, though, the sheer pain of other functions - the hard, ugly, destructive ones - will cut us at the knees and drop us to the floor. The man that cheated on you, the friend that betrayed your trust, the family member that, in one way or another, abandoned you.

What if there were no such thing as 'good' or 'bad' functions, 'good' or 'bad' relationships? What if we realised that we are always and forever summoning into our lives either what we desire, what we're subconsciously conditioned to, or what we spiritually need to grow.

*"The Universe will give you whatever experience necessary
in order for you to awaken."*
Eckhart Tolle

We must strengthen our inner environment and take responsibility for the quality of the relationships in our lives. Beyond practicing self-love, we must dig deeper, and commit to finding and embodying a level of self-respect that allows us to anchor into the core of who we are. Beginning *there*, we're able to more confidently interact in our relationships, know and own our truth (and worth), and back ourselves. But unlike downing a green juice or a five-minute dry body-brushing session, self-respect doesn't just happen. It needs to be earned through conscious choice-making, gentleness and actions that support the growth of our spirits.

Do you want radical relationships? Because radical self-respect is the almighty magnet that will enable you to hold the space for the types of connections that pepper your dreams.

Again, as we learn from *A Course In Miracles*, we will either lose ourselves in another person in our unawakened state, or consciously find ourselves by taking the journey into *their* heart, which is a gateway to *our own*.

In the order they appear in this book, Guy #1 taught me to prioritise my values, to flex my sovereignty muscles, and that empowerment can come through saying 'no' and walking away. Guy #2 taught me to value my time and my body. He also taught me the price I paid when I sacrificed my authentic nature in favour of others' approval. Were it not for the time I spent with him, perhaps I wouldn't have realised that underneath all the games lived a girl who wanted to love deeply, instead of pretending as though she didn't need to.

Lessons that we learn in relationships like these deem them priceless and divine, not unhealthy or destructive. All relationships – but particularly those that are romantic – offer us a portal through which to see ourselves, discover more about who we truly are, and to return home.

And the man through whom I made the journey back home to myself was Glen.

The snow was cold. (Novel concept, huh?) And I was fiercely unprepared. I remember one of my roommates generously offering to walk me down to my orientation, and as I jumped icy puddles in my ratty canvas shoes – my toes turning bluer by the second – I thought to myself, *"Hmmm. These shoes just won't do."* Give me red dirt, country air and coastal waves, and I'll feel right at home. But snow? I was out of my element. Completely vulnerable. Yet hypnotised by the marshmallowy beauty of the mountains.

I found comfort in solitude. Apart from smiling shyly at the folks I'd pass and making small talk with my work mates, I kept a low profile, turning my back on snowboarding lessons in favour of attempting to teach myself an appropriate way of sliding down the mountain. I was black and blue and limping in no time, and loving every second of it. Loving the bruises, loving the sensations of change in my body, loving the silence. After all, I knew myself. I knew it was only a matter of time before the mountain lifestyle gathered me up and launched me into sleepless nights of non-stop fun, so the short-lived solo silent time was deeply enjoyed and cherished.

The first night I met Glen, he was shit-faced. Gorgeous and hilarious, but blind drunk. It was kind of off-putting to be honest; to see someone so wasted through sober eyes. Looking back, though, I can see that I called into my life a man that was not only mirroring my own struggles back to me, but demonstrating a lifestyle that I didn't even know I was slowly backing away from.

We kicked off a silly, flirtatious friendship once I'd mustered enough backbone to make a return to the social circles, but he made me nervous. When I became aware of the attraction that was intensifying between us, I almost felt suffocated by uncertainty. Shorter than me. A surfer. A snowboarder. A man who'd come to the snow to ease the hurt of a failed eight-year relationship. A man in transit. A man seven years older than me. A man who could fit the contents of his life in the back of his van. There was no doubt that we shared a lot in common, but in so many ways, we were polar opposites, and because of this, he fascinated the hell out of me. But still, I held back. The way I had compromised myself in Sydney still felt red-raw. Although the ski fields were a hub of promiscuity and parties, my eyes kept settling on this man in the blue and green beanie, who made me feel alive and terrified all in one. The eyes on this guy sparkled. He would cock his head to the side when I spoke, as if there were a specific angle that enabled him to gaze into the very depths of my soul. Even the way he said *"thanks, beautiful"* after I'd serve him a gin and tonic at the bar would have me flushed with nerves. I'd smile before darting off to mindlessly wipe down a bench, pretending as though I were busy.

The moment that changed everything

Glen and I are sitting in the communal lounge room together; he's on a chair and I'm kneeling next to him, nursing a vodka. Everyone else is outside chain-smoking, and it's the first time we manage to steal some time alone together. The tension in the air is thick. My heart is pounding with such severity that it's taking every ounce of my might to simply sit, and stay, and see what happens, instead of run to my room and hide. Like magnets, I can feel the two of us being drawn together. And although I still can't quite bring myself to look in his eyes, I find myself nestled into his chest, my forehead pressing into his heartbeat with a sigh of relief at how safe it feels there.

That was the night I first kissed my future husband.

Glen wanted to be treated well. So did I. He didn't want to play games. Neither did I. We trod on vulnerable ground together, awkwardly navigating our way through unmapped terrain, fumbling around in an attempt to *feel* to the core, while trying our best to leave our expectations and past experiences at the door. Through many laughs and tears and suspended moments of quiet, we released the love lying latent within both of us, the love we had been begging to give, give, give. And the more we gave, the more we opened up to receive, and the deeper we loved.

I was able to let love in, not because I was hungry for it, not because I needed a man in order to once again feel validated or 'enough', but because my truest sense of Self had regained a little composure. The beginnings of my self-loving, self-respecting state of mind didn't materialise out of a vegan diet and hatha yoga. Rather, it unfolded naturally through presence; being present enough with myself to sit in the discomfort – both my own and others'– without judgment; taking off the masks I had been wearing in Brisbane and Sydney; tending to myself with time.

A little *time* was what I'd needed. Forget about those detoxes! I needed silence with myself and the gremlins in my head. I needed to *feel* my heart. I needed to touch back in to the *trust* I knew I could offer someone. And since those days of discovering who I am through the medium of men, every time I have re-prioritised my wellbeing and sense of inner peace, it's had a staggering impact on my friendships, on my marriage, on my family connections. I show up more whole, more joyful, more radiant.

You must be nourished physically, emotionally and spiritually in order to notice the miracles of aligned opportunities, abundance and good old-fashioned love. Showing up in your life wholeheartedly and with presence and curiosity is what transforms your relationship with yourself, and thus with other people.

Tribal power

There's barely a week that passes by that I don't see emails with sentences like the following landing in my inbox:

"I can't wait till I find my tribe, like you have."

"You're so lucky to have such strong bonds with your friends."

"Tara, the connection that you and those other bloggers have is out of this world."

First, let me say that it hasn't always been this way. I've yoyo-ed between being the outspoken, attention-seeking member of a group, to hiding behind the safe identity of an 'introvert' for years; keeping myself at an arm's reach from anybody and everybody. Until relatively recently, I always had an agenda in my friendships; a role to play, a silly little self-imposed expectation to fulfil.

It took a little time, a lot of awareness, and a willingness to do the necessary inner work for me to experience what is now an abundance of soulful friendships and connections. The women in my life today make my days rich with sweetness. The light they radiate out into the world makes me feel proud of them and strong within myself. They make me laugh like I wasn't sure I'd be able to again - like I did when I was little, trying with every inch of me not to laugh hysterically at the kid that just farted in class. (Actually, just recently, my bestie Rachel and I laughed in this very way in yoga class. Uncontrollable, red-faced giggling and shaking and chortling. Appropriate? Hell no! Bursting with happiness? Ya!)

So if you're just like those gorgeous blog readers of mine who waltz into my inbox, hoping for a nugget on how to make manifest these connections in your life, you've got to do two things, pronto. First of all, self-love (or as we distinguished above, self-respect) needs to become your number one priority (for now), as difficult or as downright impossible as it might seem. Presence, acceptance, letting go, trusting, allowing yourself to feel what you need to feel in **this** moment - self-love is about refusing to turn your back on yourself. Before you breathe a sigh of frustration, let me empathise with you. I know that at times this concept seems easier said than done, but self-love *is* an extension of your spiritual practice after all. (More on this later.) Like all practices, it gets easier with time and patience. Heck, it even becomes joyful! As my gorgeous friend, Melissa Ambrosini, so eloquently put it one night while we shared the stage at an event called *Self-Love & Sisterhood*, "A sea of angels came flocking into my life". (I just got goosebumps typing that.) And trust me on this one, when your angels start swooping on into your life (which they will - it's inevitable), you will know. Rather, you will **feel** and recognise that they're reflecting your bright light and shining your grace straight back at you.

Secondly, you'll need to start lovingly letting go of the friendships that are making you feel constricted, strangled, uncomfortable, small. I know this sounds awful and just plain *ick!* But this process, as experienced by myself and my Peace Girls, can be gentle and soulful. Rather than being a painful, hostile experience, it can instead offer you another opportunity to call up the love within you and act with integrity and authenticity. If the thought of letting go of long-held friendships is making you wriggle with tension in your seat, hold tight. In a chapter that's yet to come, we'll discuss the concept of the loving friend detox.

Self-love is the creator of a strong sisterhood

Sisterhood is the inevitable, enriching result of your ongoing commitment to *you*. Sisterhood simply cannot sidestep you if you're energetically investing in your vitality, spiritual wealth and inner joy. **It simply shows up.** The secret, in a sentence? **Treat yourself the way you'd like to be treated, and then be patient.** Before you know it, you'll be packing picnics for six, holding space for your girlfriends to grow, and helping them celebrate the beautiful lives they're creating, just as they do for you. You already have everything you will ever need, sister girl. By celebrating yourself, you give others permission to do the same. So start now, **because you're already enough.** If you've made it to here and you're still a little perplexed on all this self-love shizzle, let me rally a few of my girls so we can clear the air and instil a little clarity, because **you have to decide what self-love means to *you*.**

My beautiful, brave friend, Jess Ainscough, is a wellness warrior resolute on spreading her self-love message far and wide. Hers is a message that's simple and potent, **"Self-love is about complete and utter acceptance of who you are in this moment."**

Wham!

Not a willingness to improve who you are… Not an overarching desire to shed a few kilos or meditate a little longer… Not the cultivation of a perfect morning routine. (You already know my thoughts on this). Just… **acceptance.** And 100% of the time, that requires a *massive* mindset shift.

In the early stages of her cancer diagnosis and subsequent Gerson therapy, gorgeous Jess resented her new healing regime. The only thing that propelled her into her rigorous days of juicing, soup-eating and coffee enemas was **a fear of dying.** Everything changed for her, when instead of living from that brutal base of fear, she took ownership of her situation and instead decided that she was excited, thrilled, grateful to **be alive.** She accepted her situation: *I have cancer. I can thrive alongside this disease.* She found new enthusiasm and **zest for life.** Suddenly, hourly juices were no longer a means to an end; they became inspiring, life-giving elixirs. How's *that* for a reframe?

Amanda Rootsey is an eco-model, mentor to young women, and one of the sweetest souls I've ever met. Her definition of self-love can be summed up with these three words: **gentle, generosity, gratitude.** Be gentle with yourself. Tread lightly. Move softly. Everything's more sustainable that way; more organic. If you're unsure of where to start with self-love, or you get lost along the way, then Mandy suggests generosity is the answer. How can you give? Lend a helping hand? Be of service? Give freely, give often, contribute beyond yourself, because when you give love, you simultaneously receive it. Tenfold!

And for the love all things, **express tremendous gratitude for all that you have in this life.** Relentlessly. Melissa Ambrosini is a life and health coach, inspirational speaker and self-love ambassador. Her journey over the last five years has been one from boozing actress, model and dancer to holistic goddess. "When I got sick three years ago, I made a conscious commitment to clean up every area of my life," she says. "My thoughts, what I was putting in my mouth, my environment, my friendships. I literally did a spring clean on everything. I was using alcohol as a suppressant, and would go out on the weekends and write myself off because I was in so much pain. These days, every time I put something in my mouth I ask myself, *"Is this going to make me feel sluggish or bogged down?"* And if the answer's yes, it will make me feel bogged down, then I don't really want that. It's the same with my thoughts. I feed myself nourishing thoughts, and if I notice my inner Mean Girl start to kick in, that's when I bring in positive affirmations and my self-love mantras. Surrounding myself with amazing, inspiring, like-minded people has been crucial too. Some friends do slip away. And that's okay. It's all part of the process of closing one door and opening another. Basically, to me, **self-love is about letting yourself off the hook**, and being kind to yourself."

And how on earth can we have a conversation about sisterhood without addressing its sneaky little shadow aspect, **comparison**? "Comparison is the trap", says Melissa. "I used to feel as though I was treading water, non-stop. It was a constant battle. But the more I have accepted myself, the more all of that has disappeared. **It's about community and sisterhood now.** We need each other. We all need to do it together. We need to compare no more."

Rachel MacDonald (my giggling yogi friend) and I co-wrote an ebook entitled *Spirited: Soulful Lessons on Clarity, Connection and Coming Home (to You)*, and a sequel: *Spirited Solutions to What's Holding You Back*. In both of these books, we explore - and give options for moving through - comparison and envy. The next time you find yourself in the grip of gruelling jealousy, instead of being swallowed whole by separation and sadness, elegantly navigate out of those low-vibing states by doing the following:

1. Stop! And just... watch.

When you observe yourself comparing and feeling jealous, you're able to recognise that you are *not* the jealousy itself, and instead, that you are the one *watching* the jealousy. This distinction is crucial, because it allows you to understand that the state you're in right now is fleeting. (Nothing lasts forever.)

2. Locate the sensation.

Where is this nasty pang sitting in your body? Your heart? Your chest? Your throat? Zoom in on it and become curious about it. Is it throbbing, sinking, vibrating? Does it have a colour, shape or size? I wonder if, as you look at this emotion in your body, it's changing form rapidly?

3. Feel each sensation in its entirety.

Instead of suppressing the sensation (with distractions such as food, alcohol, Instagram), truly feel it. When we attempt to escape the energy moving through us, we do ourselves a disservice of massive proportions. **Feelings are meant to be felt** (whodathunkit?!), not pushed down, buried deep, or side-stepped. Comparison, envy, heart-tugging jealousy, these are all part of the human experience. Though they are traits of the Ego, they're completely natural states to experience from time to time. We intensify our pain when we deny ourselves the experiences of these states. The sooner you *feel*, the sooner the sensation transcends and leaves your body. There's even research proving that this process can take as little as 60 to 90 seconds. I don't know about you, but I'm more willing to sit and breathe through a minute of comparison-itis, than being knocked for six time and time again for deeply buried jealousy that's been waiting to be set free from my cells for decades. *Who needs vodka shots when you have energy alchemy at your disposal?!*

4. Take time for a reality check.

Is your jealousy warranted or logical in any sense? Use your cognitive and brilliantly functional brain to assess the situation rationally. Personally – and this is specific to my experience with comparing my creativity to others – I've found that acknowledging that the person's hard work and efforts have paid off fruitfully for them gives me hope and re-inspires me to keep going. Rather than jealously reacting to their success, I allow myself to perceive what's *possible* for me and that keeps me moving forward. Jealousy and inspiration are two totally different experiences. It all comes down to which one you choose. (Hint: choose to be inspired!)

5. See yourself in her success.

Your soul sisters, the women you look up to, the bloggers you idolise, they've all got one thing in common with you: your light. They're constantly reflecting it back at you. Remember that the Ego believes in specialness and separation, but the loving presence within you knows beyond any shadow of a doubt that we're all in this together; that what we perceive as wonderful, successful, inspiring in another, also lies latent within us. See your reflection as you star-gaze at her.

6. Celebrate the bejesus out of her.

Instead of turning your back in a jealous huff, give her a round of applause. Be the first to make the call and congratulate her. Re-tweet her stuff. Tell her you're proud of her. Remind her of how beautiful she is. Send her a text thanking her for how much she inspires you. Doesn't that just feel so damn good, when you feel your feelings and rise to the occasion in a conscious way, instead of shrink-ing into a dark and moody pit of mud and envy and goop?

7. Re-write the letter below.

You're writing this note to the person who's triggered you, but this is for **your eyes only**. Watch what happens to the state of both your mind and body as you soften and release the hostility in you.

Dear _____

I have a confession. I'm feeling really jealous about your _____
(relationship, body, success).

You have/are _____*, and it seems so far removed from*
what's possible for me right now.

My jealousy/comparison/resentment feels like _____ *in my body.*
This is not how I want to feel.

The specific things that are triggering these feelings are:
1.
*because*_____

2.
*because*_____

3.
*because*_____

So what I've decided to do, because I'm ready to release this heaviness in my heart, is
transform this comparisonitis into a celebration of you.

I'm celebrating your greatness because I know, deep, deep within me, that you rep-
resent all that's possible for me.

I'm celebrating the fact that you're in my life because you're aligned with where I'm
going. You encompass all that I'm capable of.

I'm celebrating you because you deserve to be celebrated!

Even though I might struggle to realise it from time to time, things don't always
happen as easily as they appear. In applauding you today, I'm honouring your com-
mitment and dedication to living a beautiful life.

You've inspired me to create the same.

Thank you, thank you, thank you.

Your joy is my joy.

Comparing no more,

_____

(signature)

One final note before we move on...

Forgiveness.

Oh yes. That damn 'F-word', as Gabrielle Bernstein affectionately calls it. Please, allow me to get one very important (and very loud) thing off my chest: *I think you're fantastic.* Actually, I know you are. You're perfectly unique, un-questionably fascinating, and you have a twinkle in your eye unlike anyone else on the planet. *You* are remarkable, and believe it or not, you're destined for a remarkable life.

So before we set out to plot revenge against our disappointing ex-boy-friends and bitchy ex-besties, let's take pause. Without the hurt, you wouldn't have this opportunity for a gorgeous, soul-stirring awakening. You no longer need the assistance of anyone else to help you switch on your own light. So let's show gratitude for this opportunity to un-learn, re-shuffle, and then re-learn the decisions that we want to make and the direction we want to take. Without everyone who's judged, berated and pressured you, it's likely you'd never turn toward party-fuelled, self-destructive behaviour, because let's face it, we always (unquestionably and without a doubt) fall into The Party as an attempt to escape who we are in one way or another. Without that pressure cooker you found yourself in all those years ago, you wouldn't be here, searching for the way back to the one divine person who's been ever-present, and ever-patient, just waiting for you to come back: *you.*

Let's bless every single conversation, relationship, awkward moment, rejection, anxiety, and situation that took The Party from being an expression of fun to, at times, a manifestation of hell on earth. Let's bless every hangover. Every blackout. Every regret. Every single moment that you abandoned yourself in pursuit of escape. Without these moments that smothered you in guilt and shame and embarrassment, we wouldn't be here, right now, in this moment, starting a revolution.

So now, as we move forward, promise me this. Promise yourself this. No more regrets. No more wishing that things had been different. No more self-hatred. **No more ill-feelings towards those who didn't allow your light to shine bright**; because trust me, although it mightn't seem like it, they truly did the very best job they knew how.

The Hawaiians had it sussed beautifully when they created the Zero Point - a practice of reconciliation and forgiveness. Put simply, rather than indulging in resentments, they return home - back to the truth of all things - with a mantra that sounds a little like this:

"I forgive you. I'm sorry. I love you. I release you."

One to throw in your back pocket, no? Spiritual teacher, Marianne Williamson, adds to this perfectly, "When you forgive someone, one of two things will happen. Either their behaviour will change, or you won't care anymore." And I just *love* that.

So, what's love got to do with it? Bloody everything! If there's not some semblance of balance, compassion, joy, ecstasy, trust, and passion in your relationships, then it's likely those same qualities aren't as present within you as they could be. And that - right there - is why you've 'lost yourself' to The Party. Fake joy has seduced you into chasing it down the rabbit hole of escapism and fraudulent fun. It's time to come up for air now, Party Girl. It's time to look the lie in the eye, and remember that everything you've ever wanted or desired comes from *within*. Shines from inside you.

Peace Practice

The way we relate and interact allows us to dive so divinely deeply into who we are at our core. 'Mirror work' as this is often called is profound and – I believe – *really* wonderful. Think of the process of mirror work like a playground, like an adventure. You never know what you're going to get, but it's always a surprise when you get there. Bring that lightness of spirit into this Peace Practice and enjoy getting to know yourself a little more intimately.

What attitudes am I most attracted to/do I most long for?
For example: gratitude, grace, humility, organic... etc.

These traits must be present within me, too. Here's proof...

What do I perceive to be five flaws of mine?

What can I do to cultivate appreciation and compassion for these things?

How can I begin to heal what I perceived to be flawed about myself?

What ten things do I cherish about myself? And why?

I feel like something's missing in my life and that it might have something to do with my relationship to myself. What is it?

'I've been showing up in my relationships with all kinds of agendas, like…'

And I have a hunch those agendas may be doing a disservice to both them, and me.
(List some examples.)

Who am I in quiet moments, alone, without distractions?

Here are ten reasons why that is *perfect*…

'I'm currently harbouring resentment for/about…'

'… and I'm willing to forgive them for everything I perceive they've 'done' to me. Here's why…'

What self-love means to *you*

Okay, this is it. You get to make the rules here. There are a million and one self-love definitions out there. There a million and one ways to practice it. But no-one can express your experience of it like you can. So use this space to craft a nourishing explanation of what it means to you.

*What you may discover as you let go and surrender to this self-inquiry is that self-love is less about **what you do** and more about **how you be.** It's a way of life, rather than a To-Do List of self-care rituals…*

My definition of self-love is…

Exploring self-love not only opens our hearts to other more meaningful relationships, but ensures that we have a solid base on which to build routines, rituals and practices that elevate our energy and improve our overall health and wellbeing. In the next chapter, we'll talk about making the move from a full-tilt crazy lifestyle to one that's super-nourishing on all levels.

5.

From Ballistic
to Holistic

*"What the caterpillar calls the end of the world,
the master calls a butterfly."*
Richard Bach

Glen and I married in September 2011, on a beautiful spring day in alpine Australia. Most of the snow had melted, leaving beneath it dry, golden, straw-like grass that looked rustic and picturesque against a backdrop of abundant, green hillside. I wore a short lace dress with long, belled sleeves, and a ribbon around my loosely curled hair, and he wore jeans, a black, fitted shirt with a grey vest, and his Converse sneakers. Our humble little Love Party played host only to immediate family and a very small handful of friends, and they all watched on as the two of us stood there, nervous and giddy, clutching onto one another's hands for courage and balance. As Glen cried during his vows, it took all my might not to pull him close and guide his tear-streaked face into my neck; my heart, melting. Finally, as we were announced husband and wife to our small tribe, we lost ourselves in those timeless few moments of slightly shocked, breathless, smiley kisses.

That day, I felt truly beautiful. I felt lovely, radiant, pretty. And though the years that preceded our wedding were spent in oversized t-shirts, skate shoes and snowboarding attire, I felt soft and feminine on our special day (as I'm sure most brides do). But it had nothing to do with my cute lace dress and freshly balayaged hair. I felt… *alive* and *luminous*.

The bride-to-be bug bit me *hard*. As the date approached, I found myself becoming frustrated as I tossed around ideas in my mind on what it was going to take to look my best. I was nervous as all hell about this. In their photos, brides are always aglow with beauty; practically levitating as they beam out undying love and grace. I wasn't quite sure I could pull that off, because after all, I was a self-proclaimed tomboy. I felt like a weirdo every time I wore a dress, and being that this whole shindig was going to take place smack-bang in the middle of Glen's and my backpacking adventures, resources were more than a little scarce. Oh, and I was looking less than knock-out, thanks to a booze bloat that I'd been nursing for a few years. Still. I so very badly wanted to look and feel lovely on the day. I weighed up my options. I could snowboard an extra couple of hours a day... I could put myself on a diet... I could try to restrain myself from indulging in Glen's famous chocolate fondants every so often... I could eat less… But all signs pointed to deprivation, and *ugh!* No-one knew my relationship to food better than me; if I put a restrictive box around myself, I'd be bingeing on potato wedges drenched in cheese and bacon and sour cream, and flushing it down with a few beers in no time.

"Eventually, we get so tired of trying to fix ourselves that we stop. We see that we've never been able to make ourselves good. Never been able to accomplish ourselves into being someone else. And so we stop trying. We see there is no goal, no end place, no test to take. No-one is keeping score. No-one is watching us and deciding whether we are worthy enough to ascend."
Geneen Roth, *Women Food and God*

The truth is I wasn't feeling too crash hot. Most nights, after closing my bar, I would knock off with a bottle of red wine. Living in staff accommodation and working split shifts six days a week was taking its toll on me too. Snowboarding helped; it got my blood pumping and reenergised me for a night of work, but I'd be lying if I said I was in good health.

One day, while trawling the internet for new blogs to follow, I stumbled upon a website that was curated by a 19-year-old girl from Utah. She was… *bright*, with tanned skin, long blonde hair and blue eyes, and a killer white smile. On her blog, she published recipes and reflections of her journey into the world of raw foods. In one night alone, I pored through everything she'd ever written, taking in the colours of the vibrant juices she had photographed: the purples! the oranges! the greens! The food she was eating was real, and colour-ful, and raw, and alive! And I wanted in.

As an ex-athlete, I'd tested out dietary theories for eons. Low-fat, high-protein, shakes and meal replacements, high-carb, low-carb. Hell, for a while I even ate a protein-only diet (heads up: don't do that). This approach, though – the one smacking me around the chops from Miss Utah – this seemed sustainable. It *felt* different in my body and it made plain old sense to me: eat foods that are alive, feel more alive; eat foods that are stale and old and processed, and drag your sorry, undernourished ass out of bed every day with a moan and a groan. *I'll have what she's having.*

And boom! Just like that, curiosity swept in like a gale force wind, and gave my pre-wedding jitters the shake-up of all shake-ups! I ordered a juicer from eBay immediately, and squealed when it arrived, declaring myself a mixologist of cucumbers, apples, celery and herbs. Lemon in warm water with a huge jug of green juice replaced my morning soy latte, and enormous salads loaded with fresh vegetables, nut and seeds, with a mug of peppermint tea, trumped my daily ritual of lunchtime beers. Every chance I got to head down the hill and into Melbourne, I would stock up on nutrient-dense superfoods from the health food shop – kelp noodles, coconut water, goji berries, buckwheat groats – all foods that I would spend the next few months experimenting with like a mad scientist. *I was fascinated.* I made green smoothies and chia seed puddings and salad dressing made from miso paste and avocado, often leaving a trail of destruction behind me in the kitchen, much to Glen's frustration. He became a little exasperated as I took over that space, often leaving behind coconut shreds and stray cacao nibs that failed to land in my bowl.

It wasn't just my eating habits that were getting a makeover. I was also inspired to move and sweat. I began to enthusiastically climb into my snowboard boots of a morning; not because I was thirsty for mid-ride beers (the usual focal point of the day), but because it felt vitalising to be out in the mountain air, moving my body, leaning into my joints, feeling the cold air hit my face as I threw down some long turns. It became sacred to me: silent and soul-nourishing and *fun*.

And the detoxing infrared sauna at the hotel? I began to use it. Each night, instead of clocking my usual bottle of red wine, I took my seat in the sauna, reading health articles on my smartphone, breathing deep into a guided meditation, or just being present enough to feel every bead of sweat form streams that would slide down my forehead, or slip down my spine, or run down the backs of my calves. There I was, in a desert-like inferno, not running, just feeling into it, observing myself in stillness as I allowed my body to detox, to let go, to surrender completely. **Sweating never felt so deeply spirited.**

Later on, as I'd sit on the couch, digging into a big bowl of frozen fruit laced with coconut and honey, chasing down each icy bite with warm sips of ginger tea, I revelled in feeling fresh-faced and loose within my body. Those nights were serious life-enhancers - that freeing feeling of contentment as I sat cross-legged, happy-sleepy, grateful, and vibrating on **high**. I laughed with my chicken-wing-eating friends as we got stoked up on inspiring snowboarding documentaries. Still with my people. Still belonging. And yet, making my own rules. Carving out a new vision for myself.

As I continued to devote to this new way of being, somewhere along the line I noticed that my skin - a previous breeding ground for long-standing and constant acne - started clearing up, that excess weight was melting off me, and my hair and nails had a growth spurt that I'd never before been able to cultivate. I became less reactive, less panicky, less… *angry*. What had started as simply an endeavour to look bangin' on my wedding day had quickly transformed into a commitment to a lifestyle that was rewarding me with everything I'd ever wanted: to feel whole, and to feel *here*. Instead of fear being the driving force behind the desire to look radiant, **love was**. It's as though a switch had flipped in my psyche, one that enabled me to remember, "*Oh yeah, I have a body. I should, like, probably look after it.*" The response from my body was all the proof I needed that I was onto something pretty spectacular.

Now, that's not to say that I didn't spill Jägermeister all over my white lace wedding dress in the wee hours of the morning! *Insert sheepish *gulp* here...* Clearly, I still had some work to do. But for the most part, I was well and truly hooked on health. **Changing my diet was a tangible, get-your-hands-dirty way to understand my body's responses to different foods.** Those initial days I spent in that hotel kitchen – blitzing and blending and juicing and soaking – paved the way for the coming few years of experimentation. Raw food, veganism, Ayurveda, paleo, macrobiotics, I've tried it all on for size. I threw away the Tinned Tuna With Steamed Broccoli concept that I'd worshipped as gospel in my early twenties, and instead, started paying attention to when and why my energy levels changed, what my skin was doing, and how my belly felt as it digested certain foods. Fast forward to now and I've circled back to an approach to food that is without any label. It's a tremendously lovely place to be.

My commitment to feeding myself whole, nourishing foods continues – and is one of my greatest passions – but please know this: **I am not perfect.** For the most part, I like my food whole, organic and local. My diet (for lack of a better word) iis largely plant-based, but sometimes, I eat more cheese than I'd care to admit! While I love nothing more than a big old bowl of humble quinoa salad, if the day's escaped me and I just cannot be bothered come meal time, I won't hesitate to order in from the Thai place next door. Glen and I also seem to have an occasional hankering for fish and chips and ice cream (an indulgence that we just can't seem to shake!).

More than anything, what my journey with food has taught me is that it's not necessarily *what* we're eating that's influencing us perniciously. It's *how we're eating* and *how much* of it. Food addiction doesn't stem from the food itself. No, it stems from a subconscious craving to numb out and distract ourselves from feeling the emotional states that are simply rising up to be felt, expressed and released. Sometimes, to avoid those feelings of boredom, isolation, or mild anxiety, we eat. Sometimes, we crack open a bottle of wine. *This* is what causes a dependency - when something that should bring us enjoyment instead acts as a getaway vehicle. And this is also precisely why I don't necessarily believe that everyone will find their special kind of Peace in **sobriety**. Some folks out there have an astounding amount of self-awareness; knowing what's in their highest interest by boldly declaring such statements as, *"I don't think moderation is an option for me. It feels too out of control, too risky. I just know that this is something that I have to let go of for good."* To those folks, I well and truly tip my hat. How utterly courageous and conscious. *Bravo.* I made the very same declaration with drugs. *No more. Never again. Not worth it.* But just as it would be absurd for me to give up food (one of the addictions I have absolutely struggled with over the years), laying the restaurant wine list to rest for life seems far too restrictive for me. It all feels too tense and unnatural and depriving. Personally - and I mean that, this is an individual case - it's not the chardonnay that needs to be removed from my life. Rather, it's the state in which I consume it that needs to be removed, transformed, healed.

Further, there must be an honest assessment of *how much I'm consuming* and *why*. When I figured that out, much like I did with food, it was as though I opened some inner floodgates of sweet, sweet, freedom. (More on this later.)

We'll talk about the positive effect we can have on our relationships through consistent and authentic action, but before we get there, I'd like to share an example. One of my greatest joys has been being a fly on the wall and peeking in on Glen's journey as it's unfolded right before my eyes. The dinner table, a place where our passions - fine food and wine - collide, has always been our altar. I'm sure it wasn't easy for him standing by as I waved away the foods we once bonded over, but he was patient. And I suppose that all the mess I was making in his kitchen sparked some curiosity within him. After all, I had never felt so good. And he had absolutely noticed.

Some time ago now, Glen was prepping in our kitchen for a chocolate bake-off. The man's got skills when it comes to butter, sugar and chocolate, and to be honest, I was a little nervous about this. Put a delicious dessert in front of me (not to mention in my bloody fridge) and just watch me shake in my boots while salivating like a crazy. So in an attempt to intercept any chance of extreme blood-sugar escalation, I suggested, *"Babe, why don't you try making a raw dessert? We've got all the ingredients in the cupboard."* I assumed he'd shrug off my two cents with a *that's not how a real chef does things* raised eyebrow. But the next thing I knew – after a moment or two scrolling Google – cashews were being soaked and coconut oil was being measured. The rest, as they say, was history. He was hooked.

Since then, Glen and I have collaborated on *Such Different Eats* - an ecookbook that you can download from my website - which showcases radical, real-food recipes. We're also currently in the start-up phase of launching an organic food catering business locally. Few things inspire us as much as a fridge and pantry stocked full of fresh produce and superfood staples after a big Sunday morning market haul. It goes without saying how overjoyed it makes me watching him follow his passion, all while transforming his health with gusto. **Never, ever underestimate the power of your enthusiasm** and the effect it can have not only on your own health, but in influencing others. Your health is about more than just you. It helps determine the tomorrow that you're shaping, and the way in which you can contribute to the world around you.

Enlightened Exercise

After Glen and I completed our sixth winter, we set our sights on settling in Burleigh Heads; a gorgeous coastal suburb of the Gold Coast in Australia, famous for its beautiful headland and chilled-out culture. (If you follow me on Instagram @tara_bliss, you'll know I'm a tad obsessed with this place). We were finally ready to leave our *saisonnaire* lifestyle in the mountains and reserve our holy infatuation with snowboarding for work-free holidays. The deeper the roots of our relationship ran and the higher my new coaching business soared, the more ready we were to settle a little, to plant our four feet on the earth and call somewhere 'home'. (Oh yeah, did I mention that I had the head space and creativity to launch a business when I quit bingeing?!) And so, life as we knew it was over, again. It was time for another chapter.

Once in Burleigh, I could create healthy kitchen concoctions till the cows came home, but something was unmistakably missing from my life: movement. The type of movement that rocks you, challenges you, drenches you with sweat and endorphins. I was scared to work my body out here in the real world. I had ingrained, deeply etched memories of exercise being married with suffering, with unreachable goals, with unrealistic expectations. After years of subconsciously linking exercise with torture, thanks to my party agenda, I wasn't sure if I could tread lightly with myself when it came to working up a sweat. All I knew was I didn't want it to be hard anymore. I didn't want to be at war with my body. Before snowboarding saved my ass and mellowed me out, my relationship with exercise was a caustic one, reeking of Overdoing It and self-loathing. I dead-lifted till I couldn't walk. I'd punish myself with an early morning spin class to scare away the dessert I'd eaten the night before. I trained hard. I trained angry. I'd stack too much weight while bench-pressing. I'd run my little legs out, never bothering to stretch afterwards. High energy, high stress, high hatred. And then, well, I'd just go out and get *high*.

But by now, I'd already had such effective and transformational experiences of progress within my body. I had seen - firsthand - the pay-off of a gentle and loving approach to wellness. It's as though I made an unspoken promise to myself that things would never go back to the way they once had been. My nervous system was healing. I was more present moment to moment. I had certainly become more peaceful. It's just that... with my track record of fizzing on fatigue, I wasn't quite sure if I could trust myself to enjoy exercise. Particularly without the luxury of a mountain peak covered in snow. And yet, I dug deep. Thanks to my willingness to immerse in the world of personal growth, and my commitment to my spiritual practice (which we'll discuss soon), I was now able to unhook from my attachments to words such as 'strive', 'achieve' and 'should'. These words dissolved from my vocabulary and instead, I adopted 'gentle' as my new life speed, promising my body that we'd step it up only once she was ready. No more battling. No more forcing square pegs into round holes. This time, I offered myself permission to start small and slow. I would tie my laces in the early morning and simply walk, watching the sun come up over the ocean; the active community of Burleigh jogging past me. Their energy enlivened and inspired me. It made my cells dance, until it was no longer possible for me to simply walk. I wanted to bound like a gazelle! I had energy to burn, and soon, Glen and I were doubling back, running multiple laps of our local beach with big smiles on our faces, throwing ourselves in the ocean afterwards for a cooling dip, all while most of the world was still sleeping. Whaddya know? Exercise felt *good*. And then…

Along came Brieann.

Brieann Boal shimmied her way into my life with yoga mats, boxing gloves, TRX cables and a smile that could send your soul to the moon. You know that old adage, when the student is ready, the teacher appears? Well, Brieann was one of the many teachers who arrived on my doorstep at just the right time. Adorned in qualifications including personal training, yoga, Reiki and massage, BB (as she's known around these parts) and her approach to active living was the antithesis of all I feared in the world of exercise. Holistic beyond holistic, intentional, feminine and wonderfully wabi-sabi, those months that I trained with this goddess allowed me to explore both my strength and my soul, all in one. Brieann's definition of the Japanese wabi-sabi way of life alone is enough to draw folks to her like a magnet: *"Wabi-sabi is about celebrating the cracks and flaws, the patterns and pock-marks, all signs of well-worn love. We do that when we put on our favourite pair of worn, ripped jeans, or go flea-marketing for a farm-style dining table.*

Why not when we look at ourselves?"

Essentially, this approach points to the understanding that there is profound perfection in imperfection. As you can probably imagine, this sounded incredibly attractive to me. I wanted more mess in my life, less rigidity, more freakin' flow. And I got it in droves.

Before our sessions, BB would instruct me to set an intention, and not just for our workout, but for the day or week ahead, before moving me through a few slow sun salutations. She'd then take that little intention of mine and personalise it - on the spot - into our sessions. On high-energy days, she'd have me sprinting and kick-boxing. On days I was craving a little more creativity, she'd jazzy me up with fun boxing combinations, and she'd guide me to balance the left and right hemispheres of my brain with pranayama (breath work that extends vital life force in the body). On *blah* days, I wouldn't leave the yoga mat, as she'd massage out all the *ick* from my muscles, restoring me to a happy high. And I'd return to my day, dancing on clouds. Those sessions with BB locked me into a space where my mind and my body could team up to push the boundaries from a place of present love, rather than fearful point-proving. For that, and for Brieann, I am so grateful. Consider the neural pathways in my brain officially re-conditioned!

Oh, yoga

I had a feeling yoga would crack me open. It did. From all angles. Have you ever gazed at those long, yogic limbs in posed photographs and thought, with a sigh, *"Ah shit, I'll never be able to do that. Dammit."* I have. Maybe that's what landed me on the mat in the first place; a hefty slice of a very human urge to challenge myself into perhaps, just maybe, achieving the impossible. Maybe that's the initial force that first drives most people to their yoga mats; fitness, finesse, nailing some gnarly gymnastics? Ego, check! But what I'm certain of is that, for most of us, it's not the achievement of acrobatics, or the way in which we can make pretzel shapes out of our bodies that sees us rolling out our mats most days of the week… Yoga has this stealthy way of unlocking a little depth in all of us, of holding up the mirror, of helping us to face our shadows, lean further into our light. It helps us to accept, in the moment, what we once thought we could not. If you're anything like me, yoga also has a tendency to bring you to your knees with tears of gratitude and humility.

Today, I feel the same sensation on my yoga mat that I used to feel on my snowboard. I call it my church, and to be honest, it's a little difficult to express my appreciation for it without getting a little misty-eyed. There's no running, no controlling, no excuses. And on the flip side, the practice offers each of its devotees unlimited opportunities to practice faith, patience, progress. For that relentless dance between the yin and the yang, I will forever be a student of yoga. *It cements me in my devotion.* Each time I create space in my body, spaciousness ensues in my mind. **What a groovy concept, right?** The teachings of yoga can do what no drug does, can achieve what no prescription does, can counsel like no therapist does, and that's why I jumped at the chance to complete my yoga teacher training. Those moments lying flat in savasana, after 90 minutes of sweat, deep breathing and body exploration, *those moments* are sweeter, more fulfilling, more *engulfing*, than any high on the market. *Namaste to that.*

I'd really like to encourage you to closely examine the relationship you have with exercise. It, like everything else, is a reflection of how you're living life, the speed you're operating at, and the way in which you show up. Are you sedentary? Are you aggressive? Are you maybe an overachiever who's constantly nursing injuries thanks to an inflamed Ego that doesn't know when to call in a day on the running track? Alternatively, are you playing it safe by not showing a willingness to explore the strength and edge of your body through movement? I empathise deeply with anyone out there who resists exercise. I've worked with so many women playing the *should* game; identifying that they *should* be moving their butt, they *should* be working up a sweat, that they *should* be doing XYZ, but a force greater than their desire to move keeps them glued to their couch or computer screen. Tony Robbins calls this 'should-ing all over yourself' and it's helpful to nothing but guilt and self-resentment.

If this sounds like you, Party Girl, I've got a wonderful wake-up call for you: the sheer fact that you're avoiding joyful movement is clue enough that it's a path that's calling you toward it. We resist what's most important to us; what our Soul most yearns for. You're not resisting exercise because you're not good at it, or because some people are born athletes and you're simply not. I have a hunch you're resisting it because of all the amazing opportunities that may in fact present themselves to you if you quit playing small and start showing up in service of your temple. Maybe you'll get noticed? Maybe you'll have energy to pursue your passions? Maybe you won't be able to safely nuzzle behind any more excuses? Maybe you'll start to recognise your true self in the mirror? That all sounds nice, I bet, but subconsciously these possibilities can scare us shitless because, after all, they're called comfort zones for a reason. They're kinda cosy.

There's no better time than now for me to remind you of this, Marianne Williamson's powerful quote from her incredible book, *A Return to Love*.

> *"Our deepest fear is not that we are inadequate. Our deepest fear is that we are powerful beyond measure. It is our light, not our darkness that most frightens us. We ask ourselves, 'Who am I to be brilliant, gorgeous, talented, fabulous?' Actually, who are you not to be? You are a child of God. Your playing small does not serve the world. There is nothing enlightened about shrinking so that other people won't feel insecure around you. We are all meant to shine, as children do. We were born to make manifest the glory of God that is within us. It's not just in some of us; it's in everyone. And as we let our own light shine, we unconsciously give other people permission to do the same. As we are liberated from our own fear, our presence automatically liberates others."*
> Marianne Williamson, *A Return to Love*

When we're dimming our light, or playing small, or sabotaging ourselves, Gay Hendricks calls this an Upper Limit Problem. You can start to bust through yours by starting gently from a place of love and devotion to your body, not one of fear and punishment. Start where it's easy, where the inspiration pulls you, where you can smile a little. It can be a nervous journey; this one of getting back into a rhythm of active living, but one absolutely worth taking. As one of my yoga teachers, Michelle Merrifield, says, "In the long run, it's so much easier to be consistent than inconsistent."

Healing the healer

Our poor little livers. Let's workshop this out, because I reckon your liver's in dire need of some lovin'. Ange Jackson is the director of Teapot Health Coaching. She's an exercise physiologist, holds a diploma in herbal medicine, and she's an ex-Party Girl. I interviewed her so we could get to know a little more about this extraordinary detoxing organ of ours, as well as topics such as inflammation and acid-alkaline balance.

"It's thought that inflammation underlies all chronic disease, which is a pretty big claim to make", says Ange. "Low grade, chronic inflammation is what we're talking about here, so something that's developing over years, and decades... It's really the breeding ground for more serious conditions to develop over time. Inflammation is affected by a whole range of things, not just food, but stress, over-exercising, smoking. It's an underlying systemic thing that's happening in *every* cell of the body, really. *That's* inflammation. Whereas acidity and alkalinity is referring to the pH balance." She goes on to explain, "On the pH scale, alcohol is definitely acidic, which means that the overall consensus is that alcohol has a negative effect on the body, particularly when you take into account the sugar in beer and wine, which are inflammatory. But it's the *excessive* alcohol use that has detrimental effects on the body and that's usually what we're talking about here for our Party Girls. A glass of wine of an evening is not necessarily the problem; it's when we're overwhelming the body with it... that's where the problems lie."

Still with us? Phew! So here's how the liver helps us deal with all that. "You can imagine your poor little liver is trying to process all of that stuff, and it's pretty difficult for the body to do that", she continues. "And let's be honest, it's not just alcohol that's the problem. Drugs are often involved and **they're terrible for the nervous system**. There may be junk food after a night out, and of course, the smoking... The liver is an amazing organ. It truly is just mind-blowing how much work it actually does for us. Not only does it have to deal with alcohol, cigarettes, and the like, but all the environmental toxins out there, what we're putting on our skin, what we're breathing... The liver has to work out what it is, where it's going to put it, how it's going to get rid of it (or whether it's going to hold onto it), and what it's going to do with all the proteins, carbohydrates, vitamins and minerals. Everything."

Ah, it's all coming back to me. As Ange and I chat about all this, I feel compelled to place my hand upon my liver. Poor little guy, working overtime for me all those years. I can't help but feel a little shocked at how completely unaware I was of the damage I was causing my body. We start riffing on what she mentioned about the inflammatory effect that stress has on the body. Often we're still sipping back mouthfuls of guilt and shame long after The Party's over, and those two suckers fall under the same umbrella as *stress*. "Guilt and shame are usually associated with binge eating as well, so you only have to look at the foods that we go to for comfort, the high-sugar, high-fat foods that are also inflammatory." All signs point to the body saying, *Ouch.*

I ask Ange what she'd recommend for women who are inspired and ready to take action in making positive steps towards their health and settling down their nervous system. "Herbs play a huge role there", she says. "But I think it's important that everyone seeks professional advice in this area. A lot of people self-prescribe, and that's the only reason why we see problems in herbal medicine. Herbal medicine's actually incredibly safe, but it needs to be used properly." I'm passionate about this conversation with Ange, having visited a naturopath for the first time just weeks before our chat. Ever since my consultation, I feel like I've been having a love affair with my liver. I just want it to be happy. I want to do the right thing by it. Every herb I take gets swallowed with a side serve of love, and I can't help but chuckle at the irony that the pills I take today are ones that are out to heal my liver, instead of destroy it.

"A universal issue that all Party Girls will need to address is healing their liver. There are a few ways to do that... Different herbs do different things. *Rosemary* helps *protect* the liver. Other herbs help repair it, like *milk thistle* and *globe artichoke*. Then *turmeric* assists with the detoxification process. It's also a very strong antioxidant, one of the most anti-inflammatory foods there is, and it's inexpensive."

Okay, so it's highly likely that we're inflamed on the inside and on the acidic side of the pH scale - both of which can contribute to chronic disease. What can we do today - apart from booking in to see a herbalist or naturopath - to start tidying our temples? "From a nutritional perspective, your alkaline foods like your dark leafy greens, your super-greens such as spirulina or chlorella, or some combination of those are hugely beneficial and easy to incorporate into your diet by drinking green smoothies. Healthy fats are also really important.

They're anti-inflammatory, but there's also lots of evidence now that supports the long-term health benefits of adding olive oil, flaxseed oil, avocado, nuts and seeds... all these foods form the basis of a healthy diet."

Living holistically means getting quiet enough to listen to your body. It means showing up with a willingness to live life differently, to try new things, to approach your body with a child's mind and play. And healing – though our Egos would have us belief differently – needn't be heavy. It doesn't have to feel like a tiresome concept that we lug around on our backs; one that holds within it the burdens of our pains and miseries. It doesn't have to be veiled in drama. Healing can mean whatever the hell you want it to mean; happiness, softness, awareness, forgiveness, letting go, returning to totality...

In *Free Air*, a brilliant TED talk, spoken word poet Buddy Wakefield explains that to avoid the word *healing*, he asked a close friend of his for a word to use instead. To which his friend replied simply, *presence*. I adore his friend's response. To strengthen this, modern-day mystic and my personal spiritual mentor, Belinda Davidson, explains that to heal, to spiritually evolve, to become more conscious, we do not in fact have to work through the darkness. We don't have to prepare for battle as we face our past indiscretions and regrets. Instead, **we're only to align ourselves with the light.**

How does this all tie back in with our bodies? We need to come back! We need to cut those cords from the past, reel ourselves back in from the future, let go of our significant and victimising stories, and be here, now, in this moment. The only moment we have to create change. The only moment in which healing can *really* happen. It's only in *this* moment, that we can 'align ourselves with the light' with wholesome choices. The question is: are you going to rise to the occasion, Party Girl? Are you going to nourish your body appropriately, move your body joyfully, respect your aliveness, and embrace your femininity? Because I'm willing to toast to the fact that you are. It's about time you let the world see the Holistic Goddess that's been hiding out for far too long.

Peace Practice

Describe your diet in a sentence or two.

How would you describe your energy levels?

Intuitively, what foods do you feel as though you need more of?

Are there any foods that you're willing to let go of or replace?
(Remember, this is about experimentation, rather than perfection.)

Consider keeping a food journal over the next week or so. Forget about counting calories. What we're trying to do here is establish a connection to your body, to your digestive system, otherwise known as the 'intuition of the body'. We are determining how certain foods affect you and your energy an hour or two after consuming them.

What does your current approach to exercise reveal about the way you show up in your life?

For example: are you prone to laziness, or overdoing it, or stretching beyond your limits?

What type of movement *inspires* you the most?

*For example: you may know that running is good for you, but you're not excited at the thought of it. What exercise really **lights you up?***

List five emotions or states that you experience after an awesome workout.

If you acknowledge these positive emotions, does it make regular and intentional movement seem a worthy devotion of your time and effort?

'I intend to craft my own brand of enlightened exercise, because...'

Do this now!

If resources permit, this would be a great time to book in a consultation with a naturopath, herbalist, or even a kinesiologist. Bonus points if your specialist is also trained in iridology. Every time I visit my naturopath, I get totally tripped out how much she can tell me about my body simply by looking into my eyes through a microscope. Groovy, indeed.

Also, consider:

Testing your pH, which you can do at most health food stores, and getting some blood work done. There's no time like the present to become informed (and empowered) about your health.

While we're cleaning out our bodies and minds with functioning, fulfilling self-care practices, let's up the ante and identify what else needs to go. It's time we took out a little more trash.

6.

A Clean Slate &
A New State of Being

"We must be willing to get rid of the life we've planned, so as to have
the life that is waiting for us. The old skin has to be shed
before the new one can come."
Joseph Campbell

Let me back this up a little. Those blissed-out, fresh-faced moments, complete with quinoa and carrot juice, they didn't come before navigating through some tricky terrain. In 2010, I was living in Queenstown, New Zealand, a jaw dropping corner of the world adorned with crystal clear lakes, jagged mountain ranges, and a pumping ski and snowboarding scene. In the winter, beer and cider sustains the transient population as they hop-scotch between happy hour, house parties and first tracks up the hill. In summer, when the sun's still shining at 9:30pm, tanned bodies gather for drinking marathons, and barefooted nomads balance their way across slack lines, beer in one hand, cigarette in the other. The town itself is intoxicating; in beauty and debauchery.

I had the best gig in town, working for AJ Hackett, the pioneers of modern-day bungee-jumping. I spent my days harnessing petrified jumpers who were two pelvic floor clenches from shitting themselves with sheer terror. I'd coach the tourists on how to plunge themselves out into the ether to greatest effect for the 134-metre drop, watching their hearts practically punch through their chests as I explained the process to them. It was an incredible way to earn money; high intensity, high energy, and lots of high-fiving. I loved my job. I adored the people I worked with, though I felt an arm's length from them most of the time. Their shenanigans shined a light on how far I'd travelled from mine. I recall thinking often, "*I don't know whether I'm crazy enough for this lot*", while remembering the times I was the life of the party, laughing and joking for days about the mess and chaos I'd caused on the sauce. These days, yeah, not so much. My Party Boots were getting a little too snug for my feet.

The town was abuzz most nights of the week, and while I was invited to each and every social gathering, I simply didn't have the energy to show up. **I so badly wanted to go.** I wanted to show these people what Seven Pots & A Pint Tara was really made of. I wanted to show them the type of girl I could be under the layer of introversion that seemed to be stifling the confidence I once carried with me. *If only drugs weren't so damn in expensive in this town.*

I started growing tired in Queenstown. Physically tired. Laughter would roar through the work bus as we made the trip back into town from the bungee site each day; my work friends planning a night of drinking and fun. "Tara, come along!" they'd encourage. I'd smile at them, grateful that they always made such a thoughtful effort to include me, but inside, I was craving a hot shower, my pyjamas and a home-cooked dinner. Maybe a dabble in our new veggie patch. Maybe cheese and wine on the lounge room floor with Glen. *Peace and quiet.* Of course on the nights that I did go out – which were few and far between – I totally obliterated myself, as demonstrated on the night I sank so many vodka shots that I ended up heaving in the gutter of the main road; two Fergburger burgers beside me, which I had obviously planned to devour while stumbling home in a famished frenzy. Needless to say, Glen was rather unimpressed when he finished work to find me sitting in a pile of my own vom. He lifted my floppy body off the road and then copped my drunken slander for the entirety of the journey home. Alcohol was once an addition in my life that uplifted me, brought me alive, but it was quickly becoming unflattering, like an outfit that just didn't fit quite right.

It was 12 months later. By then married, Glen and I were living in Whistler, Canada, still chasing the snow as it scattered itself on mountains around the world. Where the snow falls, the beer flows. And while New Zealand could compete with Canada in the good looks department, the Land Of The Long White Cloud had nothing on Maple Country when it came to the cost and accessibility of drugs. Since we're being honest here, I can't tell you that cheap and easy-to-find cocaine wasn't what sealed our executive decision to choose a Canadian winter over a French one. Alcohol had revealed itself as a terrorist in our relationship, but I couldn't get the images of getting to know Glen under the sweetened spell of a chemical high out of my head. We were both easy and free and affectionate while peaking, and I wanted the arguments to stop.

After a few weeks of grounding ourselves in epic Whistler, adjusting to new jobs, new friends, and a new apartment, we made our first 'order'. As line after perfectly cut line disappeared up our noses, we got sucked further into the kaleidoscopic vortex of The Coke High. At 4am, every speck of dust had landed in our cells, quickly pulling us down into a pit of post-drug emptiness I'll remember forever; a stark contrast to the weird and wild time we were having just hours before. Glen and I felt flat out awful, eventually retiring to bed for a few hours of fragile cuddles before rising like the waking dead. It wasn't pretty. We weren't pretty. Even the majestic mountains and fire-place scented air couldn't lift our spirits. Glen put it down to 'bad coke', to which I responded, "Babe, you know what? I think I'm done with this".

And to this day, that was the last time I ever touched a narcotic.

With that decision came a responsibility to walk my talk. And as is often the case when we make a decision for our highest good, The Universe presents us with opportunities to dial down on our intentions. When we make a choice, and life beckons us to step up and solidify our thoughts with action. Social invitations were hitting us left, right and centre. House warming party after work drinks after birthday party after après drinks after pot luck dinner and beers. It was endless, but so was my desire to treat myself better. Rather than hitting the clubs after finishing my shift at midnight, I'd trudge through the snowy forest to our back door, kick off my snow boots, and breathe a sigh of relief as I stepped into our toasty apartment. The thought of drinking after work rarely even occurred to me. I needed energy to snowboard and I needed energy to write.

Years earlier, I had launched my blog *Such Different Skies*, a name that had come to me while Glen and I were picking mandarins in central Queensland, living out of a camper trailer. We were in between winters, transitioning from Japan to New Zealand, and were looking for a way to make a few bucks for a few months. Picking those mandarins in the middle of nowhere, with my relatively new boyfriend working the tree beside me, I announced through twigs and ripened fruit and way too many spiders for my liking that I was tossing around a faint idea of launching a blog. Even though I didn't know a thing about blogging. **Even though I thought bloggers were losers.** Even though I was of the opinion that everyone should be out there, travelling the world, snowboarding, picking fruit between winters. Experiencing the ups and downs of life, rather than tapping away behind a keyboard. (How boring.) But this damn blog idea had drawn me in hook, line and sinker. Something about it felt expansive and full of possibility. You would think that climbing up and down ladders for 12 hours straight with 15 kilos of citrus hanging from your chest would be a special kind of hell on earth. Yet, the sun always seemed to set rather quickly out there in the country, where the only noises were the snip-snip-snipping of our tools, the rustling of leaves, the odd *"Ow!"* when we copped a spiky branch in the face, and the occasional revving of a tractor engine as we progressed down our row of mandarin trees. Time ceased to exist. Memories never before revisited would spring to our minds and they'd consume us for hours. Likewise for future projections. Hopes and dreams would scoop us up and carry us off into a silent, busy world of unlimited imagination, as our bodies robotically kept snipping, kept climbing, kept emptying our fruit into the half-tonne bins.

And this blog thing, it started to take up every inch of skull. What would I write about? Maybe… maybe stuff like this? Like backpacking? Travelling? Being a *saisonnaire*? Snowboarding in Japan? Culinary adventures? I could write about hiking trails and pub crawls and music that moves me. Maybe I could even, like, share some photos of my adventures? **But what would I call it? This blog of mine…**

One dawn, as Glen and I drive our old Ford out of the township and towards the farm, the sun peeking its head up over the valley and the morning mist slowly rising from the river, I look up at the clouds. Maxed out. Zoomed in. Fluffed up beyond fluffy. *If I was at the top of my ladder amongst the small, sun-ripened fruit, I might even be able to touch them.* The clouds are so big and gregarious and *alive* out here.

"We see such different skies…" I say to the car window, my neck still creaked up, so I can cloud-gaze. "Huh?" replies my sleepy boyfriend. "It's just…

you know… we've been to a few places around the world together… and the sky never looks the same…"

And so a blog was born that chronicled our travels, the music I was digging at the time, and written contemplations. But in Canada, after having transformed my habits on the lead up to our wedding, my writing had begun to change. It had become less about travel and music festivals, and more about exploring such topics as authenticity and self-discovery. I was pressing publish on whole-food recipes and deep contemplations, all the while encouraging my slowly growing audience to look at their own lives through a different lens, to explore their comfort zone, to become more compassionate, kinder people. At work, blog post ideas were being scribbled down on napkins between garnishing mojitos, and one-liners were waking me up in the morning.

With passion and, most importantly, this newfound sense of purpose, I naturally crowded out my destructive behaviours with healthy habits. That's not to say that I became a teetotaller. Some of my fondest memories in Canada were made complete by the drink in my hand. Like the time we took a gas cooker, a bottle of red, and dried spices to the frozen lake, and cooked up a fresh batch of mulled wine while watching our friends play ice hockey. Or the time we carried a six pack of beers in our backpacks up the chairlift and said *cheers!* in the back country, saluting Black Tusk as the sun set behind her peak. Or the bottle of British Colombian pinot noir that Glen and I shared over a three-course local-produce meal one night. These memories still make me smile ear to ear just thinking about them.

Like I've mentioned before, alcohol isn't the problem - and it never has been. It was always my approach to it, my dependency on it to transform me into someone I thought I should be, that made it a destructive presence in my life. But as you can see from these examples, it was quickly, gratefully, becoming something that intensified these experiences in a beautiful way, rather than being the sole reason, the main excuse, to participate in the first place. Channelling my energy into creative and soulful pursuits like writing and cooking, as well as learning how to project a confident 'no' were all pivotal in what turned out to be a smooth transition from *Party Girl* back to the truth of who I am.

I want to stress here, again, that this whole book is about anchoring into the understanding that we don't need strive to be *more*; better, worthier, more excellent as a being. When we consciously surrender our fears, when we create space in our lives, when we U-Haul out all that's been blocking us from receiving and expressing who we naturally are, we begin to hum with Peace. This chapter is about recognising how crucial it is to surrender what's no longer serving us; from physically clearing our space, or 'clearing the decks', to gently friend-detoxing, to locking eyes with limiting perceptions surrounding the almost-unyielding prickle of separateness and isolation, and good old FOMO.

Remember, life isn't merely happening *to* you. **It serves you**. It co-creates along-side you. It moves *through* you. So instead of being a spectator, get your ass on the field and get dirty! Here's a series of processes I went through during this transition. And while they weren't conscious at the time, the gift of hindsight allows me to chronicle them for you in a digestible and actionable way.

Clearing the Decks

Everything is energy; a flow of flux and change that's constantly in motion; unfolding, expanding, traveling with ease. And yet sometimes, it can't. Energy can become blocked and stagnant; slow-moving and stale. We experience these polarities of free flow and stuckness in our bodies too. As we move with either intensity *or* intention, we limber our joints, warm our muscles, and activate our meridians (the pathways in the body that allow vital energy to flow), allowing us to feel open, free and flexible; each cell nourished with oxygen, our organs revitalised with freshly pumped blood. But when we're sedentary and motion-less, which is oh-so-usual in a world rife with cubicle-nation-hell and social media addiction, our energy can become stagnant in our bodies. Our muscles shorten and tighten, we cramp up, we gain weight. With our lack of movement comes a lack of opportunity for bodily freedom and bliss. The same is true for our physical space. If your environment encourages energy to stay still – to ac-cumulate in corners – the weight of the room (or your car, or your fridge) will be heavy and burdensome, preventing ease and fluidity. I grew up in a house full of *stuff*. Cupboards were crammed full of excess linen, copious amounts of Christmas decorations and boxes upon boxes of Things We Might Use One

Day. Every drawer and spare shoebox played home to piles of insignificant nothings. I didn't take much notice of it as a little girl, but the simple thought of it now is enough to bring the onset of a headache. My childhood experience matched that of the state of our house; though it was tidy on the outside, beneath it all, it was frantic and full and chaotic. **The space we reside in often mirrors, or is an accurate representation of, the space within us**.

These days, I can sense when my life is about to shift gears; when I'm on the precipice of change, creative *or* destructive. It's because I intuitively feel the need to stop everything I'm doing and take to my apartment with a garbage bag and a vacuum cleaner. Energy courses through me as I cyclone my way through my home - shifting furniture, ripping up and re-doing vision boards, updating music playlists, cleaning out the fridge, the pantry, my office. I turn into a mad woman. Now, this isn't The Party Girl's Guide to Housework Mastery, but as you're about to discover, making decisions about how you want your environment to look and feel is not only a creative expression of self-love. It ushers in possibilities that may have otherwise gone unnoticed.

Everything we experience in our lives; whether it's great romance, belly laughs with friends, or the way in which we lay out our living room, it's all secondary to our inner energy field. Wayne Dyer teaches us that we create more of what we already *are*, not more of what we *want*. This tweet-worthy sound byte has helped me immensely over the years. It helps me take an inventory on *how* I'm creating my life. Our wallets - disorganised and crammed with receipts - speak volumes of our relationship to money, and thus, self-worth. How can we open ourselves up to the opportunity of financial freedom and increased cash flow if we haven't created any room in our wallets for it? The food in our fridge is obviously a direct indicator of how we value our bodies. The quality and amount of clothes in our wardrobes is often a representation of our framework of abundance. Our environments give us insight into what's really going on in our energy anatomy. What are we holding onto? What are we attached to? What are we trying to suppress in our lives by filling our space with meaningless *stuff*? And why? And how much of it is completely subconscious behaviour that you haven't even identified until reading this chapter?

Have you ever watched one of those reality TV shows about hoarders? They're uncomfortable programs to sit through. And not just because the catastrophic hoarding efforts are enough to make you break out into a clammy itch.

(Or is that just me?) Mostly, it's painful to witness the struggle of a hoarder. Deep down, they're suffering. They're burying their pain in a sea of boxes and rubbish, hand-me-downs, and sometimes even animals. Some folks find safety, comfort and value in possessions, and hinge their sense of self-worth upon how much they *have*, rather than who they *are*.

I'll admit that hoarding is a pretty extreme example, but the metaphysical message remains consistent: **the more you *have*, the less room there is in your life for what matters most**. Rather than settling into a state of *being*, the stuff in our lives distracts us into a rat-wheel of *having*. I'm not suggesting you pitch a *'Garage Sale'* sign, sell everything you own, throw your razor in the trash and run to an ashram (although, if the spirit moves you...) because dropping the Party Girl identity for that of a barefooted hippy doesn't bring you closer to yourself either. That's just yet another distraction, another layer to add to the facade.

This chapter is about the opposite of that: it's about **quality**. It's about only making room for the things, friends and experiences in your life that make you feel exceptional and electric. Quality over quantity - that's what we're shooting for. Not just so you can feel weight lift from your shoulders as you clear away physical space. On a deeper level, it's about radiating very clear, very symbolic vibes out into the cosmos that communicate to the world that you're ready to start afresh. Your arms are open. You want to try things differently. You're ready to play ball. Only thing is you can't catch brilliant, aligned opportunities if you're still clutching to the old with white knuckles. Quality is ten hangers of clothing that makes you smile at the sight of them, rather than a cupboard jammed with sale items that *still* have you waxing lyrical about how little you have to wear. Quality is choosing two squares of the most outrageous (and pricey) dark chocolate ever to have delighted your senses, and passing on two blocks of the run-of-the-mill milk chocolate version. It's about choosing to do what you feel compelled to do, rather than defaulting to your obligations.

Bring on the fresh slate

When we attach ourselves to something, sooner or later, we'll create a way to destroy it, whether we're aware of this process or not. Have you ever repelled a lover with co-dependent behaviour? Have you ever felt as though you lost a limb when you misplaced a material possession that you feel made you more of a person? How about the times when you've obsessed about your lack of money, only to be on the receiving end of a freak storm of bills and unexpected overdue payments? Detaching from the world of form is a brave move to make, and it might feel like a pretty alien concept at the beginning, but the pay-off is awesome. It gives our heart permission to lead the way through life with self-reliance and real love.

So, Party Girl, let's take out the trash!

Below, I've made a list full to the brim of ideas on how you can systemically wipe your life of space-fillers. For more creative genius on decluttering (until it hurts!) I recommend money mindset mentor, Denise Duffield-Thomas, author of *Lucky Bitch* and *Get Rich Lucky Bitch*. This exercise in clearing the decks is enthusiastically inspired by her. She uses this approach when teaching folks how to raise their income levels, which I love. I happen to believe, though, that this work can attract *anything* - from a speaking gig, to a new friend, to killer insights that help shape your immediate future. The question is: how much are you willing to let go of? How bare are you willing to strip down in the name of spaciousness? Will there be tears as you slowly but surely start disassociating who you are from your belongings, interactions and behaviours? If it resonates, take it! If not, leave it. Use these three questions as filters for your decluttering process:

:: Do I need you? :: Do I love you? :: Do you reflect the person I'm ready to be?

If the answer to all three is no, it's time to lighten up, buckle in, and bid *au revoir* to:

:: Clothes that don't fit, that are old, and that don't make you feel how you want to feel when you wear them;

:: Embarrassing underwear;

:: Anything broken around the house;

:: Half-used toiletries and old makeup that's collecting dust;

:: Furniture that's simply filling a corner - someone else needs it more than you;

:: Facebook acquaintances - you know, the peeps you barely know and hardly dig; ensure that that newsfeed of yours is squeaky clean;

:: Any food in your cupboard or fridge that isn't a representation of who you want to be;

:: Extra linen, towels, blankets - the Salvation Army is hungry for them;

:: Toxin-laden cleaning chemicals, toiletries, perfumes and room sprays - if you're transitioning to a more eco-friendly life;

:: Journals from yesteryear - are you brave enough to burn them?;

:: Half-baked projects that are past their used-by date - let 'em loose;

:: Friends who you need to let go - undertake a gentle friend detox (which we'll talk about shortly);

:: Commitments you've made previously that don't light you up - nobody likes going back on their word, but honesty and authenticity trumps obligation, every time; if you're overcommitted and running on empty, you've got two choices, burning out in order to appease everyone else, or pulling back with a sincere apology - without making excuses - and re-calibrating.

You up the decluttering the ante by:

> *:: Rearranging your furniture - you could experiment with feng shui;*

> *:: Hiring a cleaner for a few hours;*

> *:: Taking your car to get detailed;*

> *:: Adding air-enriching plants to your space;*

> *:: Putting fresh sheets on your bed;*

> *:: Hanging up your vision board and giving it centre stage;*

> *:: Celebrating your new space with a guided meditation, or a naked dance, or sex - whatever floats your boat*

Allow yourself some time to feel into the space, after you've systematically moved through your bedroom, office, pantry, kitchen, wallet, car, living space and bathroom (yep, I'm betting that you only need a quarter of those toiletries that you've been cramming into those drawers), and slowly pacing the area with an intention - perhaps your intention might be that this very process of outing the old represents your willingness to receive the new, or that this space, just like your heart, is open, spacious, and warm. It's ready to receive, not more stuff, but more deeply fulfilling experiences, more highly aligned opportunities, more good juju. Consider lighting a candle, smudging with sage, or creating an altar with crystals and photos.

Resistance smack-downs

Here's how you know *resistance* is showing up during your de-cluttering process:

'Don't throw that out! It's a waste of money.' Rubbish. You will always create ways to invite more money into your life. As Kate Northrup, author of *Money: A Love Story* says, "Money is simply a stand in for value". If you don't value what's taking up your space, get rid of it.

'It used to be special.' But it's not anymore, so *bon voyage*.

'I'll fit into it one day.' You're right. You might. You probably will. And when you lose the weight, you'll celebrate by buying an outfit much cuter than that one to flaunt in anyway, so say goodbye.

'I've had it since childhood.' Does it still hold a special place in your heart? Does it light you up with precious nostalgia? If the answer's no, let it go, with love.

'It's a family heirloom.' But is it significant to you? Would another member of your family appreciate holding onto it more than you?

'It was given to me as a gift.' And it truly is the thought that counts. Swap it at the store it came from or give it to charity. Disliking a gift has absolutely no bearing on your love for the person who gave it to you.

'But what will take its place?' Sweet space. Oxygen. Opportunities. Whatever you do, don't fill a space for no reason! Give it time to breathe.

'I can do some DIY and fix that.' Really? Will you? Be honest now.

'They're going to judge me if I back out of that commitment/dinner/collaboration.' They indeed might. But what other people think of you is none of your business.

This whole decluttering jam is legit. I can personally vouch for it. Once, within a few short days of completely clearing my life of past outfits, experiences and knick-knacks, I attracted six new clients into my calendar and got word of some pretty great speaking opportunities. Regularly, as I finish working with a client, a new one effortlessly appears. Sometimes, I swear that all I have to do is take the bins out, and by the time I make it back upstairs, there's an opportunity-rich email awaiting me in my inbox. In and out, back and forth, old and new.

It's not woo-woo. It's physics!

Sceptical? You're not the only one. Peace Girl Jaime had her reservations about the significance of clearing space too. "I wasn't totally convinced on the whole decluttering thing, until we gave the ultimatum to a house guest that had well and truly outstayed their welcome and become toxic to our home... As my partner was helping the guest pack up his car, he got a phone call from a good friend offering him a great job for the summer!" Nicole once posted a photo in our community of a table stacked high with boxes, clothing and knick-knacks. "Decluttering! Helps to know this is all going to a women's refuge for brave ladies and children who have little to nothing." Giving stuff away feels good.

It feels good to give away certain relationships, too. One of my darling friends, in love as she might be with her fiancé, was energetically holding on to a boy she loved when she was *seventeen*. I suggested she write him a letter, for her eyes only, one that she'd burn. So she did, detailing how ready she was to release him and move on with her life. The *very next day*, her Facebook feed boasted that he was now 'in a relationship'. Not only did her willingness to surrender their connection energetically permit him to move on with his life, but since then there is room in her psyche, her body, her everyday existence for the man she loves. Now, there's actually space for him to *be* her man. They are closer than ever.

The Friend Detox

Some of the most significant friendships we make are either founded in or strengthened by the thirst for partying. Alcohol and drugs enable us to lubricate our inhibitions and sign those social contracts with a fine print that says, *"We're all in this together"*. That contract binds us to each other; to relationships that are amplified by pre-drinks and drug peaks; where our collective Fear Of Missing Out means that we throw ourselves into any opportunity to create memories, laugh loudly, tear up the dance floor and maybe - just maybe - pluck Mr Right out from behind the laser beams and gnarly beats. It's in The Party that we find our wingmen and wingwomen, people with whom we feel safe sharing our hungover pain, lack of responsibility and tales from the trenches. More than anything, we feel we belong; even if our bodies are aching and our heads are pounding. At least we're not alone.

That feeling of finding resonance with the folks who went hard or went home is still fresh in my memory. I felt safe and held, despite being in a toxic environment, and it's because of the friendships I had made; the connections that had been established. I had become a part of the stories we shared and the drinks we shouted and the way we held space for one another to recover. It brought us closer. *This* is why it can be so difficult to pull away from a crowd of people that no longer represent the direction we'd like to take. During those late nights and early mornings, we signed our name on that dotted line, declaring we were part of the wolf pack. Who the hell are we to go back on our word?

In the heat of the amplifying and seemingly permanent moment, we often forget that people naturally grow and change. Relationships evolve, peak and deteriorate. Nothing stays the same; everything is always changing. Our challenge as women looking to live more spirited lives in this world is to acknowledge that this is a beautiful thing, not something to be afraid of. The impermanence of life is what propels us forward into a sea of unpredictable mystery, as is the impermanence of *friendship*. We learn most about ourselves through our interactions with other people. We can crouch down on our meditation cushions until the cows come home, but if we can't be truthful in the way we communicate, then what's the point? The people in our lives teach us who we are, who we want to be, and who we no longer wish to be - which, I think, is really special.

Distancing yourself does *not* mean that you have to un-friend, or leave your troops behind entirely. For you, a friend detox might mean having a few honest conversations with your tribe about your willingness to explore a different lifestyle. It may mean catching up for coffee and Sunday brunch instead of Thank God It's Friday write-offs. Or perhaps it means mid-week dinner and drinks instead of all-nighters. Friend detoxing isn't something that happens overnight either. It's a process that requires time, and if you're aware enough to honour and nurture that process with patience and a little compassion, it'll be easier for everyone involved.

My process of re-shuffling the influencers in my life was made easier thanks to my transience. Skipping towns and countries allowed me the ability to start again; to build my life afresh. With that also came an ability to hide behind even more masks (which requires a detoxing process of its own)! However, when I grew physically exhausted and emotionally fed up from all this shape-shifting, something pretty profound happened, and I can only explain it as a *surrendering*. I came back home, back to my body. **My body took the steering wheel.** Because of that, I started turning in for quiet nights and I started turning down invitations, without a trace of guilt or anxiety.

When you start listening and feeling into your body, and I mean really, really paying attention to it, you're automatically armed with everything you need to know. You'll understand whether you need to retreat into yourself, eat different foods, or take a break from the scene that carried you here. That may include the friends involved as well. In a later chapter, we'll chat in more detail about the tension that contrasting lifestyles can cause in your life, and ways to move through it. But for now, I want to introduce friend-detoxing in two different ways.

The first is to realise that no matter how pure and evolved and 'better' the choices are that you're making, they do *not* make you a better person. This is one of those pesky little concepts that's easier said than practiced. Un-cooking raw vegan cheesecake and nailing a headstand on your yoga mat can feel pretty enlightening, but they don't make you more significant a person than old friends who are still partying just as hard as they were five years ago. What makes you a more conscious, more caring person than you were yesterday is **recognising aspects of yourself in *others***, being compassionate, realising the profound truth that we each have a path to tread, and that no two paths are the same. And while your path at this time may be to restructure your life in a way that supports your physical body and limitless potential as a human being, those around you are walking down their very own dusty road of life too, doing the best they can with what they know. Let's not forget either that, often, it's the lowest lows that evoke earth-shattering wake-up calls. Whether you're interacting with Party contemporaries or not, you give those around you permission to grow by walking your talk, maintaining an authentic presence and – the big one – allowing them to feel into the full experience of their lows, without trying to fix them. (That will just piss them off.)

The second method of friend-detoxing is to communicate your intentions honestly, but in a way that doesn't intimidate. Having these conversations isn't just about rallying support and strengthening your intentions. **It's also a super-stealthy way for you to expand your decluttering efforts.** It's important for you to scan and sift through the relationships in your life. When you're honest with those around you about your transition and your desired lifestyle, not only are you laying a foundation of accountability that sets you up to walk your talk, but you're also given an opportunity to gauge who makes the cut when choosing your support team. This doesn't need to be an awkward process; body language and behavioural reactions will tell you everything you need to know.

Let's consider two reactions to this potentially difficult, but essential conversation.

You approach two friends for lunch and excitingly declare, "Babes, I'm super-pumped about a few things! I've felt really inspired lately to be the best version of myself, so I'm going to devote myself to putting my health and spiritual wealth first. I've been feeling a little disconnected from my body for a while and I think it's about time I lean into a new direction..."

Friend One says, "Oh, babe! That's fantastic. I totally understand, and I think it's amazing that you want to look after yourself better!"

Friend Two silently raises as eyebrow as if to say, "Who *are* you?"

It's not hard for us all to gather that Friend Two isn't on your bus. At least not yet.

What happens if a friend or family member then turns a cold shoulder on you and your vibrant visions? Or worse, what if you're not even willing to approach them, because you're on such different paths, and speak such different languages, that attempting to even have such a conversation would have *foolish* written all over it? **It's okay**. It's beyond okay. In fact, we don't have to look too far to find the blessing in this situation. **That person has done the decluttering for you**, dismissing themselves from your support network in this particular area of your life. *This particular area* being the operative words here. I still have friends that down beer bongs and guzzle bubbles from the bottle. Am I as close to them as I once was? Certainly not. But that's not to say I don't still love and respect them. Co-existing is not only possible, but it keeps you humble. Those who jump off your bus do you an incredible service, and allow you to become laser-focused and super-aware when building your Peace Tribe. You don't have to let go entirely if you don't want. That's not what this is about. Yet creating a little space between the two of you gives you both room to grow. Yes, that can be scary. It can feel a little yucky sometimes. It gets a little uncomfortable when we go through this. I've been there many times over. We're all in this together, sweet potato, and you'll emerge out of this more sovereign and more aware of yourself and your needs than ever before.

> *"Sometimes 'no' is the most loving response"*
> Gabrielle Bernstein

Meet one of my closest friends, writer and life coach, Rachel MacDonald. "I never wanted to miss an opportunity for the biggest, craziest, best story, or to meet the guy, or to be on an adventure", she says. "And now, looking back, I can see how there's an inextricable link between that and my self-worth. I really felt as though I had to validate myself by being there constantly, and if I wasn't there, then I may have been on the outer. Also, there was this emptiness that came with needing to be there for all the wrong reasons… When you're partying, it's like you've cranked yourself up to a billion decibels, to create this huge version of yourself… But what I started to realise is that huge version of myself doesn't need drugs or alcohol. It's actually who I am at my core. It was about connecting back in with that… and I guess this whole sense of living an authentic life, and living your truth, and living on purpose stems from that."

Party Girls have a default Yes Response. With FOMO calling the shots, we overextend in an attempt to prove ourselves and appease our peers. But get this, studies now prove that 'peer pressure' (for lack of a better term) lasts no longer than 72 hours - ahem - no longer than a single weekend. True freedom comes when we explore the result of a loving 'no', not from a place of obnoxiousness, but from sovereignty and Self. Few things in life feel as liberating and truly empowering as saying 'no' when you want to, even if you anticipate that those around you are willing you to choose differently. With 'no', comes creative power. And if you're holding a vision for yourself as someone who lives life by your terms, on your clock, you had better get used to saying it.

Another beauty of a sacred 'no'? It's an extra way to declutter your circumstances, using conversation as the broom. Plus, it keeps you within your Zone of Genius, a brilliant term penned by Gay Hendricks, author of *The Big Leap*.

Each and every time you pass on something, you're making the space for a more aligned experience to present itself. Another door truly does open every time you push one shut. Gabrielle Bernstein accentuates this perfectly, in her book, *Miracles Now*. She writes, *"As you begin to make the word 'no' a regular part of your vocabulary, you'll come to feel a sense of peace set in. Though it may feel odd at first, you'll learn to love the freedom you'll receive from protecting your time and energy. Most important, you'll feel better about yourself because the things you do commit to, you'll actually show up for."*

But, but, but… I want to be footloose and fancy-free!

"I'm afraid that I won't be able to enjoy music while sober as much as when I'm drunk or high."

"I'm not confident enough to dance without alcohol."

"I'll miss out on all the crazy stuff that might go down!"

I can't tell you how many times I've heard these words from the women I've worked with. Sisters, hand on heart, I hear you! Been there, felt that. Repeated the same story over and over in my own head for what felt like eons. After all, there's a reason they call that drug 'ecstasy'. There's a reason those alco-pops campaigns reel us in. We've created that many neural pathways in our brains that link being wasted with having wonderful experiences that anything interrupting those conditioned patterns can feel - quite literally - life-threatening.

Here's a short story about the first time I took drugs, why it affected me so much, and essentially why they remained the central point of my experiences for years. Even I was surprised by my shuffle toward drugs; despite having hit the bong and abusing alcohol from a young age, I was defiantly against chemical narcotics. Until, that was, I became part of a tribe who loved them, and it became my priority to fit in and belong. They were seasoned pill-poppers, *and would look after me*, they said.

It's Friday evening, the club my friends have brought me to is heaving, and it's my first time here. I'm wearing these cute little snakeskin heels and wondering why all the women around me are wearing flat shoes. Before thinking about the pill in my hand anymore, given the chance I might change my mind, I swallow half of it with a swig of Red Bull, and wait patiently, feeling a little self-conscious as I bop along awkwardly to music that everyone else seems to have living inside of them. And then I start to feel it; the fluttering sensations of the music becoming a part of me too. It felt like it was growing inside of me with a speedy *whoosh!* Euphoria raced up and down the midline of my body. I felt free. Entirely unshackled. And… *beautiful.* I look at my watch – it's 1am – and, relieved that the night is still so young, I smile big and stomp my feet into the beat, thinking *I'm dancing till the sun comes up.* Now I get it – the flat shoes thing – these folks come here to *dance.* At 5am, I leave the club. At 8am, I'm at work, my damn head still bopping.

If you're afraid you'll lose a part of yourself that you revelled in discovering through your experimentation with drugs and alcohol, I understand. I wasn't sure I even wanted to know what my life would be like if I couldn't have a connection to the music and practice being in my body like I could when I was high. Exploring what that might feel like takes courage and patience and a willingness to observe tricky emotions, like potentially feeling awkward, or out of place, or alien. It takes a willingness to expand your comfort zone.

Hayley Carr is a Life and Health Coach, Master NLP Practitioner, Confidence Expert, and dear friend of mine, with exuberant energy and an incredible brain. When I interviewed her, she had some golden nuggets of wisdom to impart. "Your comfort zone is defined only by what you've experienced so far", she says, after we start exploring the topic of loosening identities and launching into a world of uncertainty. "It's a complete fallacy. One of my mentors Peter shaw once said to me: "If it's scary and exciting, do it!" Your comfort zone expands when you do things that scare you and excite you all at the same time. Party Girls make the mistake of kidding themselves into thinking that they're leaving their comfort zones by having a really big night. **That's the trap**. The thing is, to truly grow, you've got to stretch further than that. A more scary and exciting situation would be to head to a gig or a festival or a party completely straight. Or to say no to drugs, or to pass on the invitation altogether. *That's* breaking the comfort zone."

This conversation was so timely for me. Just a few weeks after our interview, I was set to attend Big Day Out, a music festival held in the scorching Australian summer. The Red Hot Chili Peppers were headlining, and part of me was already peaking just imagining Anthony Kiedis romping around on stage, shirtless, in front of me, spitting out his absurd, completely moving lyrics. But AK's ripped torso wasn't the only thing inspiring me; I'd decided to see out this festival stone cold sober. By that stage, I had already sworn off drugs, but was determined and up for the challenge of driving home from the festival dusty and sober. I took that little tip from Hayley as a thumbs up from The Universe that I was well and truly on my way to Comfort-Zone-Expanding City.

"Once you push through the fear, you experience growth", she says. And if we don't? "If you don't grow your comfort zone, it's so detrimental to you, because you lose who you are. It's essential to discover more and more about who you are." Let's say that again. *If you don't grow your comfort zone, you lose who you are.* Holy truth-bomb. "The things that you desire are *always* the things that are going to help you grow, and they live outside of your comfort zone. I really believe that the more you can live in that zone of discomfort, where the good stuff is, the more you can inspire other people to do the same", says Hayley. This instantly reminded me of one Danielle LaPorte's mantras **'You *are* your desires.'**

Using my sober Red Hot dream as an example, Hayley then explained how I can use the power of my mind to paint a picture of success, weeks before the festival arrives. "What's the outcome that you want?" she asks. "Get a picture in your mind and hold onto it." *Got it.* "Ask yourself: who do I need to be in order to get what I want?" *I need to be a leader. I need to journey into unchartered territory.* "What three words will remind you of who you need to be?" *Brave. Radiant. Present.* "Set yourself some reminders on your phone before you head out, maybe one every couple of hours. Check in with yourself. Am I being my own leader? Am I present, radiant and brave in this experience? Who am I being? Feel it, rather than think it," she says. I love this important distinction.

I ask what we should do if a situation presents itself that creates conflict inside of us? "Ask yourself *does this choice help me to be who I need to be, or does it push me away from who I need to be?* And if you come up with the answer *no it doesn't help me get there,* then it's really easy to make a decision. Those three words that you chose light you up and speak to your soul so much, that saying no becomes easy."

I feel like dropping to my knees and offering 'I'm not worthy' gestures to my gorgeous friend. Here she is, a young woman, around my age, kicking limiting beliefs and behaviours to the kerb and explaining - with such certainty and clarity - how each of us can do the same, using nothing but our God-given minds and bodily intelligence as the compass.

So Hayley, you used to be a drunken Little Miss Muffet causing a ruckus. What's your life look like today?

"Today, I wake up and I live a life completely of choice. And when you live a life of total choice, *that's* peace", says Hayley. "It's not that I don't go out and have a great time with my friends, because I still love going out and being social, but it's choice-governed now. So I'll have a glass of wine, but it'll be a glass of beautiful, organic red wine, and I *choose* to drink that. And I also choose when to go home, and to feel good about that too. Sobriety may be in my future, and I could probably choose that right now, but I still enjoy experiences with my friends while sharing a bottle of wine."

Are you seeing a theme here? These women-on-a-mission-to-live-their-best-lives-possible aren't, in fact, missing out on *anything*. They're getting more out of life: more connection, gratitude, health, aliveness, awareness.

Just in case you need a little more proof, here's what Peace Girl Kristen had to say, "When going-away parties, welcome-home parties, engagement parties and birthdays rolled around, I knew I had to find a way to hone in on that care-free Party Girl I once was. So I started sneaking coconut water and kombucha into the pubs! I realised music sounded just as good when I was high on life as it did when I was high on drugs. My dance moves were still as bad sober as they were after seven shots, and the big smile that was permanently wiped across my face on a messy night out was making a comeback while I attended parties sober. **I had never felt more *rebellious*.** Going to a party sober, sneaking non-alcoholic drinks into the venue, asking the bartender for a green tea bag in some iced water and hitting the dance floor when my favourite songs played... I felt so alive."

Purposeful rebellion for the win.

The thing is… I'm kinda lonely

Here's an excerpt from *Spirited Solutions*, an eBook I co-wrote with Rachel:

Sometimes, we need to get a little quiet, a little still, if only to understand who we are in our own company. Whatever that force is - the one that grips our muscle to the bone, the one that moves the planets and allows birds to soar through the air - the Source Of All Things is a force of expansion and contraction. The rain comes. Then the sun shines. Money floats into your bank account. It trickles out. The tides rise, and fall.

And socially, as a human being, you too will expand, and when you do, you'll be out in the world, feeling kindred bonds with your people. But there will also come a time that you will be called upon to contract. To retreat. To become silent. Not because you're socially challenged, or broken, or need fixing, but because it's Universal Law. Your experience of life may be manifesting as wobbly or lonesome, but you are not destined for reclusiveness. You are simply aligning to your truth. Time spent solo needn't feel lonely. During this time, you have the opportunity to lay down a strong foundation of self-love and self-respect. You have the time (and if you choose, the inclination) to explore who you are – who you *really* are – by developing a spiritual practice, a connection with yourself, a connection with Mama Nature. But beyond even that, these quiet times that leave us wandering the world without a sense of belonging are the times that bring out the hero in all of us.

In *Sacred Contracts*, Caroline Myss references the late and great mythologist, Joseph Campbell and the Hero's Journey. (And by the way, there's a heroine dwelling within each and every one of us.) "The journey culminates in a descent into the abyss of self-doubt and a loss of faith in the divine, but then results in a vital transformation and a renewal of trust, which in turn leads to a revelation of some new knowledge, insight or·wisdom. The hero then returns to the tribe and imparts this insight."

Did you hear that, Party Girl? You're a heroine in the making! Keep breathing. Keep knowing that you are loved. I like to encourage all the women I work with to reframe 'loneliness' to 'sacred time with self', because *nothing* lasts forever, and that includes pockets of silence and perceived disconnection. A little silence and stillness is The Universe's way of tying a bow around a gift and express-delivering it to your doorstep. You're not being punished; you're taking the journey inward so you can emerge the valiant being that you are. Take this opportunity to start afresh and eat it right up!

You're not an alien. You're just growing.

Peace Practice

Who do you trust wholeheartedly to invite onto your Peace Bus? Who are those wonderful friends or family members that are going to hold the space for you to make this journey?

What new, nourishing environments can you place yourself in that will support these changes you're making?
For example: is there a weekend event you can attend, a tai chi class in the park, a yoga studio you've been wanting to try?

Taking into account our chat with Hayley Carr…
How can you expand your comfort zone?

***Who* do you need to be?**

What three words will remind you of that?

Peace Performance

Clear the decks. Take out the trash. Start afresh. Use the list mentioned previously in this chapter to wipe your life of anything that's gathering dust and no longer serving you.

Next up, I have an online workshop called *How to Say No Without Pissing People Off And Feeling Like A Loser.* Find it at <u>tarabliss.com.au</u> /sayingno

After all that work we just did - lightening our load and loosening up - we're about to shift the focus from outside, to within. Take a deep breathe, sister, because we're about to explore the most fascinating and bewildering thing we can possibly scrutinise (and declutter): our identities.

7.

Who Do You Think
You Are?

"Tear off the mask. Your face is glorious."
Rumi

As a meat-loving omnivore whose dream dish was a big old slab of wagyu steak – served medium rare with a side of duck fat potatoes – landing my ass (albeit temporarily) in the world of vegetarianism a number of years ago was the last place I expected to find myself. But alas, after a little exploring, and a little research, it wasn't long before I found myself poring over articles brimming with cold truths about animal cruelty, genetically modified foods and corrupt corporations. I felt at once outraged *and* liberated as a result of 'seeing the light'. And so, took it upon myself to become a woman on a mission; frantically sharing articles exposing the latest cutting-edge health research, and the big crooks who were keeping secrets about our food. As far as I was concerned, I had it all figured out. I was enraged with productive passion, and privy to the odd belief-brawl in the comments of my Facebook feed. I had rebellious energy to burn, and was terribly unapologetic about my new choices and values.

In the end, while I certainly may have inspired a few folks to re-think what they were putting on their plates, I ended up just annoying the hell out of people. I'd assumed the identity of Angry Activist, and felt the need to validate my message by coughing it up onto anyone and their dog, whether their ears were willing to listen or not. Am I saying we need to do away with protests, activism and animal rights? Absolutely not. *We need them.* But I'll tell you what: personally, my chest puffed out with inflated significance at every opportunity it had to slip into this identity in an attempt to 'right' everyone else's 'wrongs'. I put on my superhero cape and tried to blast the world into making different choices, often thinking of meat-eaters as people who were less worthy of love (or anything) than those who followed the yogic principal of *ahimsa* (non-violence) religiously. Though one could argue that my approach was a form of violence in itself.

We can spend so much time trying to craft and perfect certain aspects or per-ceptions of ourselves, that we become strangers to the beings we are as a *whole*. Personally, I've chased down the embodiment of such identities as The Party Girl, The Tomboy, The Hopeless Romantic, The Athlete, The Creative, The Rebel, The Rescuer, The Adrenaline Junkie. And then of course, there are the identities I hide behind, either as an excuse, or explanation of my perceived (but ultimately delusional) flaws: The Introvert, Complicated, Perpetually Misunderstood, The Country Girl.

We don't have to hunt all that hard to identify other 'part-time positions' that we take on in this lifetime. Perhaps some of the ones I just mentioned resonate with you? What about a few of these?

:: *The Extrovert*

:: *The Good Girl*

:: *The Perfectionist*

:: *The Overachiever*

:: *The Beauty Queen*

:: *The Centre of Attention*

:: *The Wild Child*

:: *The Love Bug*

Most of us are unwittingly trying to fulfil such a stressing amount of sub-personalities that we're often left with spinning heads and hungry hearts. *Hello, identity crisis...*

Healing the whole

Can we can hold space for ourselves, even though we may not be entirely sure who exists behind the image we've spent so many years actively crafting? *Easier said than done.* Meet mega-sweetheart and soul sister of mine, Yvette Luciano. After years of working as a professional Party Girl in the music industry, a breast cancer diagnosis uprooted her life, shook up her model of the world, and demanded she deep-dive into a holistic healing journey. "My identity was so wrapped up in being the girl who could drink anyone under the table", she says. "And I really felt as though that became an important part of me and who I was. It was really difficult to let that go, but it was worth it." Yvette has now channelled the energy she used to hand over to her stressful career and party lifestyle into her successful company - Earth Events - a platform which is setting new sacred business standards in an industry otherwise rife with gossip and lip service. She creates empowering events and collaborates solely with change agents who, like her, are out to empower the world with a message anchored in kindness, authenticity and warm, gooey love.

We ask ourselves:

> :: *Who am I, if I'm not the girl who needs a line of speed to have an intelligent conversation?*
> :: *Who am I, if I'm not the girl who needs to down two bottles of wine to feel comfortable making eye contact, or speaking from my heart, or making love?*
> :: *If I'm not the girl who can wear my hat backwards and pretend that I'm one of the boys while eating chicken wings and drinking beer, who am I?*

And am I willing to love what's left, when I'm in the throes of feeling empty and awkward and exposed and vulnerable without these identities? Here's a hint, you divine Apprentice of Peace… The answer must be: yes. **Yes, I am willing. Yes, I am ready. Yes, I will be gentle, and patient, and compassionate with**

myself. The way we identify with ourselves can offer us two results: it can empower us to extend the very essence of our being, or it can distract us from our core, persuade us into a world of smoke and mirrors, and ultimately sabotage our greatest joy. I don't know about you, but I'm tired of switching masks day in, day out. Flat-out exhausted. I'm buggered of playing games with myself, chasing my own tail, forcing myself into a model of projections and delusions and flaky fakeness. I just want to be… *me,* really. What does that mean? It means letting go of who I *think* I am, stabilising into the truth of who I *feel* I am, and canning the rest. **Daily**.

Vicki and I have been on quite a journey together. She joined the first ever live version of The Party Girl's Guide to Peace, then she welcomed me into her life as her personal coach, and now, she and I are close friends. I had the utmost honour and privilege of helping to guide Vicki through a transition from Identity Hopscotch to Embracing Her Wholeness.

To the outside, this woman had it all. A kickass, successful PR role that'd regularly have her rubbing shoulders with celebrities, a thriving social life, and that face? The woman's a true, radiant beauty. Only problem was that Vicki's lifestyle had all but brought her to her knees. With a few health scares under her belt, a career that consumed her, a supreme longing for more love and connection in her life, and an addictive personality that was in the driver's seat of her decision-making faculties, the expectations her industry placed on her to produce her Social Butterfly party persona at the snap of a finger rendered her resolutions on getting sober a failure. All she wanted on a Friday night was to curl up into a ball and sip herbal tea at home, but her world said a stern 'no' to that. After all, Vicki had a reputation to uphold.

While she was trying to create pockets of space to land on her meditation cushion, to slow down, to *be,* to ease the air of *hectic* in her life, the phone rang off the hook. The emails never ceased. *Vicki, we need you. Vicki, do this. Vicki, can you handle this press release...* I remember how exhausted she'd be during our sessions. Her actions (attending cocktail parties, fussing over celebrities, living her life purely from the space of reactivity) weren't aligned with her vision for life. From where she stood, it was difficult to see a way out. She'd often share with me her fantasies of moving back up to Byron Bay, selling everything she owned, running to the lighthouse every day, and drinking almond milk dandelion lattes as she lost herself for hours in her journal, in the corner of a quiet, artsy cafe. A beautiful vision, no doubt, but I had my suspicions that Vicki was (subconsciously) placing a little too much emphasis on what she wanted her life to look like - how she wanted to be perceived - than what she longed for on a soul level. She was substituting her obsession with one identity for another.

"Early addiction recovery is like plugging the holes of a sinking ship; once you plug one hole, another one appears."
Gabrielle Bernstein

"So what if you don't have to be defined by what you do?" I asked her. She responded with, "hmm." I could practically see little lightbulbs growing aglow in her noggin. "What if you didn't have to wait for your circumstances to change before you started embodying a more peaceful life?" Vicki was linking quiet cafe corners, cool hipster guys with beards and acoustic guitars, and a pristine self-care practice to ultimate freedom. She thought it all came down to her resources, not her soul; her one true identity. It wasn't difficult for me to see that if she kept these rules – this unrealistic model of Peace that she'd created – she'd have a hard time removing the bitter taste of dissatisfaction from her mouth.

Over the next couple of months, I coached Vicki on identifying all the false perceptions of herself that she'd collected over her lifetime. I explained that she needn't be one person at home, another at work, and yet another while on a first date. Yes, life will often ask us to fulfil temporary roles, but we certainly don't have to leave our authentic nature behind in the process. I asked Vicki to practice looking at her reflection in the mirror of a morning – her hair, falling at her shoulders after being worked with a curling iron, her attire, the way in which she was adorned in every Apple product under the sun – and see, really, truly recognise - that those *things* weren't *her*. They enabled her to get through her day, conform to certain standards and assume her PR identity (all very useful things), but her lifeblood ran deeper that than. I suspected that, for Vicki, this journey wasn't so much about making the journey from Party PR to barefooted hippy, and more about coming home to who she really was.

Anyway, her transformation was a sight to behold. She went on to implement much of what we've covered in this book: she cultivated curiosity; she got clear about how she wanted to feel; she rearranged her reward systems and began practicing the art of the sacred 'no'. But more importantly, she smudged the rigid lines that separated her sub-personalities. Instead of waiting for what Peace looked like, she plucked it out from within and radiated it from her being. She brought this energy to her work, her interactions, her spiritual practice.

She went to work, as Vicki. She lovingly declined invitations, as Vicki. She launched her blog, as Vicki. She took her seat for mediation, as Vicki. And sooner than either of us could have predicted, she respectfully resigned from her job, as Vicki.

These days, this incredible woman (who inspires the heck out of me) works for herself, from home, with brands she loves, and entrepreneurs that are aligned with her vision, just like Yvette. She's one of the sweetest, most conscientious, most grateful people I know. ('I feel so lucky' is her life mantra.)

Can you see the seismic shifts that can take place when you do as Rumi says, and 'take off the masks' that are exhausting you, and instead open your arms wide to the whole of who you are? Never settle for the false but widely accepted belief that we're each a victim of our circumstances (or a slave to our identities). It's bull. Something that I stamped to my psyche ever since I first read it is this from Tony Robbins:

> *"Your life conditions don't determine your destiny;*
> *your decisions do."*
> Tony Robbins

I'd like to come at that from a different angle and add: your life conditions **don't define you as a person.** Scrutinising these seductive identities (with the lightness of curiosity, of course) is an ongoing process. I remember on a recent trip to Sydney, for the Wanderlust Yoga Festival, I made my way into Bondi Beach to meet friends for lunch. When we arrived at the café, I came to a screaming halt, with a dropped jaw, and eyes popping out of my head. "Where the hell *are* we?!" I asked my friends, looking around. "Is this some sort of drop-dead-gorgeous Narnia?" Tanned bodies, hipsters left, right and centre, girls effortlessly pulling of the 'I've just rolled out of bed after sex' look, while wearing designer labels head to toe. English accents. Double denim. Longboards. Trendy fixed-gear bikes. Everyone with a latte in hand. *Holy shit. We're not on the Gold Coast anymore.* The place was heaving with confidence, style, sass and attitude. I looked down at my outfit and let out a nervous laugh. *Consider myself officially **triggered**,* I thought.

It can take all but a moment to lose yourself in this world of form; to lose your centre, your core understanding of who you are. Within a few seconds, my mind had conjured up outfits I needed to buy, new ways to talk, walk and carry myself, language to add to my vocabulary. This, my friends, is a little insane. We were not sent here to make cookie-cutters out of ourselves, or to appeal to a certain demographic, or culture, or trend. You came here to extend yourself, your *Self.* If that means rocking boyfriend jeans and chai tea and balayaged hair (personal favourites of mine), go right ahead. But be vigilant when it comes to detecting that stealthy Ego. Often it feels like the Ego is on a continuous mission to ensure that you fit in, fake it, and fail trying. Your job is to hold steady, knowing that you are enough exactly as you are in this moment.

So I'm supposed to be a zen robot with no sense of self...?

Not at all! My friend Alex once said to me 'life is about laughing and loving' and I really dig that. What a gorgeous statement to remember if we ever find ourselves digging our feet a little too deep into the sand of shadow work (more on this shortly). This process is allowed to be fun, and light, and beautifully buoyant. I'm simply encouraging you to see through the lie, to identify what is permanent behind the impermanence, to recognise yourself beyond our multitude of costumes.

Have you ever thought to yourself: *I have no bloody idea who I am*? Rather than perceiving this as a problem that needs solving, Eckhart Tolle views it as a divine awakening. When we're humble enough to look within before emerging with nothing but a vague statement such as, "Okay, so I can feel into the essence of who I am, but I'm not sure of what that means", well, many spiritual teachers deem that worthy of actualised celebration. In other words, **when we're a little confused, we're open and receptive to answers**. Today, I revel in allowing an air of mystery to exist inside of me, because if I view myself as a mystery, as a vessel that holds a little magic, then it's highly likely I'm going to think the same about you, and about the planet we live on. That's a blessing.

But what about those times that call upon us to purposefully project certain identities out into the world? Personally, this question presents itself to me in relation to my online platform. It's a fine line to tread, this one of effectively communicating who we are, without attaching to the achievements and circumstances that got us here. I recognise that the internet needs me to tell it who I am in 140 characters or less. Quite a task! Here we have a limitless soul that knows no bounds, and yet the world of *www.* wants me to broadcast a version of All That I Am so that it's tweet-worthy? This is the strange pursuit of a Peace Girl, a pursuit I used to struggle with a lot. It all felt very drenched in Ego and competitiveness. These days, I tend to just laugh and find the amusement in the process. Instead or harbouring frustration, I generate gratitude. And besides, if crafting an online image on platforms like this *still* doesn't sit well with you, there's always the option to remove yourself from them so that you can focus on what's most important to you. (Life goes on without Twitter, trust me.) The secret sauce of making peace with the many fractions of ourselves is to find appreciation in these identities (in my case, The Spiritual Practice Coach, The Yogini, The Writer), but to ultimately understand that they are nothing but what Tolle would call 'signposts pointing to the ultimate truth'.

Once, on a live call with my Peace Girls, Niamh posed this dilemma: "I'm feeling into and exploring identities and labels that I've created for myself over the years. While it's 'easier' to drop the connection around the 'bad' things, I find that I'm still holding onto the 'good' things a little too tightly, for example, accolades, university achievements, etc. I feel that it's time to shed these, but I'm not sure what I say or call myself, or even what I'm worth without them. These are the only things that I find bring me the feeling of recognition, acknowledgement, belonging, 'being seen', connection (though often only in a superficial way). Nevertheless, it's how I've associated them."

Just in case you're wondering the same thing, imagine I'm sitting opposite you right now. I have my hands resting gently on your shoulders. I'm smiling at you with a knowingness that reeks of conviction and certainty, and in a soft, but deliberate voice, I say this:

> *You transcend what could ever be written on your About Me page,*
> *the accomplishments listed on your CV, and what's hanging*
> *in your trophy room. Yes, acknowledge your achievements!*
> *Celebrate your successes! When it's time to allow that spotlight*
> *to shine upon you, make sure the biggest and proudest pat on your*
> *back is coming from your own hand. Yet don't get so lost in the*
> *glitter that you link your sense of Self to how long (or how*
> *bright) that light is shining upon you. Because you are*
> *more than any certificate, any gold star, any Noble Prize.*

Work it, woman.

I've noticed a pattern among many of the women I've worked with over the years as they make this incredible transition from automatic, self-destructive behaviour to considered choices. They, much like Vicki was initially aiming to do, lean into the idea of trading out their stilettos for harem pants. They feel compelled to cancel their hairdressing appointments, turn a shoulder to their cosmetics draw, and slather themselves in patchouli essential oil. I fell into this trap too. Until I woke up one morning and realised, *um, I feel a bit like a slob.* While, sure, a lot of the effort I went to in the past was to appease others, I couldn't help but deny that one of the most memorable things about being a Party Girl was the way I felt when I left the house, or entered a club. Each week I gave myself the permission and attention that allowed me to look my best. And I missed that. There I was, eating my superfoods and pounding the pavement. Yet, at the same time, I was 'letting myself go'. I fell for the limiting notion that, to be spiritual, I must look the part. Dirty feet, a naked face, bushy eyebrows, crystals in my bra. What I've come to learn, embrace and teach is that we must never back away from the small pleasures that allow us to bask divinely in our femininity. Disconnecting from this, cutting ourselves off from feeling like a woman is sacrilege.

That which we'd rather not see

*"Find that behaviour or quality you find unsavoury in others - in yourself.
This is your chance to truly, simply awaken, and it will show you the actual
meaning of the word 'compassion'. If something in another person repels us
emotionally or physically, we have that 'something' within ourselves."*
Elena Brower

In her outstanding book, *The Dark Side of the Light Chasers*, Debbie Ford explains that *white is not the absence of colour*; it's the combination of *all* colour. And that *love is not the absence of hate*; it's the summation of *all* emotion. Picture in your mind a time when you read something (perhaps even in this book), and before you had barely digested the words, you were *all in*. You became a believer. No need to research further, no need to test the waters. The *yes* within you had been illuminated; your resonance, cranked up to *full*. **That's what happened to me when I heard this definition of love.** God, *yes*.

To return to totality, to become whole, or to simply live a peaceful life, we need to embrace who we are as a whole. That's right. All of it. Not just the aspects that beam out optimism and give love freely and operate out of integrity. If there's night and day, on and off, up and down, then we *must* also be the polar opposite of all we desire. This has to be accepted and embraced.

Louise Hay is an angel of our generation, responsible for kickstarting millions of spiritual journeys (including my own) through her work with positive affirmations and gratitude practices. It's no secret that our thoughts greatly impact our reality – the brighter the thought, the brighter the manifestation of life. Sometimes, though, we need a little more depth. We need a more visceral experience of how to better understand ourselves than a sometimes-fraudulent-feeling repetition of 'I am infinitely abundant and gorgeous' can provide. *Shadow work* can most certainly provide that depth.

Often, we cannot see and easily identify with the darkness in ourselves. And how can we? After all, it's hiding behind the light in the stuffy corners of our being. In order to more accurately perceive our reflection, our shadows reveal themselves to us via our projections onto others. In other words, it's the *interaction* between two people (or a group dynamic, or a corporation) that holds up the mirror. (This isn't the first time you've heard me mention this in this book.) Or in the beautiful way Debbie explains it: **if it *affects* you, it's a *projection.***

While I was in Bali, on a writing retreat (where the first draft of this book was penned), I confided in my writing coach that *arrogance* annoys me; that it makes me feel all icky, and impatient, and ruffled up. She barely skipped a beat in locking eyes with me and saying, *"Here's your homework. Over the next three days, you're to have three conversations with three different people, in which you'll tell them* **three reasons why you're better than most people on the planet.***"* My jaw hit the floor. *You've got to be fucking kidding me, right?* She had realised, due to my reaction to this very human behaviour, that I was being triggered; someone was *expressing* a trait that I had been *suppressing.* And just quietly, she was spot on. Without a doubt, I pranced around with an air or arrogance in my teen years and early twenties. Perhaps, somewhere along the line, I decided that arrogance was an unsavoury quality. My inception into a spiritual practice most probably had something to do with that, and so, I quashed it beneath a spiritual exterior that was now often shy, quiet, even borderline socially uncomfortable. There I was again, playing games with myself.

Looking our shadow - the disowned aspects of ourselves - in the eye doesn't come without a side serve of humility. When I first endeavoured to learn more about the totality of me, and not just the good stuff I *hoped* that I embodied, I found it shocking, but at the same time immensely exhilarating. To be honest, even playful and adventurous at times. Every time I observe my reaction to others, I'm reminded of my own capacity to act out, behave and embody the exactitude that I'm witnessing; the parts of me that mould and bend to suit my environment, the parts of me that are tunnel-visioned and self-serving, the parts of me that are stubborn, strong-willed and a little pushy. And I know these traits lie within me for the simple reason that I've turned up my nose to them in others. I've found myself cringing my forehead at people online who I've labelled as 'inauthentic'. This judgment alone is reason enough for me to step back, slow down, pry myself away from my pointing finger, and ask myself: *Okay Tara, where in life are you being inauthentic? What's feeling fraudulent here?* And sure enough, I would find it. Rather than beat myself up for temporarily detouring into Fake City, I'd evoke such incredible compassion for the two of us; me *and* the judged, and my focus could quickly shift from what they were doing 'wrong' to what an incredible gift they've just given me. Humility.

One of my mentors, Mastin Kipp, taught me that, when we label something, we lessen the power of it. I could not agree more. Cultivating an optimistic disposition is damn near compulsory if you wish to amplify joy, but what's also essential is allowing your feelings to surface in the moment. When you quit running, when you feel into what's present for you instead, no matter how much it hurts or frustrates you, you allow it to transcend; dissolve; fall away.

You might be thinking, *"Hang on, you just told me to drop the labels, but now you're suggesting that labelling something will lessen its impact on me?"* Let me explain this briefly. There's a vast difference between labelling what you truthfully identify as unravelling in the moment, and *grappling* for a label by way of over-identifying with a story from your past. Presence means observing what *is*, not constructing identities that help us tell a better story. When you're courageous enough to know inwardly that anger is present somewhere in your body, your very awareness of that will swiftly dissolve it. However, if you feel the anger, and then stumble down the rabbit hole of stories that validate all the reasons you have to be angry, then you're playing games with yourself. You're no longer in (or even being affected by) the current experience. You're playing in the past. Bottom line: **when you label your current experience, you lessen its power, but when you *identify* with a label, it lessens *your* power.**

Life will continue to show us our shadow, vicariously through others, until we've embraced it as a part of who we are, until we quit it with the lies and inner games, until we desist hinging our worth on how often we smile, or how readily we swallow down a lump of resentment, or anger, or jealousy with an affirmative 'I accept myself unconditionally'. Accepting yourself unconditionally can take many shapes and forms. Like we have by now explored many times in this book, it takes a willing, curious, moment-to-moment approach of self-awareness.

:: I hate to admit this, but I'm jealous as all hell.

:: I feel so out of control and emotional right now, and I have no idea why.

:: I feel a little worthless, and invisible, and empty.

That's wholeness: acknowledging our shadowy selves and *expressing* it, not pretending as though it's not there. **When we express, we evolve.** When we look at it, we bring it to the light. The consequence of denying our shadow is that we'll be constantly (and unconsciously) plugged into the very emotion in others that triggers us. For example, if you're suffocating your anger, you'll continually be presented with situations in your life that will challenge you to acknowledge anger. Traffic jams, impatient partners, mums at the supermarket who are at their wits' end with their children. Anger will look you in the eye, until you look within and find it there too. **Remember, if it affects you, it's a projection**. If it instigates some type of electrical charge in you – an unwelcome *buzz!* – it's an invitation to own what has previously been disowned.

Let's play with this concept. As always, I'll reveal myself first.

States that trigger me (also known as words that I hope I'm not) include:

:: Scattered

:: Narcissistic

:: Aggressive

:: Boring

:: Selfish

And if we *are* what we're affected by, then folks you heard it here first: I'm scattered. I'm narcissistic. I'm aggressive, and boring, and selfish. But because I am those things, and because we live in a world of opposing forces, I must also be focused, humble, calm, engaging and generous.

Here are some states that I love and do my best to gravitate towards:

   :: *Loving*

   :: *Creative*

   :: *Authentic*

   :: *Brave*

   :: *Determined*

Which means I must also be hateful, unimaginative, fake, cowardly and wavering.

Nothing describes it better than this powerful prose from Terence: **"I am a human being. Nothing human can be alien to me."** In other words, if one human being can experience any given state, we *all* can. No exceptions. So I offer you this seed of suggestion, when it comes to recognising friction within relationships in your life: maybe the issue isn't that you're *not* resonating with someone; perhaps the opposite is true. Could you in fact be resonating so strongly that it tears at a nerve somewhere deep within, and somehow leaves you feeling a little inflamed? This might be something for you to mull over in your journal, or during a meditation next time you find yourself, for whatever reason, casting judgment on those around you. It's easy for us to judge the wasted 20-something girl who's stumbling around with greasy hair and boobs all over the place, while we're cleaning up our life. Just as it's not difficult to judge an overweight family for devouring fast food while we're blissfully savouring our quinoa and kale. But we *must* be compassionate. We've got to beam compassion out from within us as if it's going out of fashion. I'm certainly no saint at this. I bugger it up all the time – lapsing into reactions that sting. But these days, that initial burn is closely followed by a series of choices that looks a little something like this:

I close my eyes, take a breath and think, *'Thank you for showing me what's real'*. When I appreciate this new perspective, I'm able to come down off my soapbox and embody empathy and understanding. I can see a part of myself in other drunk, messy girls, just as I can see part of myself in people who eat mindlessly.

Awareness is the lighthouse. Awareness of these shadows is the tool that allows you to shift gears; from mental-attack-mode, to intrinsic contemplation. It's the catalyst for acceptance, forgiveness and knowingness of a higher truth. It allows us to step away from the war in our minds and adopt (what's that magic word?) **compassion**. Listen up to those you're judging. Listen to what your shadow has to say. And sister, judge less, for when you judge others, you condemn yourself.

A quick note on the darker side of this shadow work

Here's a handy heads-up for you. If you're not careful, your Ego will devour this experience. There's a few things that might happen. Either the Ego will convince you that these projections are showing you how perpetually damaged you are, and to fix them, you have to do *so. much. healing.* Know this: You're *not* damaged and you do *not* need fixing. That's the amazing thing about this work; it highlights our humanity, while allowing us to lift our 'flaws' in a spirited, all-embracing way. Another rogue route the Ego might take is that it could become inflamed, and self-righteous, and revel in statements like, "I'm allowed to be a bitch! It's my nature. It's part of who I am!" Be vigilant here, Party Girl. That ain't shadow work. Shadow work is about recognition, not excuse-making. It's about oneness, and softness, and wholeness. Ask your Ego ever so gently to pipe down when the snarky comments rise up (all the while acknowledging and accepting that very self-righteousness, of course).

The freedom in forgiveness

> *"Compassion becomes real when we*
> *recognise our shared humanity."*
> Brené Brown

In keeping with most personal stories in this book, the following are acutely intimate. This one in particular, though, is among the most important for me to tell. It involves the scope of my relationship with Glen, and how we journeyed through some tough times together, caused by drug and alcohol abuse. And of course, it is most important to me that you are inspired, through my experience, to examine yourself and the relationships in your life, and choose healthier habits that impact everyone in a positive way, as well as allowing you to deeply know yourself through the act of forgiveness.

As you already know, Glen and I met in an unusual Utopian environment; one where the crisp morning mountain air carried away our comedowns, where the only remedy for a Hangover From Hell was a mug of gin and mandarin, where sleep was for the weak. I believe now, with conviction, that everyone who arrives at those snow-covered mountains is running from one thing or another, most probably themselves. Imagine dozens upon dozens of lost little raging souls being thrown together in staff accommodation for a four-month party. *Yep.*

Committing to each other might seem like a pretty outrageous thing to do, considering the circumstances, but like I said, life's different in the mountains. Our bodies didn't ache. Our heads didn't pinch with pain. Somehow, we could see straight, though it barely seemed legal that we could. So when it was time for us to leave the hill, we left together. Without the distinctive crutch of a mountain lifestyle to hide behind, we truly had to get to know one another all over again. Some days, it was spectacular. We'd eat sushi and sip sake and giggle like children as we prepared for our next winter in Japan. He'd take me to Noosa headland at night, where we'd sit in silence, wrapped up in each other's arms, listening to the water hit the rocks. He'd cook me the best food I'd ever tasted. As we explored each other over dinner and bottles of fine vintage, I'd wonder how the hell I got so lucky to be sitting opposite someone who I adored, was fascinated by, and who was an artist with food. I was counting my lucky stars.

But other days, I would get a whiff of an underbelly of jealousy, of impatience, of irrationality. We click-clacked our way through awkward conversations and silly little misunderstandings, which before would've been camouflaged by pints of beer. The more time we spent together, the more it seemed he was revealing a side of him that I most certainly had not signed up for. Where had my warm little wolf gone? Who was this rigid, uppity, unpredictable creature that was now sharing my bed?

I had realised long before Glen that the lifestyle that had brought us together – the one where we fell in love – wasn't sustainable. The love I felt for him, yes, undeniably. But not the lifestyle. I wanted to investigate a more vibrant way of living. I wanted to explore total wellness. Him, not so much. His marker of fun was still stacked up against how much he could drink, the trouble we could get up to; a game I had long outgrown *out here* in the real world. Cracks started to show, and they ran deep and ugly. The man I'd met, who was charming and gentle while high, was not the same person while drunk, and I always knew when he had gone too far and lost himself in the drink, because his eyes would turn a steely black; his mood soon to follow.

I grew nervous about this. The first night it happened, I was so shocked and confused and powerless. His softness disappeared right in front of my eyes. He began spitting out words out as though they were bitter in his mouth. His eyes would dart around the room; dissatisfied with anything that they settled upon. Agitated and expressing what I can only explain as suppressed emotion, he would tailspin into an assault of accusations that didn't belong to me. It was as though, when he was drunk, he was in a bad dream full of old memories from his past. A handful of times, he called me by the name of his ex. I would gently hold him by the face and say, "Darling, I am not her. Look in my eyes, I am not her". He couldn't hear me. He couldn't see me. His gaze pierced right through me as if I wasn't even in the room, and on and on the ramblings would continue, sometimes for hours. One minute he could be furious, as though I had purposefully done something to cause him pain; the next he would be wiping away sad tears. When I tried to comfort him, he would keep me at bay with an outstretched, dismissive hand; a signal that I couldn't be trusted. He was wild, unpredictable and utterly inconsolable, and any attempt by me to ease the irrationality that rose out of him failed miserably. And as the months wore on, and the arguments continued to tire me, I'd barely have the energy to whisper, *"I'm not going to fight with you anymore"*, before waiting for him to pass out so we could be done. Sometimes, I would hide under the bed so I could be one less distraction getting in the way of him and the only thing that could heal him: sleep.

Glen wasn't violent. He didn't blow all my money on strippers and horse-racing. He cherishes monogamy. All things I am truly grateful for. But the uncensored nonsense that would spill out of his mouth while he was under the grip of a binge, often at loud volumes, *hurt me,* plain and simple. The tone of his voice cut me to pieces. His lack of consciousness and coherence destroyed my soul on those nights. And more than anything, I ached for him to be okay. This man I loved, while drunk, he was *not* okay.

On mornings after nights like these, if I woke up in Glen's arms, I'd be furious with myself. I hated that, despite having a heart in my chest that felt torn apart, I had unknowingly pulled him back into an embrace during the night. *That* was a hard pill to swallow. I'd impatiently roll out of our bind, and often stand above the bed, staring at him while he slept, hating – *hating* – that he looked so precious and peaceful and vulnerable. When he'd wake, the pounding in his head obviously offering a *'you did it again, mate'* headline, he'd look at me with soft, sorry eyes, that said *"What did I do **this** time?"* "You're out of control", I would say. "I don't deserve this bullshit. Do you know hard it is for me to see you like that?! I swear to God, get it together or I'm out of here!" "Baby", he would say, reaching out for me, "Come here". "No". "Baby…" Sometimes, there would be tears in his eyes by now. And I would melt into his arms leaving my own tears on his chest that I had been too numb and locked up to shed the night before. He would hold me tight and repeat, "I'm sorry, I'm sorry". And the beating of his heart against my cheek would remind me of how human he was and of how much I loved him.

How do you apologise for behaviour you can't remember? Behaviour that makes you feel ashamed, unworthy, *sorry?* That's precisely what Glen did for a great chunk of time. He'd brace up in the morning and take the hit for his alter ego, and I have no doubt that that was a positively painful process for him, as he tried to piece together fragments of the previous night to no avail.

As a once willing-and-able escapist, leaving Glen wasn't the issue for me. I'd been upping and leaving since I was 16, preferring to dart away from the pain than wade through it. Let it be known that I was *not* afraid of being alone, of starting again, and of never turning back. One night in Japan, we were deep in intimate conversation, and I was sharing with him what I had learnt from my failed relationships. "I think it's really important for two people that love each other to remain independent of the *need* to be with one another. Distance is good for a relationship. Loving each other is beautiful, but *needing* each other isn't. I always needed something from the men I was with, but things have changed now. I really *want* you in my life."

Like I said, leaving wasn't the issue. The issue was I'd already seen through the bullshit. I knew who he was at his core. Beyond merely sensing his *potential,* I had received the purity of his love before these opportunities to heal had presented themselves. He had shown too much of his real self for me to pretend as though this was just another guy I could walk away from. I adored the man he was underneath it all. I worshipped unapologetically his true nature. The plain and simple truth was I wanted us to work things out. And with my hands on my heart, I thank all of Life that I was blessed to fall in love with a man who could muster the determination, courage, and will to step up. And yet....

"I'm better than you. I deserve better than you. We're not on the same path anymore."

Those three punchy sentences, I repeated to Glen over and over in my mind when we were in our darkest days. Those words tore at me as a magnifying glass was placed on the differences that were cleaving our love apart, rather than the polarities that drew us together in the first place. When I interviewed Glen for this project, I wanted to understand how the learning had come to him. "What could I have done differently?" I asked him as we recorded the conversation. "I know I didn't exactly make this journey easy on you... I gave you a pretty hard time... What I could I have done in hindsight to make the transition less abrasive for you?" He's a man of few words, my Glen, but the ones he speaks are potent. "Be patient and persistent", he said. He accentuated that suggestion by adding that it's important for all of us out there on a crusade to better health and greater happiness to communicate our lifestyle with *actions,* rather than *words.* The teaching comes through consistent, demonstrated *action.* Words can fall flat in the exchange of defensive language, but no-one can take from you the message that you deliver in a *Do As I Do* medium.

Ladies, take heed. This is what communication with the masculine energy looks like. Generally – and this is a sweeping statement, I accept – men don't *do* talking. They *do* doing. It's how they learn. It's also why the mere whisper of *'we need to talk...'* is usually enough to send a fearful shudder down their spines. We've gotta quit talking about it and just get on with it! Unfortunately, those around us often misinterpret our 'higher' choices as a direct attack on their lifestyle. That's not our intention, of course, yet be mindful of this. Your friends and loved ones love you just the way you are. As far as they're concerned, you don't need to change. Remember, you signed that social contract with your tribe, and when you step out of the Party Scene, you're breaking that contract and lighting it on fire. The last thing our people need is for us to get high and mighty as we attempt to spread our message far and wide. Our well-intended enthusiasm can be mistaken for downright obnoxiousness and a message that tells our beloved, or our closest connections, that they're ever-so-slightly inadequate. *Ouch.* Rather than spreading a message with devotion, we can be quick to jump on our soapbox and let them have it. This was certainly true for Glen and me. I knew he missed the old me; the me who would throw caution to the wind in the name of adventure. The me who'd flip my middle finger in the air at the first hint of adversity. The me who would join him, and validate him, in the underworld of inebriation.

You can *tell* someone to get healthier, *or* you can come home from yoga, fresh-faced and bounding, and offer him one of your green smoothies. You can complain about his habits, his choices, his lifestyle, *or* you can positively reinforce him for every choice he makes that lights you up from within. You can whine about the fact that things aren't the same anymore, *or* you can take it upon yourself to instigate a new and refreshed onset of variety and uncertainty in the relationship. You can harbour resentments and hold onto the story, *or* you can forgive. And once you've forgiven, you can do one of two things. Let go of that person with love, *or* simply **love**. Unconditionally. Without withholding. Without expectation. You can give with a love that knows no limits. That cannot be stopped. That dissolves every morsel of doubt. Me? **I chose option two.**

Who would have thought that my love for this man – my devotion to him – was in fact the very medicine that he needed? All I had to do was take a moment to pull my head out of my own ass and **include him in my life**. I needed to allow him to actually be my man because – how's this for a thought? – all men want to be made men of. This happens when the women standing by their men are women who willingly let him in. I used to think that the most important thing in the world was self-love. These days, I'm not too sure. While I'm a true-blue advocate for it (let's not forget that it's one of the pillars of this book), the most expansive way for us to experience love is by sharing it; by being vulnerable enough to pry open our heart chakra and love fiercely, despite risking getting hurt.

I needed to show Glen that I was more worthy of his company than a carton of beer. That we could blow the type of fun we used to have out of the water, while sober. That there was no-one else in the world for me, but him. Friends, he beyond rose to the occasion. These days, the two of us lift each other up to a level of love I never even dreamt was possible. I get just as inspired watching him pass on an afternoon beer, as he does when he sees me chase down the tail of a lofty dream. When he's pacing out in front of me on our morning beach run, sucking in salty, oxygen-rich air, I smile on the inside as I press my feet into the footprints he leaves in the sand, in awe of him. And don't even get me started on that look on his face when he's walking out of the ocean with a surfboard under his arm, with eyes that sparkle every damn shade of blue. He is a sight for sore eyes; a beacon of what it means to personify transformation. And as his wife, as the woman that knew not to run away this time, I am proud - incredibly proud - of the man he has allowed himself to be. My warm little wolf has returned. *Sniff.*

To stay or to leave?

I can only speak from my own experience, but what I've observed is this: if we create our world from the inside out, then one of two things might happen. Either our behaviour (which is beaming out high-vibration health) will rub off on the people we care about, and they will begin to re-prioritise their lives, like we have, or those relationships will slowly and organically dissolve. Either way - and as painful as the latter may sound - it's divinely perfect and as it should be.

I've shared this story with you because many of my girls have battled with not feeling loved, or worthy, or respected in their relationships which, like mine, were built on the foundation of drugs and alcohol. Since embodying the practices in this book, some of them have mustered the courage to speak more openly with their partners, which has allowed them to rebuild their relationships. Others have mustered just as much courage to bravely walk away, freeing themselves of loveless connections and relationships that aren't aligned with their truth. And others found that their relationships flourished as they continued to gently chip away at enhancing the quality of their relationship with themselves first.

Love is messy and imperfect and it damn well hurts sometimes. It's almost impossible to avoid the fact that you will be slowed down by speed bumps along the way. But Party Girl, one thing will remain constant: **your body knows**. Your mind will tug-of-war you into conflicts, but your heart? She knows whether you should stay put, or tie up your shoelaces. Lean into her. Listen to her. With Glen, it was never a matter of justifying our relationship in my mind, or writing a pros and cons list on staying versus leaving. Nor was it a case of feeling as though I had to swoop on in and 'rescue' him in an effort for him to realise his potential. I'm his beloved, not his mother, and the relationship I have always sought to have with him is one of romance, intimacy, trust. I experienced those things with such intensity with this man that I was willing to stand alongside him and hold space - that space he needed - for him to grow. My head said, countless times, *"Bail"*. My heart said, *"Don't you fucking go anywhere, woman"*. Obeying this heart-command was one of the most rewarding decisions I've ever made.

If you're not sure where to start when it comes to body awareness, the next couple of chapters will help you anchor into experiences of being guided.

Peace Practice

An introduction to your identities.
(I've used personal examples here, for context.)

What personalities were you rewarded for as a child?
For example: being good at sports, being caring, keeping a space tidy…

What behaviour traits were condemned as you were growing up? Who were you 'not allowed' to be?
For example: dependent, messy, constantly told never to take drugs.

What identities are currently 'over-worked muscles'? Which ones are seemingly running the show?
For example: The Tomboy, The Party Girl, The Procrastinator

What other sub-personalities do you suspect might be a little hungry to get out and be expressed?
For example: The Wild Woman, Generosity, The Abundant Creative

What traits do you find unsavoury or unattractive in others?

Give some examples of these traits being present within you too.
(Sideline the self-judgment as you jot these down, though.)

Make a declaration right here: what two identities are you ready and willing to start gently releasing?

And what two disowned aspects of yourself are you ready to start playing with and exploring?

What two things can you do *this* week to experience these aspects of yourself?

:: If there's still someone in your life who is triggering anger, resentment or frustration in you, write them a letter (for your eyes only), forgiving them, and thus setting yourself free.

:: For the next seven days, observe what you get triggered by, observe what self-created identities you become fixated with, and breathe into those feelings and reactions. Breathe into the observation, and notice whether you can feel the always-present and never-changing aliveness that rest beneath these projections.

I'm so proud of you for willingly making it this far. We just covered some pretty heady and emotional stuff while looking at our shadows and projections. How does it sound to lighten up a little? Let's do that - quite literally - by opening up a conversation about one of my favourite things: meditation.

8

Dropping Deeper: Meditation & Soul-Level Living

"I think that anyone who meditates seriously and turns inward is going to sooner or later realise that there's help coming from a subtler or higher source that they're turning into when they're aligned in their practice"
Sally Kempton

As a young girl, I would race into new age stores in our local shopping centre, ogling at the sparkling crystals, white unicorn statues and wind chimes as mum paid for the groceries at the supermarket checkout. I could feel the magic in those stores; they had a smell about them, an unmistakable vibe, and every time I stepped inside I entered what felt like a land of secrets, myths and endless possibility. With keen eyes and an eager spirit, I would save my pennies and buy tumbled crystals, scented candles and incense, as well as little stick men who lived inside rainbow coloured cotton bags, and slept under my pillow, catching my wishes and prayers. *When I wake up, there will be two dollars under my pillow!* I would wish with all my might. *When I get home from school, a cinnamon doughnut will be waiting for me on my chest of drawers!* I never did master the fine art of materialisation, but that didn't deter my faith in all things unseen.

Growing up to movies such as *The Craft* and *Practical Magic* only amplified my obsession. I wanted to be like those girls on screen, the girls who sat around the campfire with their BFFs, repeating incantations together, casting love spells on cute boys, playing *Light As A Feather, Stiff A Board*. Instead, I would find a patch of grass, lie on my back, and breathe deeply while pretending I was a fairy in a secret garden. I'm still not sure how I even knew what meditation was as a small child - no-one else in my family practised it - but I loved cosying up in bed for hours, listening to the rainforest meditation music coming from my tape deck; journals and connector pens strewn across my room.

When I was 15, I shared a very awkward first kiss with a 17-year-old boy from out of town. The next day, instead of flipping out about it and gossiping like a love-sick teen, I taught my best friend how to meditate on my dad's lounge room floor. *Priorities, people. Priorities.*

   I've always sensed that there's more to life than living and dying; more than meets the eye anyway. *Where do I come from? Is there another girl somewhere in the world doing exactly what I'm doing right now, thinking about me as I think about her? How do the trees know how to grow?* Deep contemplations for a girl yet to hit puberty, and perhaps it's that archetypal seeker within me that made The Party so attractive in the first place. *Give me a life-altering experience. Give me answers. Let me feel enlightened.*

My first kiss may have been one to forget, but soon there would be many to remember. As a 16-year-old who was freshly declared legally independent of her parents, while navigating her way through wild hormones and an unquench-able thirst for vodka, well, big old Life had swallowed up my fascination with that which cannot be named – a world of spirit and energy and infinite love. And instead, as so many of us do, I got distracted.

My next spiritual experience was falling in love with my best friend – a girl – as an all-or-nothing 17-year-old, closely followed by my experimentation with drugs, both of which ended badly and depended on a source outside of myself to be brought alive. As you can probably imagine, this was a pretty tumultuous time. As a creature on the cusp of young womanhood, one who was trying to uphold good grades, while playing ball, paying rent, dating a girl and polish-ing off each night with a few Vodka Cruisers, it's fair to say my inner compass was more than a little rusty. I had shelved spirituality, making room for the rollercoaster ride of my early twenties, still managing to find a little grace in the simplicity of a lit candle, or a perfect, chilled-out electro beat that made me pause, and *feel.*

Thankfully, I circled back to that pull, towards a life of light and faith. My scepticism was replaced with same You've Gotta Believe It To See It wonder that lived inside of me as a little girl, but not without a little nudge (or 12!) from The Universe. Many spiritual teachers share that, often, The Universe will talk to us in whatever language we need it to in order to understand the message. In other words, it presents itself to us as a God of our own understanding. I sense the Divine was clued into the fact that if I was seriously going to explore myself as a limitless, all-loving being, then I needed to be whacked over the head with more than my fair share of miracles.

One night as I'm working in Canada, an English lady in her fifties takes a seat at my bar. She orders a serve of yam fries and a zinfandel and introduces herself as Jules. She's a regular. She's also a yogi and Reiki practitioner, and becomes one of my closest friends in Whistler. On the nights I manage to knock off early, we sit together, sipping red wine, swooning over her crystal collection. Jules insists that I soak in the world of yoga and meditation, and her warmth and well-wishing encourage me to dip my toe in. Not long afterwards, I take a Greyhound interstate to Calgary, Alberta, to visit Sarah, a close friend who I hadn't seen in years. I instantly resonate with Sarah's mother-in-law, after spying several books I've only just finished reading among her book shelves. She reveals to me that she's a channeller, someone who verbally dictates messages from the afterlife or Great Spirit. I smile as I think to myself, *"Of course you bloody are"*. I've just learnt about synchronicities – a term penned by the great Carl Jung - moments that are not merely coincidences, but cosmic hellos from the Source. "My friend's about to come round", she says. "She's a psychic. I can ask if she'll give you a reading?" *You've got to be kidding me.* "Yeah, of course. I would love that. Thank you." Never having had a reading before, my nerves are on fire in my belly. I feel alert and afloat in this place, fully aware that every moment in my entire life has accumulated to position me right here, in this lounge room, with a woman I don't know about to shed light on an unchartered corner or two. "You're a healer", the psychic says. "I can see you doing Reiki, or counselling." I lean in a little closer. "This is a huge year for you. Things are about to change. Keep committing to your practice... It's important that you find like-minded people..."

Well, I liked the sound of that. Having sworn off drugs after my coke binge a few months previously, and preferring a quiet glass of wine over a party in town, while most of the time I was energised by my lifestyle makeover, I wasn't without the odd isolation hangover of a morning. Though I was feeling better about myself, and more at home in my body, I couldn't deny that showing up in social circles just wasn't the same anymore. The more I recognised that the very scene that had held space for something of a Coming of Age for me was now making me tired, the more challenging it was. The thought of meeting like-minded people, whose idea of fun would be to get together for a potluck dinner, or take off on a hike *without* a cask of wine in our backpacks, was a beautiful thought, but one that felt far away.

"You're going to write books", the lady says. "You're definitely a writer." "I... Um... Okay... I have a blog." "Keep writing, the blog is important, but there's definitely a few books hanging around you." As I sit cross-legged on the recliner, totally gobsmacked and bamboozled and full of gratitude, I can't help but give these two women shy, warm smiles. I may have also snuck a sneaky grin or two in for The Universe. I'd heard enough to inspire a few visions, a few dreams. But most importantly, I'd heard enough to re-inspire my faith.

I sincerely believe that you will be 'reached' in a way that resonates best. For you, maybe that means copious amounts of 'coincidences'; maybe it means seeing the same combination of numbers over and over again; maybe it means feeling an invisible, nurturing force surrounding you. For me, it meant reconnecting in with the mystical; the wonder that carried me so beautifully as a child. And that mystery entered my life by way of light-working folks. I like to imagine the way that this all unfolded as a chess board, with the Divine glancing down cheekily upon it; me standing in the centre, willing to make a move, but not entirely sure how. And so, to ease the abrasiveness of confusion, I would meditate. And the more I committed to meditation, the more open and receptive I became to my next right action. The more receptive I became, the more it felt as though The Universe strategically placed those bishops and queens and castles in my life, not to compete against me, but to allow the game to be played. What's that old saying? **When the student is ready, the teacher appears?** Yeah, that. It's your *willingness* to change that will move mountains for you.

Remember how, in the last chapter, I mentioned that when you're attempting to positively influence someone's life, you can either *tell* them some facts and figures, or you can *involve* them in an engaging, interactive, gentle way? I'm going to take that very same approach in this chapter as I speak about meditation. I could give you the nuts and bolts of this practice, the ins and outs; but instead, I'll share what has transpired from my own exploration with it. Each of us experiences meditation in our own very unique and sacred way. Who am I to tell you what (amazing) consequences you can expect once you take your seat? I simply can't. I can, however, inspire you with a few stories of how radically my life changed, and how supported I began to feel as a result of my commitment to stillness. I encourage you to not attach to my stories, not to expect any of these outcomes to happen to you too. Instead, just allow yourself to open up to the endless possibilities that are available to you when you slip into the silence. Here are the reasons I'm hooked.

1. Grace-filled Guidance

In between our memorable stint in Canada and arriving back in Australia for what would be our last winter as *saisonnaires*, Glen and I travelled Mexico for a month; restoring our vitamin D levels, eating our body's weight in guacamole and, in my case, surrendering three out of the four weeks to food poisoning, thanks to a dodgy pancake in the city of Oaxaca. It was also one of the most guided times of my life so far. Though I was longing to set down roots, I was simultaneously terrified of moving back to Australia. After exhausting my options as a hairdresser, personal trainer, and cocktail bartender, I felt... *annoyed*, actually. There I was, one of the most enthusiastic, passionate people I knew, and apart from the odd slide down a mountain on a snowboard, I had nothing into which I could channel that wild bursting passion.

I knew, even as a little girl, that doing important work would be, you know, *important* to me. That's why I leapt enthusiastically into the salon all those years ago. I wanted to be creative. **I wanted to have something to do with making people feel beautiful.** It's why I picked up on the scent of personal training. **I wanted to belong to the equation of transformation in people's lives.** But *something just wasn't right*. And yet...

I just *knew* that something incredible was out there waiting for me. I didn't know the form it would take, or when it would 'happen', or when I would be 'qualified' enough, but something in me was ready to take a risk. So I did what so many of my generation do when they first start out on an inner quest to change their lives; I played Louise Hay's *I Can Do It* affirmations in my headphones on repeat. Strolling down the street in Puerto Escondido, sitting on the beach, watching Glen surf, or simply lying on the bed in the scorching heat, under the fan, I recited, *"I am infinitely abundant, I nourish my body with healthful foods, I fill my life with love, all is well"*, believing each of those potent statements a little more, each and every time they bounced around my mind. I knew I wanted to be of service; I wanted to impact people in a meaningful way, but I was unsure of what form that would take. Would I be a health coach? Would I do some type of one-on-one body work? Could the psychic have been right in predicting that one day I'd be a healer? What does that even mean, anyway, *to be a healer*? And what on earth could I write books about?! (This still makes me smile) I was apprehensive and nervous about the steepness of all that uncertainty, but everything I had learnt up until that point reminded me that the only moment I had to create change in my life was *this* one. And so, Mexico became a four-week long spiritual experiment.

On the oversized coffee table in our ramshackle penthouse, I laid out a crystal grid, full of specimens I had accumulated in Whistler. Sitting next to the grid in the morning with closed eyes, I could feel the sun touch my skin, energising both me and my circle of citrines, amethysts, and quartzes. I would sit in the glow, hearing the crash of the waves, and visualise how I wanted to feel, how I wanted to help others feel. After our sleepy bodies had walked lengths of the beach, been pummelled by waves, and devoured our daily ritual of an icy cold margarita, I would drift off for a siesta at the tail-end of a meditation, before walking up refreshed and smiley.

All the while, on my visits to the internet cafe for brief check-ins on Facebook, email and my blog, I had seen the stirrings of an eight-week entrepreneurial on-line program circling around social media. *BSchool* was its name and Marie Forleo its creator. At that stage, I'd been following Marie for a few months and loved her fresh and spunky approach to doing business in the world as a heart-centred woman. Like so many trailblazers out there, she showed me an example of what was possible if you allowed authenticity *and* hustle to marry up and lead the way.

Sign up for B-School. I heard it, loud and clear. Or maybe I didn't hear it, and rather, felt it. One thing's for sure, in between audio sessions with Louise Hay, Wayne Dyer and Danielle LaPorte, when my body was still, and my mind was quiet, those four words of guidance landed right on top of me with an unwelcome thump. *No way, I can't afford it!* was my first, and very reasonable reaction. Though Glen and I were travelling to stunning locations and living the good life, we were a far cry from affluent, often maxing out credit cards with flight bookings and cash advances. We were having experiences that dreams were made of, but as far as cash was concerned, we were constantly fighting an uphill battle. One step forward, two back, hustle, spend, repeat. But alas, this guidance was giving me a resounding, rather uncomfortable **yes**. *Do this. Do this, and it will change everything. Do this, and you'll pay the money back in no time.* There was a sense of urgency to the message. *Go, go, go, what are you waiting for?* I was utterly torn – not knowing whether to look to the heavens with deep thanks for such clear communication, or to curse it for its terrible timing. Just as I'm about to err on the side of cursing it, and calling it a day, I see it: **the payment plan option.** *Oh dear.*

I took it up with Glen. $2000 was a lot of money for us back then. It was a big risk to take. And besides, he didn't entirely understand the reason for taking the course in the first place. "So, it's for women in business, and it teaches them how to change lives, and make more money?" he asked. "Yeah, that's pretty much the gist of it", I replied. "But... **you're not in business**, babe". "I... yeah, I know", I pause for silence, completely understanding his hesitation. "I just can't help but feel that this will help move things along. It feels right. I can't explain it."

And in the first of many offerings of good - albeit apprehensive - faith, Glen threw the ball back in my court, and encouraged me to decide for myself; making it clear that regardless of my decision, I'd have his support. Like a synchronistic steam train, BSchool choo-choo-ed its way into my life. Since that day, which I remember so well, sitting in an internet cafe in Mexico, punching in my card numbers, and praying like all hell to the credit gods that my transaction wouldn't be declined, life has never been the same. I may not have had a business at the time, but I planned to use whatever insight Marie's program gave me, apply it to my little blog instead, and just hope that in itself would make a bigger impact on my readers. *It did.* I'd hoped, in and amongst blogging and connecting and spreading an empowering message, a course of passion and service would reveal itself to me. Once back in Australia, instead of snowboarding, I spent the hours between shifts toiling away on my online digs; publishing posts daily, dedicating myself to writing meaningful stuff, and of course, completing and implementing BSchool. Then, barely a month after diving into the program content, I *accidentally* became a life coach. My inbox was being inundated with emails from my readers who were connecting with what I had to say. The words I was writing were landing on them, and they were looking for a little extra support and encouragement.

One lunchtime, I tell the boys all about these beautiful emails at the pub. They're playing pool and drinking beers while I'm gulping down a green smoothie I managed to smuggle in. "Makes me feel as though one day, when I'm qualified, I might actually have a shot at being a successful coach", I say. My friend Dean scoffs, "What are you waiting for? Start helping them now and charge them $50 a month. Enough to make it worth your time." "No..." I say aloud, which is instantly backed up by an internal yes. *Yes, of course.* Within the week, I had 10 clients. Each time I would doubt my ability to make an impact on these brave women, I would slip into meditation, where I'd remember that this whole thing wasn't even about me; I was simply the vessel and these women had been carried into my life for a reason; so we could help each other grow under the umbrella of a coaching relationship. I had never felt so useful, as though I had something to contribute. Purpose woke me up in the morning, and meditation kept my feet on the ground.

Not only were incredible clients finding me, but so were my soul sisters. Women who I had spent months and years following online, admiring their words, their messages, their presence, they were becoming a part of my life. First, online connections were made; tweets, emails, love-soaked blog comments, but at lightning speed these friendships evolved. Before I knew it, those like-minded people the psychic had mentioned (the ones I had prayed were out there) starting showing up. Women who were on a mission to live vibrantly and love fully and serve from their hearts. Here they were, banging down my door, asking me to come play.

Six months later, I was a full-time, work-from-home entrepreneur, coaching clients from across the globe from my computer, writing ebooks and speaking to large groups on stage. I was also attuned to Reiki energy, became a qualified crystal healer, and was immersed deeply in the creation phase of The Party Girl's Guide to Peace online program. And my tribe of angels? Thanks to a meditative message to relocate and settle in Burleigh Heads, most of them now live within a two-hour radius of our home. Just like dreams that materialise in front of your eyes, so too had these beautiful friendships: people who were no longer just names behind a blog, but real-life, hug-able, inspirational forces in my life.

I love telling this story because it indicates the perfect marriage of guidance and action. "Spirit makes the connection", says Hiro Boga, energy alchemist and business strategist, "but it can't make the phone call". I believe wholeheartedly that the real work is done when we're still; when we quieten down and listen; when we become brave enough to open our palms with closed eyes and ask for help, or at the very least, a little light-filled advice. I also know, having lived and breathed this experiment for years now, that we need to feed our dreams with *motion*. First, we hush to turn inward, allowing the process of stillness to burn up our fears, our blockages, maybe the odd chunk of karma. And *then* we create and march forward, because guidance can reach us more easily. We get noisy, and messy, and creative, and we start to make some serious magic.

2. Synchronicities (AKA: Universal Swagger)

After running the online version of The Party Girl's Guide to Peace twice, I knew in my DNA that I wanted to tear it down and repurpose it into a real-life, place-your-hands-upon-it, turn-the-pages, pause-for-contemplation *book*. It was an intimidating vision and of course I had no idea how it would play out, but it felt right. It had only been a few weeks since confiding this vision to my friends, when one of them, Yvette (who you might remember), clued me in on a writers mastermind in Bali, hosted by Mastin Kipp. I'd been following Mastin's work for years, admiring him for being one of the only guys in what Oprah Winfrey herself declared the 'new generation of spiritual teachers'. I adored his transparency and courage to wear his heart on his sleeve while serving the masses. Not surprisingly then, I was more than a little stoked to learn he was hosting a 28-day writing retreat.

After watching the promotional clip, my heart swelled with a deep knowing. I remember thinking *I'm already there; I can feel it!* And that's exactly how I applied for the opportunity - as if I *were* already there - as if the entire retreat materialised in this world to allow my stories and teachings to manifest in the physical form of a book. I followed the very guidance that I'm teaching you here now, and on the lead-up to my interview for the retreat, added images of beautiful Bali to my vision board, decluttered my environment and cultivated a sense of alignment and commitment within me. *This opportunity is mine for the taking and I'm ready for it.* I accepted my invitation to join the 13-strong mastermind, and spent the next five months getting on with my life, knowing and feeling that the book was pacing back and forth inside of me; waiting for me. Well, October crashed into me like a ton of bricks. What was once a date in my calendar, comfortably cushioned by time, was now, um, **here!**

I'm disorganised; fumbling with flight itineraries, herbal medications, loose notes and my passport. I'm so scattered that, just hours before my flight, I – luckily – discover that I'm flying out of Brisbane and not my local airport on the Gold Coast, like I first thought. *Shit!* Rather than simply having to catch a 20-minute taxi, I now need to cab it to the train station and take the two-hour journey to the international terminal. I'm sweaty, and flustered, and giving myself rather a hard time about the whole situation, which has dialled the pressure up to high mighty quickly. On top of that, I'm starting to second guess my book outline, which I handed into my writing coach a few weeks ago. Tardy preparation, second-guessing, self-criticism, planes that are flirting with the prospect of setting flight without me. *Argh!*

I manage to secure my bulging backpack, double-check my flight details, and ensure all the doors are locked just as my taxi arrives. After I crumple into the passenger seat, I notice how shallow my breathing is - that I haven't taken a deep breath all day - so I fill my belly with fresh oxygen. The way my breath opens my body feels both relieving and exposing. There's no escaping this trip now. For better or worse, this damn book in my bones is sending me international.

The cab driver and I spend most of the drive in silence. (To be honest, I'm on my smartphone, hectically tending to last-minute emails and blog posts. You know, the uber-important stuff). Then he asks if I'm headed for the airport. "Yes, I am... I'm going to Bali for a month", and I notice there's a smile in my voice now. I put Facebook away. "By yourself?" he asks. There are parts of Bali that are notorious for danger, so I'm not surprised to hear the concern in his voice. "Not exactly. There's 13 of us all up. We're going for a writing retreat. I'm... writing a book." "Oh!" He comes alive, and his joy feels thick in the cab. "That's fantastic! Years ago, my daughter went to a writing retreat in the Blue Mountains for three weeks..." "Really? Incredible! Did she enjoy it?" "Oh yes, she loved it! And she published her book! She's currently writing her second." "No way! She's published? She must be so thrilled to have put her words out into the world like that."

He exudes a Papa Presence that reminds me of my own dad; proud as punch and full of emotion. "She just loves writing, and the retreat helped her finish her book, because she's a busy mum of two and has a full time job." *What a brilliant woman,* I think to myself, drawing inspiration from her. "She even contacted a hire car company, convinced them to sponsor her for a road-trip book-signing. She made 20 stops all over Australia so she could sign books for her readers", he boasts. "Wow! Good for her. You must be so proud of her."

As we pull up at the train station, my entire body is grinning from top to bottom. Just 30 minutes ago, I was hot and flustered and cursing my idiotic capacities that always, *always* leave things to the last minute. Next moment, here I am being a served a soothing gift from The Universe; a conversation that points to the journey I'm about to make myself. One that begins with a leap of faith. One that ends with a book. I've never felt so relieved to run late in all my life. I take my seat on the train, and can't help but laugh out loud. *Thank you,* I whisper, to the empty seat opposite me.

3. Non-reactivity

I spent 10 days, to all intents and purposes, living life as a Buddhist monk (or would that be a nun?) at a Vipassana meditation retreat. *Silence.* Noble silence in fact, which meant: no gestures, no eye contact, no laughing. Not a word was to be spoken. No wifi. No reading. No writing (ugh). No crystals or essential oils (double ugh). No yoga, or any other exercise for that matter (triple ugh). Simply 10 hours of meditation per day. Eating. Breathing. Sleeping. That's *it*.

Vipassana retreats run for 10 days, because in all truth it takes every moment of those 10 days to fully learn and grasp the technique. This style of meditation was not, in fact, about omm-ing. Not about connecting to Spirit. Not about channelling information from a higher place (although I certainly experienced moments of mega clarity). **Vipassana is all about understanding the 'truth' of the world, pertaining to the framework of this physical body**. No philosophies. No blind faith. Just awareness of the natural breath and the sensations - both 'pleasant' and 'unpleasant' and everything in between - that course through the body. All intellection was removed from the equation and, for the love of God, while on the surface this might sound torturous, I cannot even begin to express how freeing this theory was at the beginning. *You mean to tell me that I don't have to find the origin of my pain? Hell, I don't even have to feel my pain!? My only job is to acknowledge and observe it?* Rock on.

It all sounds very serene and zen. Very *right-up-my-alley*. But 100 hours of meditation in 10 days was no easy feat. It was outrageously challenging. There were times where I was so frustrated that all I could do was squeeze out a few salty tears. At other times, the compulsory one-hour sittings in the hall would melt into a buzzing frenzy in my body that I swear lasted only 10 minutes. It was easy. It was gut-wrenchingly intense. It was all of it. I learned that by observing the *pain* in me with equanimity rather than *aversion*, **I was freed from suffering.** I learned that by observing the *pleasant sensations* within me with equanimity instead of *craving*, **I was freed from suffering.** Wishing the pain away (aversion) is essentially useless, because it'll undoubtedly result in instantaneous misery. Willing the pleasant sensations to hurry up and return (craving) is, again, utterly useless, because it'll undoubtedly result in instantaneous misery. **I learnt to accept that in this present moment the Law of Nature has *impulsively* and *impersonally* placed this sensation in my body, and that it will not last. Nothing ever does. Nothing stays the same. Everything changes.**

With that in mind, you can let go of your stories, Party Girl. You can take comfort in the realisation that your fears, your insecurities, your discomforts, hardships and resistances are not here to stay. By Universal Law, it's actually impossible for them to remain. **If the world is forever changing, then why not change with it?** Life operates under a constant ebb and flow characterised by cycles and rhythms. And with life comes chaos. That's the beauty of uncertainty and the unknown. As much as we wish we could predict our circumstances, there's a constant variable playing out always. Chaos *will* come. It's inevitable. No doubt about it. Yet we have a choice about for how long and with how much intensity we attach to it. How often do we, as human beings, completely attach to a sensation that arises in our body – a niggle, a pang of jealousy, a spike of discontent? How often do we subscribe to insane stories that are cosmic light-years out from the truth? Often the women I work with experience this attachment via the emotional state of *comparison*. They feel as though it's a force in their life over which they have no control. It becomes a strangling presence in their lives, and I need to remind them that, yes, we all get triggered from time to time. Ultimately, however, the choice to really feel the breadth of that suffering is ours in its entirety. It's a choice that can be changed at any moment.

We *choose* how deeply we feel jealousy. We *choose* how deeply we feel anger. Meditation teaches us (and this transcends the modality of Vipassana, by the way) to *feel* it, but let it flit on by. Feel it, and then liberate it. Don't become a slave to these emotions! I'm not talking about intense periods of grief or loss. I'm talking about the everyday 'stuff' that simply rises up so it can fall away. And yet, we make our lives so much more difficult by getting ourselves sucked into the cyclone of it all. This guidance, which spilled its way out onto my journal one wide-awake night at 2am, captures the essence of this teaching beautifully: *You are feeling too intensely that which is only meant to be fleeting.* Meditation reminds us that **this too shall pass.**

4. The Whisper of *Enough Is Enough*

We'd all be making fools of ourselves if we thought we could drink bottle after bottle of wine, live on a diet of processed food, participate in relationships that drain us, continually watch reality television *and* expect to be able to create and maintain a beautiful, always-present, conscious intuitive connection. It is in this respect that we really *can't* have it all. As you strengthen your connection with your inner guide, with life, with God, or however you interpret the

Source, you will invariably be called upon to gently release any toxicity that may be holding you back from your greatest potential. This is an ongoing process, and what you'll most likely notice is that dropping one bad habit is often followed up by guidance to relinquish another, then another. Have you walked away from some type of toxicity before, be it a substance, a relationship or a working environment? How did it feel afterwards? Frightening, but freeing? As though another door was *just* about to open for you? As though you had a new, fresh life ahead of you?

I had the privilege of speaking alongside naturopath and angel intuitive, Robert Reeves, at an event called Body and Soul Foods in Brisbane. He gave a brilliant sermon on food sensitivities and the role they play in today's society. Something that, on the surface, may seem inconvenient and like a giant pain in the ass (let's say for instance allergies to gluten, or dairy, and sensitivities to sugar, or processed foods) are, he believes, the answer to our prayers. Clairvoyantly, Robert perceives gluten as physic *glue* that clogs the third eye. How's that for a visual! And sugar? He sees it as crystals that float in our aura and drain energy from us like vampires. I'm sure we've all felt that, right? The crippling effects of a sugar comedown? If these food products affect us so radically, it's not difficult to see how alcohol can sever our intuitive connection, too.

Robert says that many of today's sensitivities are covert answers to our deepest prayers. We've been getting down on our proverbial knees, going *alright! I'm ready! I want to live a better life now*, praying for a life rich with meaning and purpose. In response, we're being adorned with sensitivities that demand we clean up our bodies and clear the channel. You see, it's not just the accumulation of birthdays that are making you more hungover, sweet potato. It has little to do with your age. Suddenly, fewer drinks are getting you more drunk and you've started asking questions like: *What the hell is happening to me?* Now you know. You're being called upon to rise up. To shun the crap, and instead crystallise into a new, groovy way of being. Word on the street is that *radiant* is the new black.

5. Creativity, Contribution, and Answering the Call

Remember Rachel? Here she is again: "I've always had big dreams and I've always had big visions, but I wasn't in a position to be a clear channel for that creativity, and for those creative gifts", she says. "All that toxicity was holding me back from putting it to good use and that's where the self-care aspect has come in. Your level of self-care directly impacts your creativity. When you're emotionally, mentally, physically nourished, there are no limits. You really can take your vision and just run with it."

It was ultimately an inner acknowledgement of what she was truly capable of that enabled Rachel to swap out caipiroskas for Sunday morning bush-walks. "That internal voice would say 'there's more to your life that this and you can go out and change lives and connect with so many more people, if you would just connect back up with *you*', but I had to get nourished on all levels first", she says. "And you're just not when you're partying. You're sleep-deprived. You're eating crappy food. You're filling your body with toxins. You're just not a clear channel for those gifts."

I ask her what matters most. "I just want to feel good. I just want to feel joyful. I just want to be happy. And if there's things that aren't in alignment with that, I start chipping away at them until I get back to my truth", she answers. "You don't want to be doing the things that take you away from who that is."

Bring us home, Rachy. Give these Party Girls a precious pep talk to remember! "Stop looking for validation and instead connect back in with yourself. The best way to do that is to get *still*. I love the quote by Michael Singer in *The Untethered Soul,* 'Meditation is a return to the root of your being'. Happiness isn't found in the bottom of a bottle, or in the bathroom at 3am when you're looking in the mirror thinking, 'Oh my God, I'm so wasted right now'. That's not happiness. It might feel good in the moment but that whole quote about happiness being an inside job is spot on. You are *so* powerful. You don't need to turn yourself up or amp yourself up to be confident or to be beautiful or to be accepted. You just need to come back to yourself and return to the root of your being." Couldn't have said it better myself.

6. Remembering Who I Am

Here's an updated and edited excerpt from Rachel's and my book, *Spirited:*

For a while there, every time I curled up with a guided meditation, before long, I'd find myself sobbing uncontrollably over the words and music. In those tears,

I could feel a deep un-hooking in my chest; a slow and steady *clunk!* It felt vulnerable – and at first, a little strange – to be sitting in a space of stillness, yet at the same time, be having such a dynamic, heart-opening experience. It's challenging for me to explain the emotions, the tears, that unmistakable Cracking Open thing that happened to me in those first few months of meditation as an adult. The best I can do in attempting to describe it is to say that I truly felt as though I was coming home. *Finally.*

I had resisted it. I didn't understand it, didn't see how it could fit into my life. I couldn't get my head around the point of it when I already felt so bankrupt of time. After all, *things needed doing!* and perhaps that's exactly why my journey into the silence was so significant and soul-shaking. What we resist persists, and the more it persists, the more vulnerable it feels to surrender to it. I searched for Ideal Tara in 6am vodka recovery sessions, mysterious men and job after spirit-depleting job. I travelled the world, hoping I'd learn to love myself more if I could just... find the ... right... place. And yet there I was, in bed, perched on my sit bones with closed eyes, crying from my heart, feeling an all-encompassing love for *me*. So much that it hurt a little. It was the spiritual detox I didn't even know I was desperate for.

Today, I meditate for maintenance, clarity and insight. I meditate for *love*. I meditate *on* love.

I meditate because life is, without a doubt, much sweeter when I do. And easier. This has been made apparent to me countless times - when I feel as if I'm lacking direction or flow, and when my attitude of gratitude isn't dialled right the way up, a little reflection is all it takes to realise *Ah... I haven't sat for a meditation in days... Got it.* Every time I have this little *a-ha!* moment, I like to imagine that The Universe has given me a wink, as if to say, *"That's right child. Time to get back to work, now."*

But the meditative crème de la crème – for me – is being shown a world of truth and magic. A world of grace and love and wisdom beyond anything that we can experience out here, in the world of form, with our senses. I love 'touching' the unknown; the mystery of the void, which is all there, behind my eyelids. Its description defies the mere English dictionary. The mind and the soul speak different native tongues, and trying to translate one with the other is near impossible. **But this, I'm certain of:** I am grateful that Spirit insisted I drop on by and say hi.

Spiritual practice is responsible for my transformed marriage, the birth of my business, the words I publish on my blog, the abundance of opportunities that float into my life, my friendships, and indeed, this book! It was in meditation that I was guided to move to Burleigh Heads (where I finally feel at home), hire incredible mentors, work with amazing women, take risks, embrace my femininity and resiliently keep placing one foot in front of the other. It was and continues to be meditation that bridges the gap between what I can see with my eyes, and what I believe with my heart.

7. Grace Generates Generosity

Recently, I spent 10 days in Los Angeles on something of a personal spiritual pilgrimage. Before I set off, I started reading *Invisible Acts of Power* by Caroline Myss. It's a beautiful book that basically highlights the good in humanity with a collection of stories that feature generosity and compassion, which are seamlessly stirred into fundamental teachings of the chakras. Reading that book made me hungry to be a better version of me. Since I was in LA, where the homeless population is really quite staggering for this sheltered Aussie creature, I had a hunch on what it was I had to do. *Before I leave, I'll feed someone.*

You might be thinking: *yeah okay Ta's, whatever, what's the big deal?* **But damn.** Meeting someone in their pain like that. Looking in their eyes. Trying to perceive the difference between the two of you, when really, what's being illuminated is your *sameness*. It's fucking hard.

I was angry with myself. Every morning, I woke up, and declared, *Today's the day. I'm going to feed someone today.* And then I'd hit the pillow at night and scrutinise myself on why I just couldn't bring myself to extend my hand to someone so vulnerable. Toward the tail-end of my trip, I opened up Caroline's book and began reading. *Bam!* Right there on those pages were three examples of how people have outstretched a hand to the homeless. I slammed the book shut. *Right!* I stormed into my cute little kitchen, flung open the pantry doors and grabbed a good kilogram of trail mix I'd bought at Wholefoods the day before. Cashews, gojis, mulberries, walnuts. The good stuff. *This will keep someone going. Today. Is. The. Day.*

But not before a shopping trip to The Grove. (Resistance at its finest.) When I'm done, I duck into Barnes & Noble. I take the elevator up to level two and station myself in front of the personal growth section. (While writing this book, I made a habit of entering every book store I come across, so I could meditate on *High* sitting on its shelves.) When I crack my eyes open from my stealthy, upright meditation, I see a middle-aged man standing in front of me, running his hands over a few book spines.

Resting in his hand, pressing against his heart, is none other than *Invisible Acts of Power*. A lump hardens in my throat. "That's an incredible book", I spit out at him with a smile. "Is it? I'm not sure whether to get this one, or *Sacred Contracts*." (Another outstanding Myss book.) "Well it depends what mood you're in", I say. "If you feel like being reminded that humans are generally good people who know how to look after each other, read *Invisible Acts*. *Sacred Contracts* is amazing, but you'll have to study it. It requires a lot of journaling and self-enquiry." "*Invisible Acts* it is", he decides, grinning. As he walks away, I reach into my handbag and feel for the brick of trail mix, remembering why I put it there.

Traffic that day was bad. Man, it was so, so bad. The Grove was only three miles from my apartment, but friends, it took me *an hour and a half* to get home in a taxi. I spent the first half of the trip in moody silence, before my cab driver had a genius idea to take a more-than-scenic route which would essentially double our travel time, but at least we'd be moving. *Sure*, I said, a little ruffled. And when he veered off towards the side street, *I saw him*. A different shoe underneath each of his blistered feet. Filthy clothes. Bruised skin. A limp that looked uncomfortable. He started digging in the trash can, before coming up with a few cigarette butts, which he lit, for a puff or two. Our car crept towards him as we came to a red light, and without hesitating another moment, I lowered my electric window. "Are you hungry?" He glances up at me and the blue of his eyes, which burn brighter from the contrast of the dirt on his face, pierce me right through to the soul. "I have some food for you…" He just nods. With both hands, I extend him the trail mix, not breaking eye contact with him once. As the cab starts to pull away, he says, "*God bless you*". And I tremble into an awkward cry.

Spiritual practice *irons out the creases of separation* and helps you to feel the essence of you in every being that you encounter.

Okay, so here are some short and sweet cliff notes on the shape that meditation takes in my life. The styles. The signature dance moves.

Guided meditations

This is a beautiful place to start. Whenever I introduce meditation into anyone's life, I always encourage them to ease into it with the help of beautifully recorded guided versions. You can find a guided meditation for any symptom. Whether you're looking to dissolve fear, manifest dreams, forgive a past hurt, connect with angels or your highest self, or generate gratitude, the list is limitless. Beats a trip to the drug store, any day of the week. These days, I tend to turn toward guided meditations when I feel as though I need extra support; when I'm busy with work, when I'm feeling a little tender or emotional or overwhelmed. Never underestimate the power of a love-infused five-minute guided journey. You thought acid was good? You ain't seen nothing yet. You'll find a list of my recommendations in the resources section at the back on this book.

Anapana: Breath observation

Simple, profound, perspective-changing. This one sweet thing that we take for granted most moments of our life - our breath - is truly a mystery to marvel at and behold. With breath comes sensation aplenty. The cool prickle of it as it enters your nostrils. The faint sliding of it as it cascades down your throat. The gentle lift of the collarbone, the heart, the belly. The beating of the heart beneath it. The sound of it - oceanic and fluid and meditative by nature. The way it effortlessly and instantaneously seems to lengthen and deepen as soon as we place our awareness upon it. What a trip. Both spirit and science will tell us that our lives mirror the quality of our breath, which is why it's such a central focal point in both meditation and yoga. One thing I like to contemplate in my meditations as I feel the rise and fall of my breath is this: *Am I breathing right now? Or is The Universe breathing me?*

Mindfulness meditation

This is a stunning way to practice presence. We simply place our entire attention on the present moment. With eyes closed, we observe the world around us,
allowing the rest of our senses to open up and receive – the sounds, the feelings,
the smells, the breeze, the next-door neighbour's lawn mower – we welcome the
lot of it. Not pushing anything away, not succumbing to frustration, instead we
allow and accept everything as it is, in this moment, completely.

Transcendental Meditation (otherwise known as TM)

This is a technique in which you repeat a stillness sound over and over in your
mind, eventually sinking into a deep state of bliss. TM is taught at seminars and
retreats and each person is given their sacred sound, or mantra, which should
never again be repeated out loud. The mantra, once focused on with the mind,
acts a vehicle that carries you to a still mind. Google *transcendental meditation* to find an event or workshop near you. I learned TM from Tom Cronin,
founder of The Stillness Project.

Vipassana meditation

A process of scanning the entirety of the body, from the top of the head, to the
tip of the toes, and up again, continuously, observing sensations in a sweeping
manner, while practicing equanimity and non-reactivity. Check out vipassana.
org for a retreat near you. Payment is by donation only.

Chakra cleansing and balancing

Ooof. This is a lofty, gorgeous, delicious topic. Using the mind to focus on our
chakras (or energy centres), we allow them to open, and spin, and cleanse, and
heal, while empowering and enlivening them with the addition of visualisation.

I feel beyond privileged to have been mentored one-on-one by psychic,
medical intuitive and creator of the *School of the Modern Mystic*, Belinda
Davidson. If you've been following me online for a while, you'll know how
much I adore her, and how significantly the work we've done together has

impacted my existence. Under Belinda's guidance, I learned how to balance and heal my chakras, journey towards chakras eight and nine, intuit messages from them, 'download' my soul's purpose, and then express it. *(Ahem. That has something to do with the reason this book is in your hands.)*

Like I said, lofty. And there's simply no room in *this* book to discuss all this. So instead, I'll point you in the direction of a chakra workshop that Belinda and I have created for you to dive into. Head to tarabliss.com.au/chakras. There are also some guided chakra meditations that I recommend in the resources section of this book.

Suggestions for *easy* meditative experiences

Now, before I put the wrong idea in your head, you certainly don't have to wait until you've attended a meditation retreat, or read ancient scriptures at great length to start a meditation practice. No bloody way. You can begin – or deepen your current practice – right now. Here's a few ideas to get you started, pronto.

> :: *In the evening, turn the television on mute while the ads are on, and close your eyes. You can focus on your breath, or on the noises around you. If you have a family, you can get them in on the act too.*

> :: *Move your body. Notice how dynamic a few moments of stillness can feel after dancing vigorously to a song or two. Completely let go, dance your heart out, and then turn off the music, take a seat, and remain stationary for a couple of minutes. Sense the aliveness inside of you.*

> :: *If you catch public transport, listen to a guided meditation on your way to work.*

> :: *Consciously sip in big breaths at the traffic lights.*

> :: *Fall asleep at night to the visions of all that you're manifesting.*

:: Meditate on the toilet - seriously!

:: Take the first few moments of your morning to generate gratitude by placing your hands upon your heart and feeling it beat beneath your hands.

Here are three tips for creating a meditation practice worth shouting about.

1. Make a magical altar.

Creating a sacred space in which you devote to your spiritual practice is a holy experience in and of itself. I adore the process of piecing them together - deciding which items make the cut, which of them hold symbolism, which of them remind me of depth, joy, love, laughter… each piece meticulously chosen with care. The idea is that you selectively and intentionally create a space with meaningful things, that bring you a sense of reverence as you take your seat.

My altar includes: a Thai silk given to me by a dear friend a few years ago, my vision board, crystals that represent each of the chakras, a sacred geometry card gifted by a client (which acts as a centrepiece and compass), a mini statue of creative goddess Saraswati, a journal, a couple photos of me as a little girl, a pyramid made from hematite, and items that represent the elements: sage for earth, feathers attached to leather for air, a candle for fire and alchemical oil for water.

Altars are deeply personal, so enjoy the process of collecting your personal items and arranging them in a corner of your home in a way that fits your soul. Also, bigger isn't necessarily better. Maybe your altar comprises just a handful of special little somethings. And that's absolutely perfect. Meditate in front of your altar, journal there if you wish, say a few prayers – any act that you deem sacred.

2. Breathe, babe, breathe.

You know how important your breath is now, right? You know that it's the sacred place where the form and the formless mingle with one another? You can appreciate how much of a mystery it is? **Well, let's learn to appreciate it just that little bit more.**

In the yogic tradition, both asana (movement) and pranayama (breath work) traditionally come before meditation (which is why I like to move and then practice pranayama before I settle in). Mastering the mind by focusing on the breath creates an environment where you're likely to feel less distracted in your meditation.

Feel your breath fill your belly, your ribs, your back, your chest. Feel it fall out of your chest, your back, your ribs, your belly. Consciously slow the breath, keeping count of the seconds that you both inhale and exhale (ensuring that they're timed evenly).

3. Seal it with love.

Energise the closing moments of your meditation by breathing in love, and exhaling compassion. This is a technique I picked up at Vipassana, and I simply adore it. I like to imagine that I'm breathing in vibrant pink light and that, each time I exhale, I extend healing, golden, compassionate light a little further around the globe. It feels loving and dynamic in my body. It feels like I'm making a small difference to the world.

Peace Practice

Rather than prompting you with journal questions, I'm going to invite you to lean into your journal after your meditations. You can jot down how you felt before, during, or after your experience.

You could perhaps try automatic writing, a process of letting go of conscious thought and allowing your subconscious to communicate by moving the pen across the paper. If you're more of a romantic type, you might prefer to view the guidance spilling out onto your journal as wisdom from your *angels*, or *spirit guides*, rather than your *subconscious*. Sometimes, when I'm writing automatically (whether it's after I sit for meditation, or upon rising in the morning), I feel like it's my *heart* speaking to me. In any case, just sit yourself down, even if it's only for five minutes, and *see what happens*. **I promise it will be the start of something beautiful.**

There's no question that meditation not only heightens our awareness of Self and teaches us the importance and availability of stillness and inner peace, but it also reminds us of what's true underneath our crazy ideas and false beliefs about ourselves. Meditation keeps us grounded, and focused, and steady in times of chaos, resistance, and so-called 'failure'. And *presence* – a moving, walking, dynamic meditation – is not only the greatest gift we can give ourselves and others, but it's our most potent medicine when our Egos are on a mission to assume control…

9.

You Cannot Fail

*"Freedom is not worth having if it does not include the
freedom to make mistakes."*
Mahatma Gandhi

You've just cracked open your eyes. Your head is pounding. Your mouth is dry. Your body is aching all over. And – the icing on the cake – you don't know the name (let alone recognise the face) of the guy who's snoring next to you. As you cast your mind back to the night before, you can pinpoint the exact moment that one or two drinks snowballed into an *Oh, what the hell!* declaration, allowing the wine to flow freely; each sip tarnishing the promises that you had made to yourself just a week before. Promises of mindful drinking, of moderation, they're pinching at your tender temples now as you lay in bed feeling as though you've crashed into a deep pit of despair and failure.

Hold up, lady. Before I get into how to best 'recover' from this type of situation, I want to make sure we're clear on a few things. 'Only love is real' is a concept that's echoed throughout *A Course in Miracles*. And if you're anything like me, you find that very concept romantic and soul-nurturing. If 'only love is real' became a mantra of yours, and you believed in it wholeheartedly, how would that change your approach to processing your fears and failed attempts at living a life you dream of? How would your life be different if you came to understand that each and every hangover is divine, instead of a drag? (Yep, you heard right.) So too is each and every argument, or accident, or dare I say it, one-night stand?
Stay with me here.

I'm not asking you to make excuses for your behaviour, and I'm certainly not giving you the go-ahead to slack off... I'm suggesting an alternative to the way we relate to ourselves when things don't go as planned. Think of it as taking the scenic route that detours west of self-hatred, towards forgiveness. We need to stop viewing hardships as 'tests' and 'punishment'. Pain is part of the experience of existing as a human being, but can we even label pain as a test? Can we even label it as negative? If pain itself is the very experience that reminds us of what unconditional love is (through a process of dichotomies), then correct me if I'm mistaken, but is it not one of our greatest blessings as creatures who have the capacity to *feel*? Pain courses through our bodies so it can be felt; so it can be experienced; so it can move up and out, just as you would feel and express joy, gratitude, courage. We make a huge error in perceiving that The Universe is out to run through a series of rigorous exams, and in that belief, we breathe life into the fears that surround it.

Every single moment is a divine opportunity to be present. That's all it is. It's neither good nor bad. It just is what it is; totally neutral. We shape our experience of the moment by how we perceive it (good, bad, inspiring, painful, joyful), but we can utilise an awareness of the present moment to slip back into our bodies at any time, thus cultivating peace and contentment. Your body is where you belong; a semi-permanent palace with solid foundations. It's loyal – something we so often forget. And yet, instead of experiencing life in the moment, we take refuge in our minds, a place where an incessant soundtrack of self-loathing plays on repeat, distracting us from what's real.

To make sure we're all vibing together here, let me elucidate: **life isn't a test.** It's a never-ending playground of opportunities. How empowering is that? Knowing that we can choose to be in each moment as if it were a fresh slate (which it is), rather than willing ourselves out of current experience because it just feels too uncomfortable. Or disappointing. Or frustrating. Or empty. In times of perceived 'failure', I ask that you prescribe yourself a present-moment-opportunity mindset. Feel your precious body. Whether you've woken up feeling as though you've been spat out from behind a dump truck thanks to a coke bender, or you're suffering a severe case of vodka-and-Red-Bull comedown, or you've had a one-night stand, or you've over-eaten, or you've treated someone close to you poorly, feel what's happening in your body in ***this*** moment.

Stop thinking (I mean it!) and just *breathe*. Feel the energy in your hands and feet. Notice your heart beating. Draw your attention into your gut. What is your body saying to you? She could be whispering; she could be howling; she could be struggling to keep up with your antics. One thing's for certain, though, your body will forgive you long before your mind does. She's one forgiving, compassionate little minx, that bod of yours, which serves as a beautiful reminder for us all to embrace our flesh - our organs, our heartbeat, our energy field - and the indescribable intelligence that connects it all. Kinda makes you wonder why we ever set out to sabotage our health in the first place, huh?

Don't mistake this whole acknowledging-the-feelings-and-sensations-within-your-body thing as woo-woo or fluff. When we're in pain, often we feel as though the 'cure' to our problems need to be as monumental and significant as the problem itself. No way. It's simply not true. The answers you're searching for can be sought, found, implemented and embodied in a fraction of a moment. Small, incremental change equals maximum results. Hear me when I say that this does not need to be difficult.

Binge drinking is something that's repeated weekend after weekend simply because we refuse to connect in with our body! We distract ourselves! We binge (be it booze, food, relationships, shopping) because we're unconscious to the connection we were born to have with our bodies. Upon waking the following morning, we proceed to unconsciously smother our hangovers with greasy food, or a sleeping pill, or trashy television. When we're high, we go to extreme lengths to delay the coming-down process; we stock up on booze to ease the stress of the rising sun. We scramble to get our hands on more pills, more coke, more meth - whatever it will take to resist feeling the 'pain' of reality. And then, when we simply can't go on any longer, we collapse into a dishevelled, exhausted mess. The scent of food makes our stomachs churn, the normally beautiful glare of the morning makes us recoil like vampires, the faintest musical beat reverberates abrasively in our skull. We become over-sensitive and aggressive toward a life that's *really* here to be cherished and adored. **We become monsters.**

Want to know how to cure your hangover, once and for all? Brace yourself, because I've never met a solution that can stand up against this one. Here it is: **Feel it.** *Feel the damn thing.* I know what you're thinking. You're thinking:

Come on, blondie! I sure as hell know what a hangover feels like. It feels like death warmed up! It's awful! Like sweat and puke and clammy and gross and bleurgh. I'm not convinced. When you reach for that phone so you can dial a pizza, you're saying - out loud or not - *bring me this pizza so I can sideline this misery inside of me.* When you reach for that TV remote so you can fill up your space with the distraction of reality television, you're thinking - consciously or not - *give me something that takes my mind off how much I want to hurl.*

Think of your hangovers in the same way we think of our shadow when we're doing shadow work. Until you fully acknowledge and appreciate the effect that these hungover states can have on your life; until you feel the thickness of it; until you surrender to it completely (rather than trying to manipulate it and lessen it and cover it up), you cannot heal it. The bingeing will continue. The Sunday Sadtimes will continue. The destructive cycle of excess and detox and self-hatred will continue.

In this way, hangovers become a part of our spiritual practice. Yes, they're unideal. They're wildly inconvenient. They - quite frankly - blow. They're a little reckless and a lot disrespectful to these bodies of ours. Yet ultimately, when you have a hangover, you *have* a hangover. No Vedic chant or liver tonic will take away from fact that, this morning, you woke up with a hangover. A hangover! Just as no amount of guilt, self-shaming or attack thoughts will lessen the agony.

This chapter isn't about writing yourself a post-Party checklist of 'self-care'. *Have a cold shower. Eat a salad. Drink lots of water. Sleep it off...* It's not about that. We're not going to continue to mask anything anymore. In fact, we're doing the opposite here - we're getting honest with ourselves and we're prying off the very masks that have been keeping us stuck. Are you sensing a theme here? *Seems I have a vendetta against these masks, huh?*

Your body is your truth-speaker. When you live from a space of body awareness, you experience presence. When you're present, your energy centres (chakras) open and expand and start spinning. When your chakras are spinning, and moving energy freely around your body, guess what's happening? You're healing. Healing what, exactly? Take your pick: physical ailments, a closed heart, financial blocks, past resentments, back pain, acne, the big toe you stubbed this morning getting out of bed (most likely thanks to that bleeping hangover). The list is limitless.

When we live presently - which is most certainly a spiritual practice in and of itself - we learn that the moment is here to teach us. We remember what we've forgotten. The *a-ha!* moment arrives. A soft whisper from your heart is much more potent than just another compassionate-less voice that clip-clops around your in your mind. So again, **feel what's going on.** If you experience guilt thanks to a relapse of sorts, can the guilt. Instead, intend to adopt a little compassion and apologise to your body (and listen to her as she forgives you). The sooner you actually *feel* that hangover, the sooner you'll be inspired to make lasting change. Like I said, the pain (and for our purposes, let's talk specifically about self-inflicted pain in the shape of hangovers) is a blessing.

When I made the decision to start drinking more mindfully, my relationship to hangovers changed completely. I became more and more sensitive to alcohol, feeling rusty in the morning after just two or three glasses of red wine. Whereas months before, I would have moped around the house cursing myself for not being able to handle my booze anymore - *What's happening to me? I'm getting old! I used to be able to drink so much more!* - I'll never forget the first time I felt true and total gratitude for a red wine headache. I sat up in bed, acknowledging the ache with a gentle temple massage. This headache, this churning belly of mine, was a divine message communicating that three glasses of wine was now beyond my capacity. I was becoming more sensitive. My body was consequently speaking up to let me know, and I was grateful in that moment that I could sit there in my bed and *feel* my body communicating to me. Yeah, I was a little uncomfortable – because hey, headaches aren't fun – but strangely, I also felt really empowered. I truly grasped the message behind the migraine. **I was listening.**

When we think about it, how else are we going to know when it's time to change our behaviour? Drinking and drugging are both rubbish for our bodies, minds and spirits – there's no doubt about that – but we continue to dip our toes into the mess of it all until our bodies begin to speak up. Hangovers are hell for a reason, Party Girl. The next time you experience one (*if* you experience one again), with a little mindset shift, you can redirect your focus from how much it sucks, to how interesting a gift it is to unwrap, this opportunity to heal. To release a shadow. To stop the saboteur in its tracks. Before long, you might find yourself in the throes of a statement such as thing one, from Jaime:

*"Well, I've done it. I've had my **last ever** hangover. It had been a good eight to ten months since my last hangover. While my drinking was in hand, it was creeping back up on me - still not drinking a lot, but drinking more often. Can't say that I enjoyed any of the hangover I dealt with yesterday, but I did enjoy the knowledge that it would never happen again! No, not one of those 'I'll never drink again' moments. It was truly a moment of clarity. I've got better things to do in my life than waste days hungover! So tonight I'll be celebrating with a big fat juice and I can't wait!"*

The only intention worth setting

Why is it that so often when we attend a wedding or party, we become hot messes, el pronto, despite our best intentions? **It's because we place limitations and restrictions on ourselves.**

:: *I'll stop at two.*

:: *I'll drink wine, and not spirits.*

:: *I'll be designated driver so I don't drink. Ah. Actually...On second thoughts, I might just drink and then cab it home...*

I think we all underestimate how primitively rebellious we are by nature. No matter the size or shape or strength of the box that's placed around us, we'll always find a way to pole vault out, even if we're the ones who put it there. (*Especially* if we put it there.) What if, the next time you were headed for an event, your intention instead was simply: **I'm going to be present tonight.** If that were your intention, then perhaps you'd be able to actually taste and savour your beverage of choice. Enjoy it even! (*Imagine.*) Perhaps you'd sip slower. Maybe you'd hold eye contact and exude a grace that's impossible to exude when you're guzzling away happy hour. You could **decide** whether in fact you truly wanted another drink, after checking in with your body.

You know what? (And I really mean this.) After all's said and done, all you have to do is be present. **That is your only job.** And not just when there's a risk you might hit the piss. I'm talking about the entirety of your existence. Present in your relationships. Present in your interactions at work. Present while you're on the phone to your telecommunications agent. Present in the traffic. In the bank queue. While making love. While bending into sun salutations. While sipping hot cacao with almond milk and maple syrup. Presence is the most profound thing we can desire for our lives, because it's the only space in which we can properly give to and receive from Life. It's the only place where a miracle can unfold, where guidance can be glimpsed, where questions become answers. You and I can sit here and mull over our pasts; all the mistakes we made, the men who hurt us, the severe pain we've caused others. We can blush at the cheeks as we replay cringe-worthy memories in our mind. We can reboot such fierce, sheer hatred that we haven't felt in *decades* by indulging in and reliving the burn of What Happened Back Then. Sounds crazy fun, right?

We can also work ourselves up into such an anxious, panicked tizzy over the future that we render ourselves stuck and fearful in *this* moment. We remember all the ways in which we've experienced 'failure' in the past, and we assume that the future is riddled with identical torments. (Here's a newsflash: the past does *not* equal the future.) We amp up such stress in our nervous systems because of the uncertainty of the future that we escape to our minds in an attempt to manipulate and grapple for perfect outcomes, often numbing ourselves from the life that's laid out in front of us *right now.* Man, I don't know about you, but that all sounds exhausting, and… rather *balls*, really.

Or we can ditch both of those (non-productive, spirit-depleting) approaches and instead aim for something much more groovy. We set our intentions upon *playing* in the present moment. Notice how I didn't say 'do the work' in the present moment, or 'toil away' in the present moment, or 'ride it out' in the present moment. Each experience of pure *now* gives us an opportunity to play with it, to explore it, to cock our heads to one side and watch in wonder as it unfolds. Ask yourself for a moment how different life might be if you chose to see it as an amusement park, rather than a classroom. Perhaps you'd be open, ecstatic, raw with authentic emotion, no? You wouldn't miss a beat. You'd take any opportunity to stretch yourself, to embrace variety, to overcome your fears (and maybe even have a lil' giggle at their expense).

So next time you get on out there into the big wide world, feel the energy in your body and take Life into your senses as if you're in a 3D theatre. Get out of your own way, Party Girl! Life is here to serve you; it's not *out to get you.*

Please remember that. Feel the aliveness in you when you're in the presence of others. Notice the space you're filling energetically. Notice if your chest puffs out a little, or your aura feels as though it's pulsating. Notice if you start looking people in the eye more, and how you carry yourself through conversations. Notice if you begin to feel the ever-present love that's available to you, when you're mindful and really, truly *here*. Let's do away with the notion that this is all a big fat exam of some kind, and get back to enjoying these moments, these blessings.

Here are three questions you can ask yourself before hitting the town that should inspire a few cogs in your mind to spin in your favour. The first is: **what part of me wants to get drunk tonight?** *Hmm.* Does your soul want to get drunk tonight? Your highest self? Is it your inspired self? Or is the part of you that needs to rely on something outside of yourself to feel validated, beautiful, engaging, *enough*. Is it the insecure, small part of you that craves finding some way to become bigger? Is it the part of you that fears missing out... on anything? Something for you to consider: *what part of me wants to get drunk tonight?*

The second question is: **do I want to have a grateful heart when my head hits the pillow tonight?** I remember the prep process of going out so very well. Gorgeous friends, pre-drinks, rad tunes playing in the background, limbering our bodies and inhibitions. Gosh, it was so much fun. But on a deeper level, how might the trajectory of your night change if you asked yourself: *do I want to feel grateful, or do I want to feel drunk and messy and blacked-out, maybe a little regretful, perhaps a bit out of my body?* Am I doing this to cultivate gratitude, or am I doing this to escape myself? Consider this a stealthy little permission slip reminding you that *gratitude* is a legitimate option.

And the third: **what can I do tonight to get outside of my comfort zone?** Remember our earlier advice from Hayley Carr? Dancing on a table or getting blind rotten drunk, they're not comfort zone expanding endeavours. For Party Girls, that is the epitome of comfortable. Getting out of your comfort zone doesn't mean having an all-night bender or approaching a guy with a nose full of coke. *Oh, no.* That's comfortable. For you, discomfort (which ultimately points to freedom) can mean *not* responding to the booty call. It could mean politely saying 'no' to the next round of drinks. It could simply mean trying out this *presence* thing I've been banging on about for a whole chapter!

This is the stuff that **helps you grow**. It shifts and widens that soul container we spoke about way back in the beginning.

But.. it's too late. I already feel like shit.

If present-moment awareness isn't enough to instigate a lightbulb moment of compassion or two, read on. In times of perceived failure, ask yourself:

1. Have my rituals been setting me up for success?

Hayley was in a space where so many of us have been countless times in our lives. One day, in a rush of frustration and anger, she shared this with our community:

"I am so pissed off with myself! I just know how much of a negative impact alcohol has on my life so how do I stop? I'm sporting a nice bruise as a consequence of drinking ridiculous amounts of alcohol. What more of a wake-up call do I need? Sorry ladies… I just needed to be able to vent my frustrations somewhere other than my head." Sound familiar?

Take a step back, zoom out, turn down the volume… and before we lose ourselves in self-attack and helplessness, let's look at this differently. So often, when in the grip of a perceived failure, it feels immensely, painstakingly personal. Kind of like we're perpetually flawed and forever destined to screw things up. But if we take the emotion out of it and glance back quickly at the events that preceded our disappointment, we can definitely connect more than a few dots.

I asked the Peace Girls if they noticed a correlation between their day-to-day rituals and their experience of 'success'. *If you're making wholesome food choices, moving your body regularly, sitting for meditation a few times a week and spending time in nature now and then, are you more likely to make conscious choices when it comes to The Party as well?* Like a chain reaction, their answers flooded in:

Belinda: "When I look back at some of my biggest slip-ups, it's been when I'd been slack with personal rituals, and bad habits snuck in again."

Cassandra: "Yep! I think the good practice makes it easier, as we are more aware of taking care of ourselves and treating our bodies well, so we don't cave in to more drinks. But I think it works in reverse too. When we have hangovers and work is overwhelming, it's such a societal and social thing to turn to more drink, food and late nights. And it really does snowball."

Sarah: "Hell yes!"

Claire: "Absolutely. Big ones for me are change in environment (travel), not exercising, and definitely if I haven't been managing my stress levels with meditation, relaxation or yoga."

Sam: "Yes! When the self-care is flowing, the rest of my world flows. If there's a lapse, then the chaos starts to creep in."

Jaime: "I never realised how strongly these 'failures' were tied to lack of routine. The *ah-stuff-it* attitude of *yeah, let's go have a drink and I'll worry about everything else later.* Sitting back and looking at it now, every time I opt for the lazy way, my successes in health, relationships, and work suffer markedly."

Jess: "Yes, I do believe that the snowball reaction occurs. I can say, if I am loving myself and attending to daily ritual, 'slip-ups' are less likely to occur..."

A resounding *affirmative!* wouldn't you say? The phrase 'get back on the horse' springs to mind here. Become present to the moment, return to softness, and then get back on the horse by navigating your way gently towards the practices and daily rituals that *you know* keep you grounded, devoted to your body and spiritual wealth, and anchored into your vision for your life. Neither 'success' nor 'failure' simply *happen.* They're both a result of the choices that we make and the actions that we take consistently. You know the answer. You know the medicine that you need to prescribe yourself. If you detour out of those practices, dust yourself off, and with a loving and kind heart, take a U-turn and come on back.

2. Have I been competing with anyone?

Is your head buried in your Instagram feed? Are you toggling Facebook like a madwoman? Are you bookmarking blogs left, right and centre? It might be time to gently close the laptop, unplug and find your centre again. These days, a parallel world is available at our fingertips, and because of that, we're all susceptible to feelings of intense comparison as we stack up our own lives against what's projected onto our smartphones by others. While this also offers us access to unlimited inspiration, social media is super-skilled at hacking away at our sense of real Self, if we're not switched on (in the head department!) when we access it. You could be giving your body and mind the wholesome upheaval it's been craving for an age. Yet, all it can take is one moment - spotting that babe's bodacious bod at the beach, for example – to flip you out into a state of the Not Good Enoughs. This isn't about them, remember. This is, finally, about you. Compete only with *yourself*. Attempt to only outdo *yourself*. And even then, only lovingly. Remain resolute on surpassing and delighting *yourself*.

3. Do I need to revisit my definition of sobriety?

It's been a fascinating dynamic watching some of my Peace Girls transition to a completely sober life. That the program helped guide them to do this, well, I'm grateful. And I'm just as proud of the girls who still enjoy their chosen drop, yet still live vibrantly on their Sundays, rather that hiding away from the sun.

For me, sobriety means:

:: *Abstaining from binge drinking. Period.*

:: *Abstaining from drugs.*

:: *Listening to my body, always. If my body says no to a drink and I go right ahead and take a sip anyway, before I know it I'm waving hello to a decent dose of self-betrayal. If my body gives me the green light, and I sip slowly on my drink of choice, it tastes so incredibly divine; like a real treat.*

For me, sobriety does not mean:

> :: *Never having another drink again. That actually feels totally constricting to my energy. (It took me quite some time to make peace with this.)*

> :: *Becoming a teetotaller.*

My relationship to The Party has changed, because I've come to understand that the 'Party' is subjective. The 'Party' is what you say it is, sister. 'Party' can mean earl grey tea and cucumber sandwiches. It can mean sober raves on the beach in your bikini, listening to a wireless radio. It can mean you and your honey curled up in the corner of a swanky jazz bar, letting those angelic sounds permeate you between sips of mineral water. *Or cognac.* No-one knows you like you.

Take Belinda for example:

"A few months back on one of our calls, we were talking about what sobriety means to us. I said that I was being more mindful when I drink, being more conscious of what my body tells me and when I've had enough. However, I've come to realise that my style of drinking doesn't like that. It's all or nothing. Now, to me, sobriety means complete abstinence. Not saying that being mindful and aware is not a good thing, it's just not enough for me. Trying to control my drinking is harder than trying to stop! So I've chosen to stop, quit, cease all together. And so far so good! I can see relationships shifting, my mind un-fogging and doors opening. It's fucking terrifying and exciting at the same time!"

While Amber had the complete opposite experience:

"To stop drinking seemed to be the only option for me, so I went from one extreme to the other. Now, after two years of no alcohol, I can finally make the conscious choice to drink alcohol when it feels right. And I know I've done it with full awareness. I never thought I'd want to drink again but, to me, right now, it means freedom and having a more relaxed approach to life. I couldn't have figured this out when I first made the decision to stop binge drinking, but abstinence seemed to clarify things and calm everything down in my mind."

Remember this isn't about fitting a mould, it's about crafting your own. I didn't reach this point of contentedness by projecting beefy sobriety goals. I did it by making in-the-moment decisions, each one dictating the type of person I want to be; the type of person I know I am underneath all the distractions. I 'failed' along the way. And who knows? I may very well 'fail' again. Maybe one day, I'll attend a friend's wedding and wipe myself out on free sparkling wine and shots of tequila. **It's possible that I might!** I certainly hope I don't, but if I do, I'll be present with my hangover, dust myself off, and get on with it. No self-hatred. No coulda-woulda-shouldas. Like Dory from *Finding Nemo*, I'll just keep swimming. **And so will you.**

If these probing questions aren't enough to evoke empowering answers, then **try Emotional Freedom Technique** or 'tapping'. Tapping has become a fixture in my practice because, along with yoga, few things shift stagnant, limiting energy as effectively! It's also making a huge difference in my clients' lives. A convenient, easy, do-it-yourself spin-off from acupressure, tapping can trim the fat of limiting beliefs and stucknesses in a matter of moments. I tap on anything. I tap on *everything*.

:: *If I wake up achy and sore, I tap on the tension in my body.*

:: *If I wake up feeling an immediate sense of stress, I tap on the sensations of overwhelm.*

:: *If there's a relationship in my life that's bothering me, I tap on it.*

:: *If I feel sluggish, I tap on laziness.*

:: *If I'm busting through some huge limiting beliefs (fears of success, of tuning into abundance, of expanding my business), I tap on the discomfort of it all.*

:: *If I'm resisting any of my projects, I tap on procrastination.*

You get the idea. 'Better out than in' is a mantra of mine. Consciously vocalising what feels truthful to me in the moment, while tapping on specific acupressure points, not only tells my fight-or-flighty amygdala to calm the hell down, but it unlocks emotional and energetic patterns that hold me back. And as a bonus (I've seen this happen in the moment with both myself and my clients), eventually, a more empowering truth starts to surface.

'This neck pain is driving me crazy' becomes *'I can feel the tension easing'*. *'I'm overwhelmed at everything I have to do today'* becomes *'My To-Do List serves me, not the other way around. I'll take it one item at a time'*. And *'I'm not good enough to follow my dreams'* becomes *'I can do anything I set my mind to'*.

For more on this transformational practice, log onto *tarabliss.com/tapping*: There's a range of videos I've created for you to heal – in the moment – blockages that are holding you back.

Going head-to-head with resistance

There I was, sitting rather un-pretty, in Bitchville. I was acting irrationally and picking fights with Glen. When I looked in mirror, I thought I looked angular and ugly. I was hormonal, moody; utterly pissed, actually. Not even the blue skies and crystal clear ocean could cheer me up. I honest-to-goodness wanted to scream obscenities to the world, break things, crawl under a rock, and sob. And *then...* I read this incredible passage in *The War of Art* from Steven Pressfield:

"What does Resistance feel like?

First, unhappiness. We feel like hell. A low-grade misery pervades everything. We're bored. We're restless. We can't get no satisfaction. There's guilt but we can't put our finger on the source. We want to go back to bed; we want to get up and party. We feel unloved and unlovable. We're disgusted. We hate our lives. We hate ourselves.

Unalleviated, Resistance mounts to a pith that becomes unendurable.
At this point vices kick in. Dope, adultery, web surfing.

Beyond that, Resistance becomes clinical. Depression, aggression, dysfunction.
Then actual crime and physical self-destruction. Sounds like life, I know.
It isn't. It's Resistance."

Clarity hit me like a tidal wave. The reason for my *prickliness*. I was resisting writing the outline for this book like a motherfucker. Rather than tend to it lovingly, with curiosity and an open heart and a Let's Just See What Happens mindset, I had been distracting myself relentlessly. With emails, dish-washing, updating my vision board, unnecessary re-organising of nothings. Anything to avoid that *thing* that was so important to me.

So after reading Steve's passage, I took a deep, emotional, fed-up breath. I knew that starting that outline meant that I had to finish it. And that finishing the outline meant that I had to start the book. And finishing the book meant that I'd have to have... well... written a book. It all felt so risky and uncertain and scary and *big!* But I stood back, zoomed out, and saw what a disastrous effect my negligence of this project was having on me. It was getting under my skin, making me itchy and unsettled and scattered. I thought that writing the book would be difficult, but as it turns out, *not* writing it was unquestionably Hell On Earth. And so that day, I *started*.

Each chapter was contained on one A4 sheet, which was carefully BluTac-ed to my full-length mirror, in between the chapters that surrounded it. Ideas that were sitting in my head, tearing at me with threats to seek out another writer, were finally freed onto Sticky Notes and placed together in groups, in themes, in chapters. The process had begun. I had moved through the frustrating goop of Resistance.

Did I write this book because I love to write? Can I be honest? No, I didn't. I adore writing. I believe I was sent here to do it. But I sincerely feel as though I didn't have a choice with this project. I *had* to write this book; not for the purpose of being an author, but because the book, the idea, the message, the project *chose me*. Until I set aside the time, energy and resources to answer its call, it would continue to rattle around inside my head and haunt me. I didn't want to feel haunted by that which I'm most passionate about. I wanted to feel liberated by it!

The same can absolutely be said about you and your journey, now. You don't want to be enslaved to those thoughts that tease you with scares of how much you might fail. You want to stand victorious in and amongst the process of change, right?

Most days, I simply *must* write. Most days, I simply must make it to my yoga mat. I must sit in stillness. And not because I'm a sucker for punishment and I insist on boxing myself in with rigid guidelines and must-dos. I must do these things *most* days for the simple reason that they're the very things that I resist the most, and yet ironically, they bring me the most freedom. They're a form of spiritual, creative breakfast. They sustain me.

You'll remember in Chapter Two we learnt that understanding our fears is crucial to living brilliant lives. It's the *lean into them* that enriches our experiences and results in courageous evolution. It's why I moved out of home when I was 16. Why I journeyed to Japan with a man I'd spent only a few months getting to know. It's why I launched myself into the online entrepreneurial planet as a coach, on zero experience. It's why you picked up this book. **Fears point to where we're supposed to go next**. The same's true for Resistance. We resist what matters most; what pays out the biggest lump sums of joy. Resistance is self-protection at its finest and most stealthy. It's *fear*, disguised as laziness, procrastination and excuse-making.

There's no better time than right now to take an inventory on what it is that you're resisting in your life. What are your Resistance triggers? Pressing publish on a post or video blog? A mind-blowing exercise regime? A morning meditation practice? Intimacy with your partner? Quitting sugar? Good! **I'm glad you're resisting!** Sometimes, it's that raging burn of unbearable Resistance that gets us to that moment of emotional threshold where we realise we simply cannot go on like this any longer! *This is good.* When Resistance becomes furious fuel. *This is very, very good.*

When you're in the grip of Resistance, you are being gripped by something that is so profoundly important to you on a soul level that it's dizzying you. It's time to take a little of that power back, Party Girl. It's time you went head-to-head with that inner conflict, and walked towards it. It's *yours* for the gripping; not the other way around.

"When you're ready to manifest change in the world, just know this: it's the human condition to resist change. No matter what you want to transform, from the smallest improvement to the greatest evolution, there will be opposition."
Joseph Pierce Farrell

So, to drink or not to drink?

How does it feel when you repeat the words 'I'm never gonna have another drink ever again' out loud? Does it feel restrictive? Suffocating? Like total hell? Or does it sing a chorus of glowing freedom? How about if you ditched the pledge, and instead took a moment-to-moment approach? It's easy for us to rebel against our own limitations, so if you're accustomed to breaking your own promises, you've got to ask: *why set them in the first place?* I'm not saying don't go out on a limb and make a few bold declarations. After all, The Universe moves when you go out on a limb, and addiction recovery will demand you to, so if you feel compelled to, go ahead. I myself have made pledges in the name of change.

I've declared my body an energy-drink-free zone. No minuscule amount even of liquid sugar and caffeine in a can is welcome in my sphere of influence. *Bon voyage.* I've given recreational drugs the permanent flick. I can't unlearn what I know now. I simply *can't* go back. Walking past a night club in the middle of the day is enough to make my heart beat anxiously as if it's the first 10 minutes of a pill. That's not a feeling I enjoy anymore. You'll also never see me suck on a cigarette. If we bumped into each other at a Party - and you can hold me to this - I would not be drunk. I'd give you a big cuddle. We'd share a little about ourselves, have a great time together. And when I go to text you sometime the next day to say 'It was fan-freaking-tastic to meet you, let's catch up soon!' I'd do so remembering your face, your name, our conversation.

Before launching the online program, I knew, without a shadow of a doubt, that I was through with the feeling of being of being drunk and the consequences that came with it. The vision of a life of infinite clear-headedness filled my chest with hope and felt plain lovely. What a relief. But committing to never having a drink again? It just doesn't feel right, or even – to be honest – necessary. So I've decided not to make that promise.

For the most part, I believe in taking life one experience at a time, rather than making big, rash projections that set up a platform of likely failure. Swearing off cigarettes, drugs and drunkenness was a no-brainer for me; something that felt like an unspoken done-deal already. I chose to speak up and share it with my online community so I could create a space where I could bring anyone with similar aspirations along with me. So we could stand shoulder to shoulder; solidifying our collective intention to get high on life; to get drunk on love.

As I mentioned, society's definition of *sobriety* is not my priority here. It's not a word that takes centre stage on my vision board. It's not a state of being that owns my heart, but I do respect it for everything it's taught me, even in the short-lived pockets of it. And I respect it for its power to heal and transform the addicted. Let it be known: I salute the sober. But just as I've worked at dissolving identities, I've been conscious not to latch my once label-loving personality onto yet another one: The Sober Girl.

Are you suppressing your desires or just plain devoted?

Words have a huge impact on my life. One word could make or break the way I filter in any moment in space and time. As an illustration of this, to me, the word 'devotion' outplays words like 'discipline' and 'determination' any day of the week. *Devotion* dissolves the rigidity and rules and toughness of those other words, replacing them with softness, fluidity and femininity instead. So when women come to me, asking, "How do you stay motivated?" I'm always a little taken aback. I don't see this journey as an inquest into motivation. It's not about willpower. It's not about slaying your beasts and reigning supreme. It's about asking yourself, "Am I devoted to myself?"

Another question you can ask yourself is, "Am I suppressing my desires right now?" We want to give this journey buoyancy - we want it to feel exploratory and fascinating, not as though we're locking away all the *fun* and throwing away the key.

There are many, many paths up the same mountain. What this book strives to do is ignite the light in you. I'm not here to nullify your desires; to dim down your fun, to make life feel muddy and beige and bland. I'm here to inspire devotion into your days, and a new way of being, where your body is your church, meditation is your prayer and joy is your living song. Know that willpower is *irrelevant*, and the only thing that truly matters is whether you can draw on the wisdom that reminds you that, with each fresh morning comes a chance to celebrate, rather than spectate. A chance to rise. To try again. No matter how deep the depths, no matter how grubby your knees, or how marred your face, your willingness to return to softness is what will weave the tapestry of your wonderful life.

Stephanie Dowrick can put it like no other: "Spiritual practice is returning again and again, to softness." We recover from hangovers by remembering that, actually, we're devoted to vitality. So, we refocus. We sideline comparison by remembering that, actually, we're devoted to recognising our light in others. So, we perceive radiance. We forgive ourselves and others by remembering that, actually, we're devoted to being beacons of compassion and understanding. So, we come home, to the truth, always. Again, and again, and again. Maybe it's time you traded the word 'discipline' for 'devotion' too? Maybe it's time to make presence your preference, rather than future-tripping? To swap out 'failure', and instead perceive those experiences as divine teachings of the most intimate nature?

Rock Bottom is somewhat optional

It's just before 7am when I open the door to my apartment. My housemate is getting ready for work and *that* visual – that it's that time of day where people are *getting ready for work* – is making me feel nauseated beyond ripping out my eyeballs. "Hey", I mumble, avoiding eye contact. She says nothing. I flop onto the bed, my heart thumping, my head buzzing. Ashleigh must have needed a few moments to collect her strength because, just as I'm about to doze off, she appears in my room and says, "You have to go". "Hmpf?" I groan into my pillow, raising an ear to her. "You've got to pack your things and leave", she says, deadpan.

Oh right, it's moving day. And seeing as I've burnt my bridges with everyone else in this city a few days before I make my great escape to the snow, it appears as though I'm suddenly homeless. "Just a little sleep..." "No. Now.

Before I leave for work."

The poor girl. This isn't the first time my behaviour has made her feel so uncomfortable. After what feels like a lifetime of effort, my car sits loaded, containing the contents of my life. My forearms are resting on my steering wheel and my head weighs a tonne. I've got nowhere to go and there's no way in hell I should be turning on the ignition, but I do, and I drive. I've got $70 to my name so I sleep in my car on a side street in Bondi.

Each of us can probably recall a moment or many where we felt at our lowest. That short story is one of mine. The story that opened this book is another. And the time I found myself in a high-speed car crash on the highway thanks to too many drugs and too little sleep is yet another. The way we each remember and store these experiences in us will be different. Some of us believe that we 'deserve' to get what we're given; others of us wake up and finally realise *fuck this, I deserve better, and no-one's going to make my life happen but me*. You don't need to have hit Rock Bottom to invite change into your life. What's more, I don't believe that hitting bottom is the only rite of passage that acts as the portal to peace. You don't need to be in the depths, you gorgeous creature. You don't need to wish an addiction upon yourself in order to tell a better story. You don't need to have lost everything and everyone prior to pivoting into a more fulfilling life. If the catalyst to inspire change within you was simply waking up on New Year's Day with the worst hangover of your life, then great, that's your story. If it's been witnessing a member of your family lose themselves forever to the drink, then that's the exact messenger you needed. What matters is that you're here now, blazing a trail of sovereignty and choice.

And for that – for you – I am grateful. One more time - just to seal the deal here – just to really punctuate the point I'm trying to make...

You cannot (cannot, cannot, cannot) fail.

Peace Practice

An (ex-)Party Girl Pledge

I, _____, promise I will be gentle with myself through this process. If I 'fail' (which is 100% okay), I will return to self-care by _____, _____, and _____.

The person I will take consolation in is _____.

I hereby commit to simultaneously apologising to my body and forgiving my choices whenever I feel blanketed by regret.

In times of doubt, I will remind myself why I'm on this journey by _____.

I can find solace in books such as _____ and listen to music like _____.

I feel most alive when I eat foods such as _____, _____ and drink _____, _____.

I promise my body herbal tea, a warm shower, and a few extra hours' sleep if I need it.

Compassion is my religion. Love is my prayer.

I promise, that when Life gets crazy, I'll breathe. I'll return to presence. I'll come back home to my heart.

Signed,

_____

Just for today, devote to remaining as present as possible, particularly in relation to your interactions. Open your heart to the people that cross your path today - lovers, acquaintances, strangers. **Listen with your whole body. Look into the depths of their eyes. Be there, where you are, 100%.**

Consider spending some time in nature and take it all in with each of your senses. Study a tree with your gaze. Try to feel each blade of grass, or each grain of sand, under your feet.

When I was in the mountains, I used to consciously *feel* the chilly air brush my face when I was on my snowboard. It's as though Mama Nature is always communicating with us, always reminding us that miracles are everywhere. Your Peace Practice for this chapter is to start noticing them. **Start now.**

How does it feel when your fingertips reach for this page (or this screen) to turn it?

That
is
presence.

This
is
where
you
belong.

10.

Sober Stories To Ignite
A Revolution

"Peace comes from within. Do not seek it without."
Buddha

I'm standing at the bar having spent all day watching presentations at the ProBlogger event, which is being held on the Gold Coast, where I live. I'm a little sleepy from a day of taking in tricks of the trade and sponging up information. Before my friends and I take off to the after-party, we head to the gorgeous bar in the hotel lobby for a drink. As I wait for the barkeep to mix my cocktail, I'm flooded with a feeling of nostalgia for the world from which I came. Handsome men dance around beautiful women as they poetically fling ice into Boston glasses, flick lime muddlers over their knuckles with theatre; tasting a pinch of their finished product from a straw before serving. I remember what that feels like; to bring a sense of passion and art to something so simple as mixing drinks. He presents me my margarita with a smile on his face. I thank him profusely, truly appreciating his effort, and noticing for the first time how thirsty I am for this holy combination of tequila, Cointreau, lemon juice and salt.

There's almost a pang of guilt as I pick up my glass. After all, I'm the creator of *The Party Girl's Guide to Peace*, and this is a *blogging* conference. Beating the ex-Party drum has become part of my online presence, and here I am salivating over alcohol. But as I take my first sip, I remind myself that *this* is what my project is all about. It's not about deprivation and limitations; it's about making choices, without the acidity of regret. It's about enjoying the taste and experience of a drink, without having to need or depend upon it anymore.

It's a bloody good margarita; sour and strong, just the way I like them. Every sip is heavenly and appreciated. I feel a sense of quality as I nurse it in my hands. Who'd have thought that anchoring into the moment instead of careering into escapism could feel so good?

Every now and then when I enjoy a glass of wine or a cocktail, my inner Party Girl archetype finds a few vulnerable moments where she tries to convince me that staying out - having a few more, *indulging* - is a good idea. She's insidious and so-very-close-to-convincing. Memories flood back to me of sharing deep and meaningful conversations with dear friends, a mountain of empty glasses between us as we continually circled back to conversations of how much we loved and adored each other. Memories of heart confessions, made possible by beverage bravery. Memories of that moment when the final grain of inhibition dissolved, permitting me to move onto the dance floor. They're all memories that bring a smile to my face.

But even in that momentary seduction – beyond that whisper to stay out – *I know better now*. What first arrives as enthusiasm to keep the night alive quickly lessens to a sudden sleepiness; something I would have remedied with a Jagerbomb in the past. Today, instead of uppers, *sleep* is my cure to mid-cocktail yawns. After driving home, turning my key in the door, washing off my makeup, brushing my teeth and letting my head hit the pillow, I feel grateful, relieved, excited to wake up fresh. And when I rise naturally before the sun does, I do so with a silent thank you and a happy yawn that tells me that *I didn't miss out on anything.*

Throughout this book, I've used my stories as a way to create an honest relationship between you and me. To earn your trust, to give you faith and understanding and empathy, before you could decide whether I was worth taking advice from. I hope what I've shared with you so far has acted as a mirror to your own experiences, and that you can now see a legitimate alternative path thanks to what you've read in these pages, living vicariously through me for a short while. This is the final chapter, and though we're coming close to the end of our time together (at least for now), the stories aren't ceasing just yet. But they are about to change direction, drastically.

So far, you've learnt how crucial is it to reactivate and totally engage in your curious nature. You've looked your fears in the eye and watched them dissolve into dust. You've acknowledged the madness of your current reward system and shaken it upside-down so it serves *you*, not the other way around! You've seen – perhaps for the very first time – the impact that self-love has on *everything*; from your relationships, to your daily routines, and into your creativity. You've glimpsed a life that's possible for you if you take the journey from a ballistic life, to a holistic one; the health, happiness and sheer energy that can rise out of you when you eat wholesome foods, move your muscles and bones in an inspiring way, and cultivate a more intimate connection with the whole of your body. You've promised yourself a clean slate, so that you can live from a fresh state. You're bidding so long to *stuff* that's cramming your space, people who are unkind to you, and you're ready to transform your FOMO into JOMO (Joy Of Missing Out). You've cultivated compassion and oneness by courageously stepping *towards* your shadow, rather than away from it. You've marvelled at the identities that have had you chasing your tail for a decade or more. You're re-membering who you *really* are through meditation practices. And you've made peace with the fact that this journey is not a one-trick pony; it's a never-ending mindfulness experiment taking place in the greatest amusement park there is: your Life.

So now, as we look to tie a bow around this adventure, I want to share a couple more stories with you. The theory's over. There's no more philosophis-ing. Just a few recounts of golden, heart-expanding moments of mine that you can return to when you feel the unwelcome pinch of *so how the hell do I have fun with drugs and alcohol, again?* After reading these stories, you'll know why I always raise an eyebrow when I get asked that question. The fun I've had over the last couple of years has outshone any chemical high I've ever induced in myself. The conversations I've had have lodged themselves in my being more than any drunken deep and meaningful. The love I've given and received? It's been unencumbered and completely unmatched.

But the fun. This last piece is all about The Fun. It's about giving you the confidence in knowing that joy beyond your wildest dreams is waiting for you right behind *that* door. All that's left for you to do now is gently walk out of the room you're in, and close that door behind you.

Sweat, Scar Tissue and Sobriety

Keen to hear how it all went down at the Big Day Out? In short, I had the time of my life. Obviously, there's a whole different vibe to it when you're doing a festival sober. Hours that are normally spent in high-as-a-kite conversation, instead can feel a little naked, particularly when most of those around you are drunk or high. For my friend Ally and I, debaucherous trips to the portaloos were replaced with plenty of people-watching - a fascinating time-filler between gigs.

I found myself smiling at folks throughout the day. I could see the old me in them; in the girl that was spread out on the ground with her eyes closed, tripping, and clearly having a very, very good time, not at all aware of the world of pain she'd be in tomorrow, and the day after that, and most likely the day after that too. I could see me in the girls who were dancing around like crazy banshees with their friends. That was me a few short years ago, and watching them was like looking in a nostalgic mirror that reflected back non-judgment and contentment, rather than a pinch of FOMO.

Dancing at the back of the Boiler Room, listening to Nicky Romano drop ridiculous beats, I turned to Ally and yelled, "Everyone who's fucked up will be having a *really* good time right now!" She just laughed, nodded and continued stomping into her dance moves, as if to say, "Hello!? So are we!"

One of my greatest fears in peeling away from The Party has been that my connection to music and movement might become altered forever. After all, it's what happens to our bodies when we combine drinks or drugs with music that's the major catalyst for what keeps us going back for more, isn't it? The godliness that enters our blood, the possessed-by-light feelings that swoop over us and make us move with inspiration. I was scared to lose that. But at Big Day Out, the epiphany hit me: I **can** still dance. I **can** still feel the music in my body. I **can** still predict when the beat's going to bounce and when the crowd's going to go insane. (Always an amazing moment!) And I can do all of this with nothing in my system but water and delicious, deep-fried garlic Hungarian bread. (One day they'll start selling healthy food at these types of gigs, I hope.) And you know what? Let's not beat around the bush here - I can dance *better,* without thinking that I'm, like, so amazing. *Good riddance to that.* Give Ally and me a 2×1 metre space, and we'll be rocking it, owning it, going hard as we ever have, without trying to tell the whole world about it.

The next morning, as I woke up, I half expected to feel rotten. (I'm going to put that down to habit). When I realised that, actually, I didn't, holy smokes Batman, it was a realisation worth an *hallelujah!* For breakfast, Ally and I tucked into leftover kale quinoa and ginger kombucha. Limiting beliefs - quashed. Standards - raised. Liver - humming along quite nicely, thank you very much.

Gather 'round the fire

After weaving our way through the lush Byron Bay hinterland, our car load of four arrives at The Burrow, the nickname our friend has affectionately tagged her property with. Two beautiful timber houses sit perched on what we all sense is sacred land. Immediately, our shoes come off and we enjoy the feel of the earth beneath us as we walk towards the back yard, where we find a number of 20-something and 30-something women sprawled out on picnic blankets snacking on hummus and halloumi and throw-it-all-in salads. Some of the girls we know. Some we recognise. But most we don't. It's always environments like this one, ones where Mother Nature is the icebreaker, that it doesn't even matter. Consciously or not, we're all here to connect to one another, and most likely ourselves a little deeper too. So we marvel at the property, and sip in the country air, and then adventure around the nooks and crannies of the land, together, gathering flowers and pinecones and pretty little somethings in preparation for tonight. These little treasures filling our foraging basket will soon form an altar for - wait for it - a cacao ceremony.

With full bellies and souls that are high on the aliveness of the hinterland, we move inside, pair up, and proceed to give each other oracle card readings. There's laughter, there's whispering, there's hugs. There's 'I just know you're going to pull through this' prophecies and 'that was exactly what I needed to hear' resonating.

What is it about this sense of mystery and femininity and intuition that brings women together like this? That animates us to the frequency of children? We may not be playing *Light As A Feather, Stiff As A Board* now, but we're pretty bloody close to it.

As the sun starts to set, we snack on leftovers, and there's an unmistakable chill of anticipation in the air, particularly from us cacao ceremony virgins. My friends and I have been craving this: communion and collective ritual, and an excuse to leave the house. It's Friday night after all, and just a few years ago I'd be cracking open a third or fourth bottle of wine by this time in the evening. But here we are, champing at the bit to experience sacred hot chocolate! It feels perfect and ridiculous and enlivening and humbling all in one, and I'm not quite sure whether I should assume the position of reverence, or piss myself laughing.

We watch the fire burn brighter and the altar breathe a little more beauty into the backyard with each moment as it sits in front of the flames. People by the dozens are arriving to share in the experience. I look up and see the stars twinkle above us. Why does that feel so good - to look up at the stars in the night sky? Maybe it's because we remember the vastness of The Universe, or because there's a covert comfort that comes with knowing that we'll never truly figure everything out. It doesn't even matter. It just feels good.

Our guides for the night are Jemma and Chris, a couple who look as though they've just stepped out of a shamanic version of *Vogue*. Jemma, draped in white, with tumbling blonde curls and a face that exudes love of the unconditional kind. Chris, rugged and muscular, with a delicious hybrid accent, adorned in musical instruments. Together, they're the perfect team, set to give us a night to remember.

Jem's standing by the fire, looking like an angel. (I'm convinced she is, by the way.) She explains that the dance the planets have been doing lately is why life for many of us has a real *intensity* to it. And all it takes is a moment - just a brief moment in time - for her to take in a breath and the heavens open. Actually, the heavens *heave* open. Rain slams down on our circle with such force that, for a moment, we all freeze in shock. And then, as though we all get jolted back to life with the same on switch, we jump to our feet, grabbing blankets and yoga mats and altar pieces and whatever else we can manage, before finally gathering around the house, some of us, damp, some of us, drenched.

No-one seems surprised at the rain that fell from the clear, starlit sky. What, for a few moments, felt like chaos has now begun being a cosy blessing as the rain has crammed us all into the living room; the fire crackling, extra candles being lit, sage being smudged. We huddle together, and start again. Back to the chat about the planets. Back to the story of the sacred cacao. (It's intuitively gathered from shamans in South America.) Back to the importance of being a lightworker in this world; of using the *good* in us to manifest wonder.

And then the ceremony begins. Jemma strikes her drum as we all face to the east. There's such power and strength in her voice as she calls on the spirits, the animals, and the wisdom in each direction. Our eyes are closed, one palm is facing out, the other is holding a bio-degradable cup of hot cacao to our hearts. At each point of our human compass, we let go of a little more bullshit that we've been carrying. We honour those we have lost and we summon in what's rightfully ours, before bringing our hands to our mouths, and taking a sip from our decadently rich and bitter cups. We turn to the north, and do the same. And then to the west. Then the south. Once our circle is closed and our cups are empty, there's a few fragments of silence that hovers in the space.

"Just allow yourself to feel the spirit of the cacao", Chris says. "You may feel like dancing. You may just simply sit with your eyes closed and feel into it. Just surrender to it". My friends and I remain sitting, taking in the sound from the guitars, the rattles, the drums. Drinking in the laughter and the smiles of the people around us, whose names we don't know, and yet they're anything but strangers. We take our empty cups - lined with remnants of cacao - and Jemma fills them with freshly brewed chai. It's the sweetest, most divine elixir I've ever tasted, so I go back for seconds. And so here we are: amidst a *new* type of inebriation, a clean pulse of energy pumping through our veins; drunk on mindfulness and presence and clear-headedness. Peaking on real laughter, real conversations, real heart-opening, soul-bearing, perception-widening *fun*.

The stuff we were *made* to experience.

Are you here to experience love, sex or desire?

I have an amazing friend named Susana Frioni. She's a deep living coach, an embodiment teacher, and she has *actual* magical powers. Whenever you're in the presence of this dynamite, you feel compelled to bring forth more of the *woman* that you are. I've never met anyone so grounded in their body, so keenly aware of themselves, than Susana. And we're all here tonight – all sixty of us or so - gathered in this yoga studio, after hours, in central Brisbane both to bear witness to and take active part in her latest project: the first ever Love Sex Desire EMBODIED Sacred Dance Party.

She's electric and spicy and sensual – the way she talks, carries herself, dances. She speaks with her *shoulders,* with her wrists. She *wriggles* words out of her with her body. She's fiercely feminine and has a very, very special inner power that can easily tip between inspiring as all hell, and a little intimidating. We're all about to give these bodies of ours over to her for the next three hours, and I think I can speak for everyone in the room when I say – just quietly – that we're all trembling in our boots just a little. There's nothing like being in the presence of a woman who shamelessly owns and projects her power to trigger your insecurities. And this woman - this dazzling creature that I get the privilege to call my friend – she means business. In a long, revealing red dress, her divinity demands attention from us - her students for the next short while. *She gets it from us.* She gets every last drop of it. We all gaze at her for direction and guidance, possibly because we're like scared little sheep that need herding, but mostly, I think, we're all just so entranced when she speaks. *The woman knows how to hold a space!* At first, we take our seat. Dozens of women sit perched on their yoga mats, eyes fixated on our very own red lady. We open our journals. There's always deep, introspective work when Susana's involved. She asks us: *What do you want to experience in your body tonight? Love, Sex or Desire.* I write: *Desire.* She asks us: *What could prevent you from feeling it?* I write: *The stories in my mind of who I think I am. Beliefs that I cannot do this. Self-criticism and comparing myself to others in the room. Judging myself for the way I'm moving.* She asks us: *What is your intention for tonight? Why are you here?* I write: *To beam joy out from within me. To trust my body and LET IT ALL OUT. Freedom.* Finally, she asks us: *What do you give yourself permission to do tonight?* I write: *To completely let go of my inhibitions and be ecstatic!*

And with that, I'm ready. We all are. The journaling has created space between our nerves and insecurities. Now we're ready to shake ourselves free of it all completely. But not before a little more foreplay from Susana.

She asks us to stand, to ground ourselves, to connect to our inner energy field; to feel the height and width and depth of our bodies, all with closed eyes, all with open awareness. Suddenly, she presses Play on a track, and the beat is met with hoots and hollers from a few in the crowd, including me. "Don't move", Susana says sternly, into her microphone. "Just feel. Don't move a muscle. *Receive* the music. Is it coming up through your feet? Is it in your hands, your heart, your head? Where are you feeling it?" She stops the song after a minute or so, and changes the track, and asks us again. Our bodies fight the urge to release the floodgates of movement for another half a dozen sound bites of electro, hip hop, rock, indie; each genre being felt in a different part of my body, with differing intensity, bringing me alive in a completely unique way. Never mind Sunday church, this *thing* going on right now, in this room, in our bodies, is all kinds of holy. Awareness - laser sharp. Presence - *here and now*. Curiosity - *check!* Intense waves of self-love and acceptance? Oh God, yes!

After what feels like forever, Susana finally relinquishes the Pause button and sets her Sacred Dance Party Playlist free. She cranks the volume, dims the lights, and away we go. Each song offers us an opportunity to explore every corner of our being with freshness and such irrational femininity that it becomes an experience to which these words could never do justice. We sway, uninhibited, to the beat of our own drum. We bounce around like Energiser bunnies. We fiercely connect to each and every accent in the music as though it comes from us, out of us. The sweat pours, and like wild lost little things, we dance on. Following occasional prompts from Susana, we close our eyes and move intuitively around the room dancing with whatever body we bumped up against in the blindness. At one stage, when she drops a gnarly remix of Icona Pop, we engulf her in a circle of bouncing, sweaty bodies, screaming the lyrics at the top of our lungs, to her, smothering her in our passion, in our earth-shaking gratitude, barely able to contain ourselves from leaping out of our own skins. She's a sight to behold - a goddess laced in red, laughing, fist-pumping, moving her body in every which way. I don't know whether to let out little yelps of joy, or to cry with joy. Look - just look - what she has done to us. She has evoked the spirits of women who, just moments earlier, felt shackled by their own expectations. Now, we are wild animals, and as we engulf her in our circle, as if we are an ancient tribe worshipping a sacred deity, she looks **glorious**.

Eventually, after more than two hours, the music slows, as do our heartbeats. We find the stillness, the volume lowers, the lights begin to glow a little brighter, and instead of wine, or vodka, or cocktails, we fill up our tanks with raspberries (Susana's favourite!) and raw chocolate and green tea. As we all unite for chats and cuddles, we attempt to explain our experience in words to each other, but we fall short. Words fail, but we are forever changed.

I should take a pause here to remind you that this isn't The Party Girl's Guide to Perfection, or Sobriety, or Teetotalling. It's a Guide to Whatever The Hell You Need It To Be, a guide that helps short-circuit the synapses that leave you hungover and riddled with guilt before you've even had a chance to say 'my shout'. This is a transformational journey that puts you and your very essence back in the driver's seat. When you're steering the wheel, you naturally get the privilege of making clarified decisions that stem from the wisdom of your truth-speaking body. And after all is said and done, one of those decisions may in fact be, "You know what? I really, really feel like a drink tonight". Who can condemn you for that? Not a single soul. It's your right as a human being to make such a choice. Harness your power of will and make that choice. With awareness.

Maybe you need the pulse of a loud, dirty beat reverberating through your bones? Maybe you feel cultured and connected in a dark corner of a jazz bar, sitting alongside beautiful company? Maybe wineries feel like the true home of your soul? Again, this is your right as a human being on this planet. To decide who you want to be, how you want to live your life, and in what way you long to express yourself.

So now, it's time. It's time for you to **head back out into the world again**. It's time for you to instigate communion. To keep your values close to your heart and choose quality. Instead of the usual 10 vodka and sodas that you may have downed without a thought in the past, why don't you order the most expensive, most fabulous glass of pinot noir on the menu, and sip it very, very slowly? Instead of ordering a laden-with-fruit-juice-and-sugar cocktail, be brave: try a top-shelf gin martini. With olives. Make it dirty if you feel like living on the edge. Expanding your consciousness doesn't just happen on your meditation cushion, it happens any time you stretch yourself. Stop at one if you feel inclined. Or two. **The choice is yours.** You don't have to be a hermit and hide away (unless of course you want to - I certainly embrace hermitage regularly!). I only want you to be able to stand by your choices. *Decide* to have a drink at the best lounge in town. *Decide* to head to the winery on a girls trip. *Decide* to sip slowly on a digestif after a beautiful meal. And decide wholly that, in those experiences, you are going to remain the leader. In those decisions - the ones where you savour the art of a fine cocktail or wine - you are showcasing what being *High* is all about:

Quitting it with the excuses, putting an end to self-loathing and destructive behaviour, releasing the identities you've spent years crafting, and polishing up your levels of awareness.

Can an ex-Party Girl have her cake and eat it too? Yeah, I really think she can. So get back out there, be yourself and, for the love of God, *enjoy* yourself! Your body knows when to stop; you know now how to tune into your body, when to puff your chest out and say 'No, thanks'. This is a gift; one you've worked hard for; one you deserve to hold onto for life. Keep it in your back pocket.

Tips for Stepping Back Out into the World Again

1. All Hail Mineral Water

When you're seated at the table and the server takes your order - *boom!* - 'mineral water please'. You'll be chipping away at the autopilot craving that's whispering to you *Oh thank Christ we're here, get me a friggin' drink!* The world isn't going to end if you get comfortable before downing a Corona, so order a mineral water - or a tea, or whatever non-alcoholic jive they've got going on - and chill.

2. Explore the Menu

Sushi and red wine? Ah, no. Pizza with an espresso martini? Bleurgh. Traipse the food menu with detail. Like, *really* dive into it. Then once you've decided what meal has your name on it, peruse the drinks list and consciously match the two. Again, it's about stepping away from the habitual longing to drink Anything On Offer, and instead, creating a real event out of your experience.

3. Explore the Conversation

What type of night are you having, conversationally? Are the chats flowing like fine wine itself, or is one of those nurse-your-balloon-of-top-shelf-liqueur-for-hours type of nights? Is the conversation light, and hilarious, and sauvignon blanc-y, or is it contemplative, and full of depth, like a shiraz? Be patient. Feel out your night. Sense it and taste it, and only then allow the drink to step in, as if it's one of those friends who always arrives fashionably late.

4. Permission to be Awkward

I really want to have a quick chat about your wonderful weirdness. Remember, for so very long, you've turned to the drink as a means of getting closer to what you perceived to be your ideal self. Only catch is: that whole perception was a load of bull. So naturally, there may be a few fleeting moments of anxiety, tension, and discomfort, when you're flirting with this new way of being. Particularly in social situations.

Something I like to remind myself of often is that my one true role in this life, each and every moment, is to **get to know myself.** *Oh hey, I'm feeling pretty awkward right now.* An inner statement like that allows me to own the moment for what it is, not how I wish it were. No sugar-coating, no beating around the bush. Just a truthful statement, lessened by my very labelling it. Rather than trying to suppress that, or trying to grapple for something to ease it, or leaving the situation entirely because awkward 'isn't a 'good feeling', instead just try to remain centred in that awkwardness for a smidge. Can you find the humour in it? Can you just notice yourself as you allow the sensation of an awkward moment to pass through you? You don't have to change. You don't have to strive to become more confident. You don't have to beg to be different to what you are.

This is awkward.
I'm feeling a bit weird.
I don't fit in here.

It's all good, sister. Accept these fleeting thoughts and emotions in the moment, and before you know it, they'll rise up and out of you. The next moment, it may be altered. An hour from now, you could be a completely different woman in the same room. You're not broken and you don't need fixing. This is all just about cultivating that awareness of Self, and meeting that Self compassionately in the heart.

5. Permission to be Dazzling...

Go out and absolutely rock this new way of life. Own your choices. Share your joy. Radiate that intoxicating beauty within you. That is how life feels when we take off all those masks and allow our true nature to reveal itself: Dazzling. Three dimensional. Extraordinary.

I forbid you to dim any longer - no more denying yourself! Come out, out, out of your hollow and into your own glorious greatness, and do it with a million-dollar smile. We are all so very pleased to be seeing you – *really* seeing you – for the first time. Welcome home, star light.

6. Permission to Exude Dream-Worthy Peace

You already know how to do this. You do it by opening your heart to the moment and giving someone your presence; your undivided attention. You do it by gently breathing through those insane Ego thoughts. You breathe those thoughts away with ease and grace and tune back into your secret weapon - the Now.

When I first launched The Party Girl's Guide to Peace, I was making a declarative statement. I wanted The Universe to understand – loud and clear – that something in me had changed and rearranged. All I wanted was to start aiming true. I was Done with a capital 'D' with what was tried and tested. And now – *dammit!* – I wanted to experience *innovation* within me. I was done with the binge-drinking, the drugging, the shared accommodation, the split shifts, the drama. Done with the guilt, the ridiculous detoxing. Done with the all-or-nothing approach. Much like you have by picking up and tuning into the words of this book, I prescribed myself a self-revolution.

Today, these teachings are so deeply integrated into my being, that All Of This has become a way of life for me. **I live, breathe and love it.** My hope for you is that you'll recognise that this process transcends merely un-identifying with the Party Girl. It is, more than anything, a guide to showing up authentically for yourself, for the world you grace, and exploring the sensations of deep self-respect.

So here we are. The end. Although, it's not really, is it? The possibilities from here on out are absolutely endless, Peace Girl. You deserve the peace you've been seeking, so go and embody the shizzle out of it. Go set the world ablaze with your bright intentions and *enough is enough!* 'tude. Go set your own heart on fire, and *burn, burn, burn*, as Rumi would say. It's time to embrace self-love. Seize adventure. Revel in unconventionality. Pole-vault out of the limitations. Grab life by scruff of the neck. Tear down the walls and create a new existence brick by beautiful brick.

Can I get a *hells yeah*?
Thought so.

Peace Journaling

Let's reflect.

'Before I picked up this book, I felt…'

'And now, as I near the end of it, something's changed. I feel…'

'I'm starting to realise that…'

'Some relationships in my life are changing. This makes me feel…'

'I'm starting to make different decisions now, like…'

'I wasn't expecting this experience to deepen my connection to Spirit to this extent, but sure enough, it has. Here's proof…'

'I am most grateful for…'

The time is *now*.

Your *tribe* is waiting for you.

A new brand of *fun* is calling your name.

Go on. Go get *high*.

Life, today.

It's the little things that feel monumental. It's the tiny little stirrings of sweet insignificant nothings that nourish me most.

Those moments of a morning, when I crack my eyes open after a meditation down on the sand, to find rays of gold and pink light stretching through the clouds and kissing the oceanic horizon. They leave me breathless, and teary.

Those moments when one by one, my vertebrae flattens to the mat beneath me, followed by my shoulders, and finally my head. There's a last little wriggle of my joints before I arrive in the sweet space of savasana, feeling my cells hum, my breath lift and lower my belly. My mind, spacious. They remind me of my resolute desire to never abandon my body again, and that we always reap what we sow. *Be good to your body, and your body will be good to you. Be good to life, and life will be good to you.*

Those moments Glen and I take our seat at a beautiful restaurant and both the food and wine menus fill us with excitement that could out-do a kid in a candy store. They remind me that life is for enjoying, and lapping up, and savouring with wonder.

Those moments when I open my gratitude journal before bed, and I'm so overwhelmed with emotion that all I can manage to write is *'Just… thank you… for… everything'.* They remind me of how much I'm able to feel *held* by life when I appreciate it with passion.

Those moments where a drink is offered my way, and I smile and raise my hand in a *no, thank you* gesture. They remind me that I'm the captain of my own ship.

When I spend time with children, such maternal emotion is evoked in me as I gaze into and beyond their soulful little eyes, sensing the impact that motherhood will make on my life. I am not scared anymore, like I once was, and this is a miracle.

The tingle of sun on my cheek. That speck of silence when my friends and I are in a fit of uproarious laughter, and we all *gasp* for breath at the same time.

The touch of my man's hand on my skin. The fraction of meditation where *form* feels like it dissolves. **This is what makes life worth living.** The emails that floats into my inbox daily.

:: *Thank you for that blog post.*

:: *Thank you for our coaching session.*

:: *Thank you for The Party Girl's Guide to Peace.*

It's impossible for me to truly receive the precious praise infused into these notes without seeing my life flash a little before my eyes. All that turbulence and insecurity and escapism - it was all so divinely worth it. When we heal, we're able to help. When we make it out the other side of confusion, suddenly we realise that we've been jolted by clarity so electric that we're *shocked!* wide awake. To me, clarity isn't about knowing the finer details; it's about sensing intuitively what we're here to do. And friends, with my hand on my heart, I know what I'm here to do:

Inhabit this body.

Love unconditionally.

Live gratefully.

Be a guide, a lighthouse for anyone who's willing to listen.

Surrender to creativity.

Enjoy and revel in this human experience…

…and step a little deeper into the spiritual one.

That's it!
That's the magic bullet.
The secret potion.
That's my answer.
And that's my prescription for Peace.

I hope - sincerely - that you write yourself a similar script.

Just... thank you... for... everything.

The Deepest of Gratitude

First up, I must bow to Yvette Luciano. Without your fervent belief in this message, this book mightn't be here today. Your enthusiasm kept me writing, beautiful. Thank you for your faith and most importantly, your friendship.

Belinda Davidson – my personal chakra Yoda, and cherished friend – your teachings have enhanced my life on every level. Words fail me. (They really, really do)

Niamh Beirne for being the backbone of my visions and dreams. You make business (and launching) better. I often feel as though I would be lost without you, my Irish Beauty.

Kris Emery, the fan-freaking-tastic wordsmith who edited this book, gracias. (I mean it, you made *High* 73 times better.) You're a total pro, and have been invaluable to this process. Your expertise, your cheeky little words of encouragement... thank you.

Tahl Rinsky, Sarah Hickey, Dani Hunt, Tahlee Rouillon and Emma Shields, and Sue Balcer, for your creative gifts in photography, videography, design, audio, project assisting, and typesetting. You made this a collaboration from heaven.

To Mastin Kipp, Kelly Notaras, Nicola Newman and my Bali sisters: what a ride! I will never forget that month in Indonesia when the first draft of this book awkwardly found its way onto the pages. A memory for the grandkids one day. Special shout out goes to Rach: #samebrain.

To Rachel MacDonald, Susana Frioni, Jess Ainscough, Melissa Ambrosini, Claire Obeid, Connie Chapman, Amanda Rootsey, Alice Nicholls and Claire Baker – my home-grown Aussie heroines that I feel blessed to call Soul Sisters. Please, never stop kicking ass and taking names. How did a girl get so lucky to have you all as friends? It's a pleasure to laugh with you, celebrate with you, and to do this important work alongside you.

My family, who I have grown to cherish and worship more than I thought was possible – it feels like we've been to the ends of the earth and back again. I just love you all so much. Dad, for your heart of caramel, and for being my biggest fan. Mama, for being the divinest mirror in my life, and for growing into my best friend, you inspire me.

To all the people that wove the fabric of my past: old friends, ex-lovers, the lot of you. Thank you for gracing me with the lessons and revelations that I needed in order to grow.

My Glen. I simply adore you. There's not a day that goes by that my heart doesn't explode with love for you. Every now and then I contemplate the notion that I still have decades upon decades of memories to create with you, and… *wow*. I look forward to each and every one.

My incredible readers over at TaraBliss.com.au, my clients, and my Peace Girls; the lovely beings that allowed me to introduce this experiment into their lives in the beginning - you all give my life so much meaning. It has been, and will continue to be, my greatest pleasure to serve you.

And to you, my succulent and sweet (ex-)Party Girl. Thanks for stepping this way, for taking this journey with me. I hope it's been a scenic, profound and beautiful one.

My hope is that this book has lifted you, given you hope, and inspired you into action. If it has, please share it with the women in your life. Buy a copy for your best friend, your cousin, your work colleague. Recommend it to your clients. Write a review about it on your website…

With your help, we can allow this seed to sprout all over the world.

May you devote your days to the Peace that has always dwelled within you.

Namaste.

About the Author

As a former hair-dresser, bungee-jumping teacher and martini shaking bartender, Tara Bliss has always loved one thing: pushing herself and other people to go beyond what they think is appropriate.

These days, as a coach, author and yoga teacher (with swagger), she's *still* deeply passionate about guiding women to stretch beyond what is reasonable, or what feels possible.

Named a 'self-help guru' by ELLE magazine, her teachings have been featured in Cleo, The Sunday Mail, The Daily Love and Mind Body Green.

When she's not jamming with her clients or immersed in writing projects, you'll find her making shapes on her yoga mat, planning a snowboarding trip with her man, hanging by the sea (channeling her inner mermaid), or thinking about Mexican food.

Meet Tara and stay in-the-know at tarabliss.com.au, and follow her yoga adventures on Instagram: @tara_bliss

Resources

Subscribe to my (awesome) weekly newsletter:
http://tarabliss.com.au/free-coaching/

I put myself into yoga shapes and share inspiration on Instagram:
http://instagram.com/tara_bliss

If, after reading this book, you're feeling a real pull to dive deeper into a spiritual practice, you'll love my online project -
Still, Sweet & Sweaty: 28 Days to a Spiritual Practice That Sticks.
Find it here (it launches 3 times a year):
http://tarabliss.com.au/still-sweet-sweaty/

To enquire about 1:1 coaching:
http://tarabliss.com.au/work/

Visit my online store for other titles I've collaborated on:

Spirited: Soulful Lessons on Clarity, Connection and Coming Home (to You)

Such Different Eats: Radical Real Food Recipes

http://tarabliss.com.au/books/

Life-changing programs and experiences

Marie Forleo's *BSchool*
http://tarabliss.com.au/bschool/

Belinda Davidson's *School of the Modern Mystic*
http://tarabliss.com.au/modern-mystic/

Rachel MacDonald's *Bright-Eyed and Blog-Hearted*
http://tarabliss.com.au/bloghearted/

Danielle LaPorte's *Desire Map*
http://www.daniellelaporte.com/thedesiremap/

Meditations

Sonesence Meditones
http://bit.ly/meditones

Belinda Davidson: Chakra Cleanse Meditation
http://bit.ly/chakramedi

Gabrielle Bernstein
http://gabbyb.tv/meditate

Sally Kempton
http://yogaglo.com

Connie Chapman: Guided Meditations for Inner Transformation
http://conniechapman.com/meditate/

My friend Claire Obeid regularly launches The Meditation Project:
http://claireobeid.com/

**Also, you can also find a list of my favourite books and
resources at my Amazon store:
http://bit.ly/amazontara**

17103621R00158

Made in the USA
San Bernardino, CA
30 November 2014